LA Lite™
Cookbook

Simple Recipes

Simply Delicious

The collection of recipes in this book come mainly from clients who have had great success with the L A Weight Loss program. We'd like to send out a special thank you to those clients who, over the years, have contributed the cherished recipes that helped them to achieve their own weight loss goals. If you have a favorite "lite" recipe you would like to share for future editions of the cookbook, please submit them to recipes@la-weightloss.com.

LA WEIGHT LOSS CENTERS®

LA LITE™

Cookbook

▶ *Simple Recipes*

Simply Delicious

The joy of the L A Weight Loss program is the variety of foods available to you while you're losing weight. With the L A Lite Cookbook you now have new and unique ways to prepare the wide array of food choices found in each program. Your entire family will enjoy these light and naturally delicious meals that range from steaming beef vegetable and french onion soup to succulent entrees such as soy-glazed chicken and beef stroganoff, to tantalizing desserts including chocolate truffles and apple crisps. Plus, you'll find hundreds of other recipes for drinks, entrees, vegetable preparations, ethnic meals and sweet delights. Each recipe represents a collection of the best preparations from our centers and clients. You can be certain that all recipes work with your L A Weight Loss program as exchanges are provided for each recipe.

So enjoy and happy eating!

Exclusively distributed by L A Weight Loss Franchise Company.
All exchanges provided are specific to L A Weight Loss Program.
6-55958-35002-0

©2007 L A Weight Loss Franchise Company

Contents

Jump ♣ Start

Breakfast is an essential part of your day. Experts believe that eating breakfast each morning may help you to have better concentration throughout the day. Also, people who skip breakfast are more likely to eat more at the next meal and therefore may have trouble controlling or losing weight in the long run. It is not essential to sit down to a three-course meal at breakfast, but it is important to have a small meal to get you, and your metabolism, running efficiently. The following section will give you some ideas, whether you're eating on the run or have time for a leisurely Sunday breakfast.

Strawberry Cheesecake Crepe recipe can be found on page 11

Basic Methods of Cooking Eggs

- **Poached** — Whole eggs are simmered gently in water; a small amount of vinegar may be added to keep the egg together.
- **Scrambled** — Eggs are whisked until fluffy and cooked over medium heat.
- **Fried** — Whole eggs are fried in butter on a griddle; the yolks may be runny (over easy) or cooked through (over hard).
- **Sunny-side up** — Whole eggs are fried in butter on a griddle; the egg is not flipped over in the cooking process, leaving the yolk, and sometimes the white, slightly runny.
- **Hard-boiled** — Whole eggs boiled in water in the shell until cooked through with a firm yolk and white, about 20 minutes.
- **Soft-boiled** — Whole eggs boiled in water in the shell until white is cooked through and yolk is almost set.
- **Coddled** — Similar to a poached egg; a whole egg, without shell, is placed in simmering water in a porcelain or glass dish for 1-2 minutes until soft.

Breakfast Terms

- **Quiche** — A classic breakfast or lunch item; eggs are beaten with milk or cream and typically combined with vegetables or meats and cheese; the egg mixture is poured into a savory pie crust and baked.
- **Eggs Benedict** — A restaurant favorite; poached eggs are served atop Canadian bacon and toasted English muffin; it is finished with a rich hollandaise sauce.
- **Strata** — A baked egg and milk mixture with vegetables, cheese and/or meats; the mixture is poured over layers of bread before baking.
- **Frittata** — A baked omelet of eggs and desired fillings; the omelet is cooked on the stovetop and then baked until set; sometimes pasta may be added as well.
- **Omelet** — A classic French menu item; eggs are cooked in a sauté pan and folded over any desired fillings.
- **Crepe** — A very thin pancake that is cooked in a sauté-like pan and wrapped around either sweet or savory fillings.

Food Safety

Though there is very low risk of food-borne illness with consumption of eggs, you should still make sure eggs are of high quality and fresh, and are cooked thoroughly in order to prevent salmonella. If you are concerned about consuming undercooked egg whites, you may use pasteurized liquid egg whites, or powder or pasteurized liquid egg substitute.

TIP!

Eating breakfast in the morning promotes blood sugar level stability, better concentration, and more energy. Your body depends on breakfast to keep your energy levels high throughout the day.

Scrambled Egg

1 *serving*

- SERVING SIZE: 1 RECIPE
- COUNTS AS:
  1 PROTEIN

☀ Ingredients

2 eggs

1 Tbsp (15mL) skim milk

dash of lite salt

freshly ground pepper

nonfat cooking spray

1. In a bowl, whisk eggs, milk, salt and pepper thoroughly until they have reached a uniform yellow color.

2. Coat skillet with nonfat cooking spray. Heat skillet over medium flame.

3. Pour egg mixture into skillet.

4. As mixture begins to set at bottom and sides, gently lift cooked portion with spatula so that the thin, uncooked portion can flow to the bottom.

5. Cook until eggs are thickened throughout, but still moist, about 3-5 minutes.

Cheesy Scrambled Egg

1 *serving*

- SERVING SIZE: 1 RECIPE
- COUNTS AS:
  1 PROTEIN
  1/2 DAIRY

good source of calcium

☀ Ingredients

1 whole egg

4 egg whites

1oz (30g) reduced-fat cheddar or swiss cheese

1/4 tsp (1mL) snipped parsley

1/4 tsp (1mL) snipped chives

nonfat cooking spray

dash of lite salt

freshly ground pepper

1. Break egg into a medium mixing bowl; add egg whites. Mix until well blended.

2. Add cheese, parsley, chives, salt and pepper.

3. Coat skillet with nonfat cooking spray and heat over medium flame.

4. Add egg mixture to skillet.

5. As mixture begins to set at bottom and sides, gently lift cooked portion with spatula so that thin, uncooked portion can flow to bottom.

6. Cook until eggs are thickened throughout, but still moist, approximately 3-5 minutes.

Jump
❖ Start

Puffy Omelet

1 *serving*

- **SERVING SIZE: 1 OMELET**
- **COUNTS AS:**
  1 PROTEIN

☀ Ingredients

2 eggs, separated

1 Tbsp (15mL) water

1/4 tsp (1mL) lite salt

1/8 tsp (.5mL) freshly ground pepper

nonfat cooking spray

1 Preheat oven to 325°F (160°C).

2 With a mixer, beat egg whites, water and salt on high speed until stiff, but not dry.

3 In a separate bowl, beat egg yolks and pepper on high speed until very thick and lemon-colored. Fold yolks into egg whites.

4 Coat 10-inch (25cm) ovenproof skillet with nonfat cooking spray. Heat skillet over medium heat.

5 Pour egg mixture into skillet; reduce heat.

6 Cook over low heat until puffy and light brown on bottom, about 5 minutes.

7 Bake, uncovered, in oven, until knife inserted in the center comes out clean, about 10-15 minutes.

8 Fold omelet in half; slip onto a plate.

Broccoli Omelet Bake

1 *serving*

- **SERVING SIZE: 1 OMELET**
- **COUNTS AS:**
  1 PROTEIN
  2 VEGETABLES
  1/2 DAIRY

good source of fiber

☀ Ingredients

2 eggs

1/2 cup (125mL) cooked broccoli, chopped

1 tsp (5mL) dried onion

1oz (30g) reduced-fat cheddar or swiss cheese

2 Tbsp (30mL) skim milk

1/4 tsp (1mL) lite salt

1/4 tsp (1mL) dried basil

1/2 tsp (2mL) garlic powder

1 tomato cut into 6 slices

1 Preheat oven to 325°F (160°C).

2 Beat eggs until light and fluffy.

3 Stir in broccoli, onion, half of the cheese, milk, salt, basil and garlic powder.

4 Pour into ungreased baking dish.

5 Arrange tomato slices on top.

6 Bake, uncovered, for 20 minutes.

7 Top with the remaining cheese; bake for an additional 3-5 minutes.

Jump
♣ Start

Apple Pancake

1 *serving*

- SERVING SIZE: 1 PANCAKE
- COUNTS AS:
  1 PROTEIN
  1 STARCH
  1 FRUIT

☀ Ingredients

1 cup (250mL) egg substitute

6 slices Melba rounds, crushed

1 small apple, peeled and grated

1/2 tsp (2mL) cinnamon

1 packet sugar substitute

nonfat cooking spray

1 Combine all ingredients in a small bowl; mix well.

2 Coat skillet with nonfat cooking spray and heat over medium-low heat. Pour mixture into skillet. Heat until lightly browned; flip over and brown on other side. Serve.

> "Talk about something new and unusual. This is definitely it. No more plain old pancakes. They are absolutely delicious."
>
> *- Michael G.*

French Toast

1 *serving*

- SERVING SIZE: 1 SLICE
- COUNTS AS:
  1/2 PROTEIN
  1 STARCH
  1 FRUIT

meals in minutes

☀ Ingredients

1/2 cup (125mL) egg substitute

1 Tbsp (15mL) skim milk

dash of cinnamon

dash of nutmeg

dash of sugar substitute

2 slices lite bread

nonfat cooking spray

12 medium strawberries, sliced

1 Combine egg substitute, milk, spices and sugar substitute in a shallow bowl; mix well.

2 Add slices of lite bread to egg mixture and let stand until egg mixture is absorbed.

3 Coat skillet with nonfat cooking spray and heat over medium heat. Place bread in skillet and brown on both sides.

4 Place on serving dish; top with sliced strawberries.

Jump
❖ Start

Greek Omelet

1 *serving*

- **SERVING SIZE: 1 OMELET**
- **COUNTS AS:**
  1 PROTEIN
  1 FAT
  1 VEGETABLE
  1/2 DAIRY

meals in minutes

✳ Ingredients

2 Tbsp (30mL) chopped red onion

1/4 cup (50mL) fresh spinach

2 Tbsp (30mL) skim milk

1/4 tsp (1mL) garlic powder

1 cup (250mL) egg substitute
nonfat cooking spray

1oz (30g) lite feta cheese

10 black olives, diced

1. Coat medium skillet with nonfat cooking spray; heat over medium heat.

2. Sauté onions and spinach until onions are tender and spinach has wilted down.

3. Remove vegetables from skillet and place in small mixing bowl; cool for 5 minutes.

4. Add milk, garlic powder and egg substitute to vegetable mixture. Mix well.

5. Coat skillet with nonfat cooking spray and heat over medium heat. Add egg mixture to skillet and cook over low heat until brown.

6. Flip egg mixture over and brown on other side. Turn heat to low and sprinkle with cheese and olives, cover skillet and cook 1-2 minutes or until cheese is softened.

Bran Muffins

2 *servings*

- **SERVING SIZE: 1 MUFFIN**
- **COUNTS AS:**
  2 STARCHES
  1 FRUIT

good source of fiber

✳ Ingredients

1/2 cup (125mL) egg substitute

2 Tbsp (30mL) water

2 Tbsp (30mL) skim milk

1 tsp (5mL) vanilla

1/2 tsp (2mL) cinnamon

1 Tbsp (15mL) flour

1/2 tsp (2mL) baking soda

pinch nutmeg

1/2 cup (125mL)
unprocessed bran

3 packets sugar substitute

3/4 cup (175mL) blueberries

nonfat cooking spray

1. Preheat oven to 350°F (180°C).

2. In a large bowl, combine egg substitute, water, milk, vanilla, cinnamon, flour, baking soda, nutmeg, bran and sugar substitute.

3. Add blueberries to mixture.

4. Coat muffin pan with nonfat cooking spray.

5. Divide batter between 2 muffin cups.

6. Bake in oven for 15 minutes.

Jump
✤ Start

Crepes

 servings

- **SERVING SIZE: 1 CREPE**
- **COUNTS AS:**
  1 STARCH

☀ Ingredients

1/2 cup (125mL) whole wheat flour

1/2 cup (125mL) white flour

1/4 tsp (1mL) lite salt

1 packet sugar substitute

1/2 cup (125mL) egg substitute

3/4 cup (175mL) skim milk

1 Tbsp (15mL) margarine, melted

2 tsp (10mL) vanilla extract

nonfat cooking spray

Batter

1 Combine flour, salt and sugar substitute in small bowl. Set aside.

2 In a separate bowl, beat eggs and milk together with an electric mixer.

3 Beat flour mixture slowly into eggs.

4 Once flour is combined into eggs, slowly stir in melted margarine and vanilla extract.

Crepes

1 Coat small skillet, or crepe pan, with nonfat cooking spray and heat over medium-high heat.

2 Scoop 2 Tbsp (30mL) of batter into skillet.

3 Tip and rotate the skillet to help spread the batter, as thinly as possible, over bottom of pan.

4 Cook 30-60 seconds, or until bottom is lightly browned.

5 Carefully flip over and cook 15-20 more seconds.

6 Remove from pan. Set aside.

7 Continue to cook crepes until all batter is used. Place a piece of wax paper between each cooked crepe to prevent them from sticking together. (Cool skillet for 1-2 minutes periodically during cooking to prevent burning.)

Crepes can be frozen in wax paper for up to one month.

Strawberry Cheesecake Crepe

1 serving

- **SERVING SIZE: 1 CREPE**
- **COUNTS AS:**
  1 DAIRY
  1 STARCH
  1 FRUIT

☀ Ingredients

2oz (60g) reduced-fat ricotta cheese

1 packet sugar substitute

6 small strawberries diced

1/4 tsp (1mL) vanilla extract

1 crepe (see crepe recipe above)

6 medium strawberries, sliced

1 Tbsp (15mL) fat-free whipped topping

1 In small mixing bowl combine cheese, sweetener, diced berries and vanilla extract; mix well.

2 Place filling over one half of the crepe and fold crepe over filling.

3 Top with sliced strawberries and whipped topping.

Jump
✿ Start

Banana Nut Crepe

1 *serving*

- **SERVING SIZE: 1 CREPE**
- **COUNTS AS:**
  1 STARCH
  1 FRUIT
  1 FAT

✳ Ingredients

1 4oz (120g) small banana, thinly sliced

4 walnut halves, finely chopped (2 whole walnuts)

1/2 packet sugar substitute

1/4 tsp (1mL) cinnamon

1 crepe (see crepe recipe on page 11)

2 tsp (10mL) sugar-free apricot spread

1 Spread 2 tsp of sugar-free apricot spread over crepe.

2 Place banana slices over half of the crepe.

3 Sprinkle walnuts, sugar substitute and cinnamon over bananas.

4 Fold crepe over filling.

5 If desired, heat in microwave 30 seconds to soften banana.

Mushroom & Spinach Crepe

1 *serving*

- **SERVING SIZE: 1 CREPE**
- **COUNTS AS:**
  1 STARCH
  1 VEGETABLE
  1 CONDIMENT

✳ Ingredients

nonfat cooking spray

2 Tbsp (30mL) chopped sweet onions

1/4 tsp (1mL) lite salt

1/4 cup (50mL) chopped white mushrooms

2 tsp (10mL) garlic powder

1/4 cup (50mL) fresh spinach, chopped

2 Tbsp (30mL) fat-free ricotta cheese

1 crepe (see crepe recipe on page 11)

freshly ground pepper

1 Coat small skillet with nonfat cooking spray.

2 Place onions in skillet, add salt and sauté on high heat for 1-2 minutes until onions begin to soften.

3 Add mushrooms and garlic powder; sauté 3 minutes, or until mushrooms are tender.

4 Add spinach; cook additional 2-3 minutes, until all vegetables are cooked. Remove from heat. Stir in ricotta cheese.

5 Reheat crepe for 10-15 seconds in microwave (medium heat).

6 Place vegetable mixture over one half of the crepe. Fold crepe over filling.

7 Sprinkle with freshly ground pepper. Serve hot.

Mexican Omelet

1 *serving*

meals in minutes

- **SERVING SIZE: 1 OMELET**
- **COUNTS AS:**
  1 PROTEIN
  2 VEGETABLES

❋ Ingredients

1 cup (250mL) egg substitute

2 tsp (10mL) hot sauce

1/4 tsp (1mL) lite salt

1 Tbsp (15mL) skim milk

nonfat cooking spray

1 Tbsp (15mL) diced red peppers

1 Tbsp (15mL) diced green peppers

1 Tbsp (15mL) diced white onion

1 tsp (5mL) cilantro

1 Tbsp (15mL) diced tomato

1 Tbsp (15mL) salsa

1 Tbsp (15mL) fat-free sour cream

1 Tbsp (15mL) chopped green onion

chili powder (optional)

1. Combine egg substitute, hot sauce, salt and milk in mixing bowl. Whisk together vigorously; set aside.

2. Coat medium skillet with nonfat cooking spray. Heat over high heat.

3. Add peppers, onion and cilantro to skillet. Sauté 2-3 minutes or until vegetables start to soften.

4. Remove vegetables from skillet, allow skillet to cool 2-3 minutes.

5. Coat skillet again with nonfat cooking spray, return to heat over medium heat.

6. Pour egg mixture into skillet, distributing evenly.

7. Continue to cook over medium heat; use a spatula to gently lift the edges of the omelet, allowing uncooked egg to move underneath.

8. Once egg mixture is almost cooked through, add the pepper mixture and tomatoes. Cover skillet with a lid and cook additional 2-3 minutes over low heat, or until egg mixture is fully cooked.

9. Use spatula to remove omelet from pan, flipping in half while transferring to plate.

10. Top with salsa, sour cream and green onion.

11. To spice things up…sprinkle chili powder over your omelet!

Matzoh Brei

1 *serving*

meals in minutes

- **SERVING SIZE: 1 RECIPE**
- **COUNTS AS:**
  1 PROTEIN
  1 STARCH

❋ Ingredients

1 sheet of matzoh

1 cup (250mL) warm water

1 cup (250mL) egg substitute

nonfat cooking spray

freshly ground pepper (optional)

cinnamon (optional)

sugar substitute (optional)

1. Break matzoh into pieces. In small bowl, soak the matzoh in water for 1-2 minutes, or until soft. Drain matzoh well.

2. Add egg substitute to matzoh mixture.

3. Coat medium skillet with nonfat cooking spray. Heat over medium heat.

4. Pour egg mixture into skillet. Cook until lightly brown on one side; flip over and brown on other side.

5. Season with pepper, or cinnamon and sugar substitute.

Jump
❧ Start

Buttermilk Scones

12 *servings*

- SERVING SIZE: 1 SCONE
- COUNTS AS:
  1 STARCH
  1 FRUIT
  1 FAT

family fare

❋ Ingredients

1 1/2 cups (375mL) flour

1 1/2 cups (375mL) old-fashioned oats

2 packets sugar substitute

1 Tbsp (15mL) baking powder

1 tsp (5mL) cream of tartar

1/2 tsp (2mL) salt

1/3 cup (75mL) unsalted margarine, melted

2/3 cup (150mL) nonfat buttermilk

1/2 cup (125mL) egg substitute

1/2 cup (125mL) raisins or currants

flour

nonfat cooking spray

1. Preheat oven to 425°F (220°C).
2. Combine flour, oats, sugar substitute, baking powder, cream of tartar and lite salt in a large bowl.
3. Add margarine, buttermilk and egg substitute.
4. Mix just until batter is moistened.
5. Stir in raisins.
6. With your hands, shape the dough to form a ball.
7. Pat out on a lightly floured surface to form an 8-inch circle.
8. Cut into 12 wedges.
9. Bake on a cookie sheet coated with nonfat cooking spray for 12-15 minutes, or until light brown.

Breakfast Burrito

1 *serving*

- SERVING SIZE: 1 BURRITO
- COUNTS AS:
  1 PROTEIN
  1 STARCH
  1 VEGETABLE
  1/2 DAIRY

good source of calcium

❋ Ingredients

nonfat cooking spray

1 Tbsp (15mL) diced green pepper

1 Tbsp (15mL) chopped green onion

1 cup (250mL) egg substitute

1/4 tsp (1mL) lite salt

1 Tbsp (15mL) diced tomato

1/2 whole wheat tortilla

1oz (30g) reduced-fat pepper jack cheese

1 Tbsp (15mL) fat-free sour cream

1. Coat medium skillet with nonfat cooking spray. Heat over high heat.
2. Add pepper and onion to skillet. Sauté 2-3 minutes, or until vegetables start to soften.
3. Pour egg substitute into skillet, distributing evenly. Sprinkle with lite salt.
4. Once eggs are cooked through, turn down heat; add tomatoes, cook 1 minute until tomatoes are warm.
5. Place egg in middle of tortilla; top with cheese.
6. Roll up tortilla into a burrito.
7. Top with fat-free sour cream.

Jump
❖ Start

Country Sausage Patties

12 *servings*

family fare

- SERVING SIZE: 1 PATTY
- COUNTS AS:
  1/2 PROTEIN
  2 FATS

❋ Ingredients

nonfat cooking spray

10 green onions, finely chopped

1/2 cup (125mL) bread crumbs
(see recipe on page 154)

1/2 cup (125mL) skim milk

1/2 tsp (2mL) freshly ground
pepper

1/4 tsp (1mL) cayenne

1 tsp (5mL) finely chopped fresh
thyme

1 Tbsp (15mL) finely chopped
fresh sage

2 tsp (10mL) lite salt

2 pounds (900g) ground lean
pork

1 Preheat oven to 250°F (120°C).

2 Coat skillet with nonfat cooking spray and heat over
medium heat.

3 Cook onions, stirring occasionally, until softened and
beginning to brown. Remove from heat and cool for
10 minutes.

4 While onions are cooling, stir together bread crumbs
and milk in a large bowl and let stand until crumbs
absorb the milk.

5 Add onions and remaining ingredients to crumb
mixture and stir with a fork until blended well.

6 Form sausage patties into 1/2-inch thick patties with
dampened hands and arrange on a tray lined with wax
paper lined tray.

7 Form into 12 patties.

8 Spray heavy skillet with nonfat cooking spray; heat
over medium-high heat, cook patties, turning once,
until browned and just cooked through, 4-6 minutes
per batch.

9 Transfer to shallow baking pan and keep warm,
covered with foil, in oven while cooking remaining
batches.

Uncooked patties may be frozen.

Turkey Sausage

4 *servings*

family fare

- SERVING SIZE: 1 PATTY
- COUNTS AS:
  1 PROTEIN

❋ Ingredients

20oz (600g) ground turkey
breast

1/2 tsp (2mL) dried sage

1/4 tsp (1mL) freshly ground
pepper

1/4 tsp (1mL) cayenne pepper

1/4 tsp (1mL) lite salt

nonfat cooking spray

1 In large bowl, combine turkey and seasonings. Mix
thoroughly.

2 Shape into 4oz (120g) patties.

3 Heat skillet, coated with nonfat cooking spray, over a
medium heat.

4 Add patties to skillet and cook thoroughly on each
side, or to an internal temperature of 165°F (75°C).

Uncooked patties may be frozen.

Jump
❖ Start

Savory
Soups&
Salads

Many of us think of soups as a type of comfort food; the kind of dish that warms us inside and out. Salad, of course, is an old meal-starter favorite. There are several varieties of soups and salads such as broth-based or cream-based soups and tossed or Caesar salads. Unfortunately, canned and pre-made soups can be very high in sodium and/or fat. Salad dressing and cheese can also add a lot of extra fat and calories. However, you'll find lots of ways to eliminate fat without sacrificing flavor and all the basic methods of preparing your own soups and salads inside.

Waldorf Salad recipe can be found on page 32

Cooking Methods

Broth or stock is one of the simplest cooking methods. This soup base starts with water and incorporates the meat or bones, as well as vegetables and herbs. The mixture is simmered for a moderately long amount of time to infuse the water with flavor; eventually, the solids are strained out of the broth or stock before use. Broths and stocks are the base of any soup and provide added flavor.

Canned stock and bouillon cubes may be used for ease, but fresh stock will provide optimum flavor. If using canned stock, choose a low-sodium variety! Bouillon cubes can be found also in a "very low-sodium" variety with less than 35mg sodium per serving; this method is quite easy and requires you only to reconstitute the broth by adding warm water.

Cream-based soups can be high in fat and calories, but there are methods to reduce the fat and calories. Cream-based soups or chowders typically start as a broth-based soup and cream or milk may be added at the end of the recipe to allow the flavors to meld. Vegetable-cream soups are commonly pureed together for serving to achieve a velvety texture. The cream used in soups may be replaced by fat-free half and half, evaporated skim milk, regular skim or reduced-fat milk, to cut back on calories.

Other Cooking Tips

When making broth-based soups, or other soups that will not be pureed, it is important to cut or chop the vegetables and protein in uniform pieces so that it may cook quickly and in the same amount of time. You may also use leftover proteins and vegetables that are already prepared in order to shorten cooking times even further.

If a thicker soup is desired for texture, you have several options. Eggs provide a rich and creamy texture to soup, but they can scramble in the hot broth. The best method is to beat 1 or 2 eggs in a small bowl and add a small amount of hot soup or broth, whisking together, then gradually incorporate this mixture back into the soup.

Flour may also be used in the early stages of the soup by lightly sprinkling over the vegetables as they sauté or in the final stages by adding a tablespoon of cornstarch (mixed with 1-2 tablespoon of water) into the soup or broth. To thicken pureed soups, you may want to add a half-cup of rice or potatoes or a slice or two of bread before pureeing in a blender or food processor.

TIP!

The cream used in soups may be replaced by fat-free half and half, evaporated skim milk, or regular skim or reduced-fat milk, to reduce the amount of calories.

Greens Dictionary

- **Endive** — Also known as Belgian endive; a small, cigar-shaped head of pale yellow-green lettuce, with a bitter taste, well paired with nuts and cheese.

- **Frisée** — Also known as curly endive; a member of the chicory family; thin, curly leaves appear to be frizzy with a slightly bitter taste; commonly found in "spring mix" salads.

- **Romaine** — Also known as cos lettuce; a common lettuce in the US, with dark green, long leaves that are coarse; inner leaves are paler in color and have a more delicate flavor.

- **Iceberg** — This lettuce got its name from its original shipping method—growers packed the heads in ice, it was previously known as crisphead lettuce; this particular head of lettuce has 90% water content, one of the highest of all lettuces.

- **Looseleaf** — Examples of this variety includes red leaf, green leaf and oak leaf lettuces; the leaves vary in flavor, red lettuces tend to be more sharp or bitter; the oak variety tends to be more coarse than leaf lettuce.

- **Escarole** — Also a member of the chicory family, though with a milder flavor; leaves are broad and wavy, though smaller than a leaf lettuce; most commonly mixed with other lettuces in salads due to its sharp taste; also used cooked, commonly in Italian cuisine.

- **Watercress** — A member of the mustard family; has small leaves and thin stems, with a slightly bitter and peppery flavor; also commonly used in soups and sandwiches.

- **Spring Mix** — Also known as field greens, micro greens, or mesclun; may include a variety of baby lettuces, such as spinach, frisée, oak leaf, radicchio, etc; of growing popularity over the past few years.

- **Butterhead** — This includes Boston and Bibb lettuces; Bibb lettuce is a smaller head of lettuce with loose, true green leaves with more flavor; Boston lettuce is commonly a larger head of lettuce with leaves lighter in color and flavor.

- **Spinach** — A dark leafy green, high in fiber, that can be used raw or cooked; approximately 1 pound raw equals 1 cup cooked; choose spinach with smaller leaves and stems, also known as baby spinach, because it will be delicate and tender.

- **Radicchio** — Also known as red chicory; appears as a red cabbage; coarse, crisp leaves with bitter leaves, commonly mixed with other greens, may be grilled to enhance flavor or used as colorful garnish.

- **Arugula** — Also known as rocket; peppery flavored delicate green leaves, similar in shape to spinach.

- **Kale** — A type of cabbage with curly, wrinkled leaves, which are hardy and coarse; most commonly used cooked, but may be used raw as a garnish or mixed into salads with other greens.

- **Mustard Greens** — A dark leafy green that can be found with red or green leaves; common in the Southern states; known for its sharp, peppery taste.

Cheesy Taco Salad
Garlic Tomato Salad
Cucumber & Shrimp Salad
Fruited Chicken Salad
Oriental-Style Shrimp Salad
Grilled Chicken Cobb Salad
Eggplant & Pepper Salad
Sirloin Caesar Salad
Blackened Portabella Salad
Carrot Salad
Chicken Broccoli Pasta Salad
Sweet Potato Salad
Asparagus Salad
Strawberry & Melon Salad
Tomato Basil & Mozzarella Salad
Ginger Apple Slaw
Citrus Salad
Dilled Pasta Salad
Cucumber & Tomato Salad
Sesame Ginger Chicken Salad
Tomato Pasta Salad
Cantaloupe with Chicken Salad
Spinach Tossed Salad
Coleslaw
Grilled Chicken Caesar Salad
Grilled Asparagus, Tomato & Carrot Salad
Shrimp Salad
Oriental Bean Salad
Chicken Salad
Tuna Pasta Salad
Strawberry Spinach Salad
Fresh Vegetable Salad
Sweet & Sour Dressing
Lite Vinaigrette
Chicken Salad with Orange Vinaigrette
Poppy Seed Vinaigrette
Yogurt-Dill Dressing

Chicken Stock

6 *servings*

- **SERVING SIZE: 1 CUP (250ML)**
- **COUNTS AS:**
  1 FAT

✳ Ingredients

1 1/4 pounds (560g) chicken bones

2 Tbsp (30mL) olive oil

1 red onion, sliced

1/2 celery stalk

1 carrot, diced

4 cups (1L) water, or as needed

1/3 tsp (1.5mL) dried parsley

1/4 tsp (1mL) dried thyme

1/3 tsp (1.5mL) dried basil

1 1/2 tsp (7.5mL) cracked black peppercorns

1 Preheat oven to 450°F (230°C). Arrange chicken bones on a baking sheet.

2 Roast 45 minutes until well browned.

3 Heat olive oil in a stock pot over medium heat. Add onion, celery and carrot; cook and stir until browned. If they scorch, add a little water and scrape up bits.

4 Add roasted chicken bones to the pot, fill with water to cover the bones by 2 inches (5cm). Bring to a boil.

5 Add thyme, parsley, basil and peppercorns. Reduce heat to low, and simmer uncovered for 2 hours. Add more water if needed.

6 Strain out the solids from the broth, drain the fat and refrigerate. You can also remove the fat after it has chilled. The stock will be thick. Use full strength for soups and gravies, or dilute with water for a milder flavor. Use freezer bags for longer storage.

Shrimp Soup

1 *serving*

good source of fiber

- **SERVING SIZE: 1 RECIPE**
- **COUNTS AS:**
  1 PROTEIN
  1 DAIRY
  1 LA LITE

✳ Ingredients

5oz (150g) shrimp

1 tsp (5mL) onion, finely minced

1 Tbsp (15mL) red pepper, diced

1 garlic clove, finely minced

1 L A Lite Cream of Mushroom soup mix

8oz (250mL) skim milk

1 Tbsp (15mL) fat-free half & half

hot pepper sauce (optional) to taste

nonfat cooking spray

1 In a small saucepan coated with nonfat cooking spray, add shrimp, onion, pepper and garlic. Sauté until shrimp is cooked.

2 Add soup mix, milk and half & half; stir until smooth.

3 Heat well.

4 Season with hot pepper sauce (optional).

Savory
Soups&
✤ Salads

Broccoli Soup

 4 *servings*

- **SERVING SIZE:**
  1 CUP (250ML)
- **COUNTS AS:**
  1 STARCH
  1 VEGETABLE
  1 FAT

good source of fiber

☀ Ingredients

2 Tbsp (30mL) olive oil

1 medium onion, sliced

1 garlic clove, smashed

1 potato (russet), peeled and diced

1/4 tsp (1mL) thyme

4 cups (1L) chicken stock
(see recipe on page 20) or very
low-sodium broth

1 pound (450g) frozen broccoli,
thawed

4 Tbsp (60mL) fat-free half & half

freshly ground pepper, to taste

1. In a saucepan add olive oil, onion and garlic. Cook over medium heat until translucent, about 5 minutes.
2. Add the potato, thyme and broth and bring to a boil.
3. Adjust the heat to maintain a gentle simmer, and cook uncovered until the potato is fork tender, about 10 minutes.
4. Add the broccoli and simmer for 10 to 12 minutes or until broccoli is tender.
5. Puree the soup in batches in a blender.
6. Return the soup to the pot and add the half & half.
7. Bring to a simmer, season with pepper to taste.

Cream of Spinach Soup

 **1** *serving*

- **SERVING SIZE: 1 RECIPE**
- **COUNTS AS:**
  1 VEGETABLE
  1 DAIRY
  1 LA LITE

meals in minutes

☀ Ingredients

8oz (250mL) skim milk

1 L A Lite Cream of Mushroom
soup mix

1 tsp (5mL) finely minced onion

1/2 cup (125mL) steamed fresh
spinach

1 tsp (5mL) fresh lemon juice

freshly ground pepper, to taste

1. Add milk into a saucepan, warm over medium heat.
2. Empty one envelope of the mushroom soup into saucepan.
3. Add remaining ingredients and stir.
4. Heat until desired temperature, serve.

"There's no extra food. I just made the servings I needed according to my plan."

- Paula R.

Savory
Soups&
❖Salads

Cream of Chicken & Rice Soup

1 *serving*

- **SERVING SIZE: 1 RECIPE**
- **COUNTS AS:**
  1 PROTEIN
  1 STARCH
  1 VEGETABLE
  1 DAIRY
  1 LA LITE

good source of fiber

✳ Ingredients

5oz (150g) chicken breast, chopped into bite-size pieces

1 tsp (5mL) finely minced onion

8oz (250mL) skim milk

1 L A Lite Cream of Chicken soup mix

1 cup (250mL) fresh broccoli florets

1/4 cup (50mL) cooked brown rice

freshly ground pepper, to taste

nonfat cooking spray

1. In a small sauce pan sprayed with nonfat cooking spray, sauté chicken and onion.

2. Add milk and soup into saucepan or Dutch oven; stir until blended.

3. Add broccoli; simmer for 10 minutes.

4. Add cooked rice. Heat through. Season to taste with pepper.

"No leftovers to go bad."

- Paula R.

New England-Style Clam Chowder

8 *servings*

- **SERVING SIZE: 1 1/2 CUPS (375ML)**
- **COUNTS AS:**
  1 PROTEIN
  1 STARCH
  1 DAIRY

✳ Ingredients

1/4 cup (50mL) lite margarine

1 1/2 large onions, chopped

3/4 cup (175mL) all-purpose flour

1 quart (1L) shucked clams, with liquid

48oz (1.5L) clam juice

1 pound (450g) boiling potatoes, peeled and cubed

1 cup (250mL) skim milk

2 cups (500mL) evaporated skim milk

lite salt and freshly ground pepper, to taste

1/2 tsp (2mL) chopped fresh dill

1. Melt margarine in a large saucepan or pot over medium heat. Add onions and sauté until soft and translucent. Add flour, stirring constantly, for 4-5 minutes until lightly brown. Remove from heat and cool to room temperature.

2. In a separate saucepan, add clams with liquid and clam juice. Bring to a boil, reduce heat and simmer for 15-20 minutes.

3. Meanwhile, in a another pot, cover potatoes with cold water by one inch; bring to a boil and cook until fork tender, about 15 minutes.

4. Slowly whisk warmed clam-broth mixture into flour mixture, stirring constantly. Bring to a boil, stirring occasionally. Reduce heat, add potatoes, skim milk, evaporated skim milk, salt, pepper and dill. Simmer 5-10 minutes, until heated through.

Savory Soups & Salads

Minestrone Soup

8 servings

- **SERVING SIZE:**
  1 CUP (250ML)
- **COUNTS AS:**
  1 STARCH
  2 VEGETABLES
  1 CONDIMENT

family fare

☀ Ingredients

2 cups (500mL) chopped onion

2 Tbsp (30mL) low-sodium tomato paste

1/4 cup (50mL) chopped fresh parsley

4 garlic cloves, chopped

1 carrot, diced

1 celery stalk, diced

1 cup (250mL) chopped fresh spinach

1 cup (250mL) lentils, rinsed

2 bay leaves

8 sprigs parsley and 6 sprigs fresh thyme, tied together

9 cups (2.25L) low-sodium vegetable broth

1 tomato, diced

2 cups (500mL) cooked pasta

1/2 cup (125mL) grated parmesan cheese

lite salt and freshly ground pepper, to taste

nonfat cooking spray

1. In a large stock pot sprayed with nonfat cooking spray, sauté onions until brown.

2. Add tomato paste, chopped parsley, garlic, carrot, celery and spinach and cook for 3 minutes.

3. Add lentils, bay leaves, parsley-thyme sprigs and broth and bring to a boil.

4. Lower heat and simmer, partially covered, for 20 minutes.

5. Add tomato and season with pepper and salt.

6. Simmer for 10 minutes.

7. Remove bay leaves and parsley-thyme sprigs and discard.

8. Stir in pasta, and parmesan cheese: heat through and serve.

Potato & Leek Soup

1 serving

- **SERVING SIZE: 1 RECIPE**
- **COUNTS AS:**
  1 STARCH
  1 VEGETABLE
  1 DAIRY
  1 LA LITE

good source of calcium

☀ Ingredients

8oz (250mL) skim milk

1 L A Lite Cream of Chicken or Cream of Mushroom soup mix

1/2 small potato, chopped

1/2 cup (125mL) chopped fresh leeks

1 tsp (5mL) onion, finely minced

1 garlic clove, finely minced

1. Add milk to small sauce pan.

2. Add the soup mix, potato, leeks, onion and garlic.

3. Heat to a boil; lower heat and cook over low heat until potatoes are tender. About 15 minutes.

Savory
Soups&
❖ Salads

Cream of Mushroom Pasta Soup

1 *serving*

- SERVING SIZE: 1 RECIPE
- COUNTS AS:
  1 STARCH
  1 VEGETABLE
  1 DAIRY
  1 LA LITE

good source of fiber

☀ Ingredients

1 L A Lite Cream of Mushroom soup mix

8oz (250mL) skim milk

1/3 cup (75mL) cooked pasta of choice

1 tsp (5mL) onion, finely minced

1 garlic clove, finely minced

1/2 small tomato, chopped

1/4 green pepper, chopped

parsley, oregano, basil to taste

nonfat cooking spray

1 In a small saucepan coated with nonfat cooking spray, sauté onion, garlic, tomato, pepper and seasonings until tender.

2 Combine milk and soup mix and add to saucepan; heat through.

3 Pour over pasta; stir well and serve immediately.

Chicken Gumbo

6 *servings*

- SERVING SIZE:
  2 CUPS (500ML)
- COUNTS AS:
  1 PROTEIN
  1 STARCH

☀ Ingredients

6 cups (1.5L) low-sodium chicken broth

4-6 cups (1-1.5L) water

3 pounds (1.3kg) chicken breast, boneless and skinless, cut into bite size pieces

1 1/2 pounds (675g) fresh or frozen okra, 1/4-inch (1/2cm) slices

2 Tbsp (30mL) canola oil

1/4 cup (50mL) all-purpose flour

1 tomato, seeded and chopped

1 large onion, chopped

2 garlic cloves, minced

1/2 tsp (2mL) freshly ground pepper

1/4 tsp (1mL) cayenne pepper

2 cups (500mL) rice, cooked

nonfat cooking spray

1 In large soup pot, over medium heat, combine chicken broth and water.

2 Meanwhile, heat skillet coated with nonfat cooking spray. Sauté chicken pieces until lightly brown, about 10 minutes. Set aside and keep warm.

3 Add oil to skillet; heat over medium heat for 2-3 minutes. Add flour, stirring constantly to create roux. Reduce heat to medium-low and continue to cook, stirring, until golden brown, about 15-20 minutes.

4 Add tomatoes, onions, garlic and seasonings to roux mixture, stirring constantly. Stir roux-tomato mixture into heated broth. Bring to a boil; reduce heat to low and add chicken and okra.

5 Cover and cook another 30-40 minutes, before serving. Add more water or broth to reach desired thickness throughout the final cooking process.

6 Pour over rice and serve.

Savory
Soups&
❦ Salads

Pasta e Fagioli

4 servings

family fare

- **SERVING SIZE:** 1/4 RECIPE
- **COUNTS AS:**
  1/2 DAIRY
  3 STARCHES
  1 VEGETABLE

✳ Ingredients

1 tomato, diced

1 celery stalk, diced

1 small onion, diced

2 garlic cloves, minced

2 cans (8oz each) low-sodium tomato sauce

2 cups (500mL) low-sodium chicken broth

freshly ground pepper, to taste

1 Tbsp (15mL) dried parsley

2 tsp (10mL) dried basil leaves

15oz (450g) can cannelloni beans, drained and rinsed

3 cups (750mL) ditalini pasta, cooked

nonfat cooking spray

1/2 cup (125mL) parmesan

1 Heat a Dutch oven coated with nonfat cooking spray over low heat. Sauté celery and onion until soft.

2 Add garlic and sauté briefly.

3 Stir in tomato sauce, chicken broth, pepper, parsley and basil; simmer for 20 minutes.

4 Add beans and tomato and simmer for 5 minutes.

5 Stir in pasta and parmesan. Serve immediately.

Bean Soup

4 servings

good source of fiber

- **SERVING SIZE:** 1/4 RECIPE
- **COUNTS AS:**
  1 PROTEIN
  2 STARCHES
  1 VEGETABLE

✳ Ingredients

3 cups (675g) Great Northern Beans, cooked

1 small onion, minced

2 small potatoes, quartered and sliced

28oz (840g) low-sodium canned tomatoes, diced

6 cups (1.5L) water

1/2 tsp (2mL) dried basil

1/2 tsp (2mL) dried thyme

1 bay leaf

freshly ground pepper, to taste

nonfat cooking spray

1 In a large stock pot coated with nonfat cooking spray, sauté onion over medium heat until brown.

2 Add remaining ingredients and bring to a boil.

3 Reduce heat; simmer for 30 minutes or until potatoes are tender; serve.

Savory Soups & ✣ Salads

Creamy Vegetable Soup

1 *serving*

- **SERVING SIZE: 1 RECIPE**
- **COUNTS AS:**
  2 VEGETABLES
  1 DAIRY
  1 LA LITE

☀ Ingredients

1 L A Lite Cream of Mushroom soup mix

8oz (250mL) skim milk

1 cup (250mL) cooked of any of the following vegetables or 2 vegetables, 1/2 cup (125mL) cooked each: cauliflower florets, broccoli florets, celery, spinach, asparagus, cabbage, carrot, mushrooms

1 tsp (5mL) onion, finely chopped

1 garlic clove, finely minced

2 Tbsp (30mL) fat-free half & half

nonfat cooking spray

1 In a small saucepan coated with nonfat cooking spray, sauté onion and garlic.

2 Add milk, fat-free half & half, soup mix; blend; heat through.

3 Add vegetables. Bring to a simmer and cook 5 minutes.

4 Serve immediately.

Sweet Potato Soup

4 *servings*

- **SERVING SIZE: 3/4 CUP (175ML)**
- **COUNTS AS:**
  1 STARCH
  1 VEGETABLE
  1/2 DAIRY

☀ Ingredients

2 garlic cloves, crushed

1 small onion, chopped

1 tsp (5mL) curry powder

3 cups (750mL) water

1 1/2 cup (375mL) skim milk

12oz (360g) sweet potato, peeled and chopped

2 low-sodium vegetable broth cubes, crumbled

nonfat cooking spray

1 Spray a large stock pot with nonfat cooking spray; sauté garlic, onion and curry powder until soft.

2 Add sweet potato, water and broth cubes.

3 Simmer, covered, for 15 minutes or until vegetables are cooked. Cool.

4 Blend or process sweet potato mixture until smooth.

5 Gradually add the milk, processing until well combined.

6 Return to stock pot and heat well, do not boil.

Savory
Soups&
❖ Salads

Beef Vegetable Soup

1 *serving*

- **SERVING SIZE: 1 RECIPE**
- **COUNTS AS:**
  - 1 PROTEIN
  - 3 VEGETABLES

❄ Ingredients

4oz (120g) chuck roast

2 cups (500mL) very low-sodium beef broth, prepared from bouillon

1/2 medium carrot, thinly sliced

1/2 large celery stalk, sliced

1/2 cup (125mL) fresh green beans, trimmed and cut into 1/2-inch (1cm) pieces

1 small tomato, seeded and diced

nonfat cooking spray

dash of salt and freshly ground pepper, to taste

1. Rinse roast and pat dry; cut into 1/4 inch (.6cm) pieces. Season with salt and pepper.

2. Coat a Dutch oven with nonfat cooking spray. Add beef and cook over a medium flame until lightly browned.

3. Add beef broth; bring to boil. Reduce to a simmer, cover and cook for 10 minutes.

4. Add remaining ingredients to pot. Return soup to a boil.

5. Reduce heat; cover and simmer until beef and vegetables are tender, approximately 20 minutes.

6. Serve immediately or store in refrigerator up to 24 hours.

Cheddar Cheese Soup

4 *servings*

meals in minutes

- **SERVING SIZE: 1/4 RECIPE**
- **COUNTS AS:**
  - 1 DAIRY
  - 1 FAT

❄ Ingredients

2 Tbsp (30mL) minced green onion

2 Tbsp (30mL) lite margarine

3 Tbsp (45mL) flour

3 cups (750mL) low-sodium chicken broth

2 cups (500mL) skim milk

3/4 cup (175mL) light or reduced-fat cheddar cheese, grated

1/2 tsp (2mL) freshly ground pepper

paprika and parsley for garnish

1. Sauté the onion in margarine until softened; add flour, pepper and blend.

2. Gradually stir in the broth and add the milk.

3. Bring to a boil, reduce the heat and simmer for 15 minutes.

4. Remove from heat. Add in the cheese, stirring until melted.

5. Sprinkle with paprika and chopped parsley.

Savory
Soups&
❖ Salads

Split Pea Soup

6 *servings*

- **SERVING SIZE: 3/4 CUP (175ML)**
- **COUNTS AS:**
  1 STARCH
  3 VEGETABLES

✳ Ingredients

2 cups (500mL) split peas, uncooked

6 cups (1.5L) water

1 bay leaf

2 cups (500mL) carrots, chopped

1 cup (250mL) celery, chopped

1 cup (250mL) onion, chopped

1 tsp (5mL) thyme

1/2 tsp (2mL) freshly ground pepper

1 tsp (5mL) garlic powder

1 Rinse and drain split peas.

2 Combine dried split peas, water and bay leaf in a large stock pot.

3 Bring to a boil, then reduce heat and simmer for 1 hour. Stir occasionally to prevent the split peas from sticking and to make sure there is enough water. Add water if necessary.

4 Add carrots, celery, onions and seasoning.

5 Continue to simmer for 30 minutes or longer.

6 Add more water if a thinner soup is desired.

French Onion Soup

1 *serving*

- **SERVING SIZE: 1 RECIPE**
- **COUNTS AS:**
  1 STARCH
  1 VEGETABLE
  1/2 DAIRY

✳ Ingredients

1/2 cup (125mL) raw white onion slices

1 packet low-sodium beef bouillon

1 cup (250mL) water

1 bay leaf

1/4 tsp (1mL) onion powder

1/4 tsp (1mL) lite salt

6 melba toast rounds

1oz (30g) reduced-fat or part skim cheese or mozzarella

freshly ground pepper, to taste

dash of parsley

nonfat cooking spray

1 Sauté onions in skillet with nonfat cooking spray.

2 Add beef bouillon to onions.

3 Add water, salt, pepper, bay leaf and onion powder.

4 Bring to a boil and allow to simmer 10-15 minutes.

5 Remove bay leaf.

6 Place soup in a bowl. Top with melba toast.

7 Sprinkle cheese over melba toast.

8 Microwave soup until cheese is melted.

9 Sprinkle with parsley and serve hot.

Savory
Soups&
❖ Salads

Sweet Red Pepper Soup

4 *servings*

- **SERVING SIZE:**
  1/2 CUP (125ML)
- **COUNTS AS:**
  3 VEGETABLES

☀ Ingredients

4 roasted red peppers, halved
and deseeded

1 tsp (5mL) olive oil

1 red chili, seeded and finely
chopped

3 garlic cloves, chopped

20 green onions, chopped

4 tomatoes, chopped

2 cups (500mL) very low-
sodium vegetable stock

freshly ground pepper, to taste

lite salt, to taste

1 Tbsp (15mL) freshly chopped
parsley or oregano

2 Tbsp (30mL) freshly chopped
chives or basil

1. Preheat the grill to high.

2. When very hot, place red peppers, skin-side up, for about 15-20 minutes or until the skin is charred and blistered.

3. Remove and place in a paper bag until cool enough to handle.

4. Heat the oil in a large pot and add the chili, garlic and green onions and sauté for 4-5 minutes. Meanwhile, peel and roughly chop the roasted peppers.

5. Add the tomatoes and stock and simmer for 10 minutes, then add the roasted peppers.

6. Cover and cook over low heat for about 5-10 minutes, then remove from the heat and allow to cool.

7. Puree the soup in a food processor or blender until smooth.

8. Return the soup to a clean pan and gently warm through.

9. Season to taste with salt and pepper. Sprinkle with fresh herbs and serve.

Egg Drop Soup

1 *serving*

- **SERVING SIZE: 1 RECIPE**
- **COUNTS AS:**
  1 PROTEIN
  1 VEGETABLE
  1 CONDIMENT

☀ Ingredients

2 cups (500mL) very low-
sodium chicken broth,
prepared from bouillon

1 tsp (5mL) low-sodium soy
sauce

dash of white pepper

5 green onions, sliced

2 eggs

1. In a medium saucepan, add chicken broth, soy sauce and pepper. Bring to a boil; reduce heat.

2. In a small bowl, lightly beat eggs. Stir in onions.

3. Pour egg mixture slowly into broth, stirring constantly with a fork, until the eggs form strands.

Savory
Soups&
❀ Salads

Garden Vegetable Soup

1 *serving*

- SERVING SIZE: 1 RECIPE
- COUNTS AS:
  3 VEGETABLES
  1 CONDIMENT

good source of fiber

☀ Ingredients

3 green onions, chopped

1/2 medium carrot, chopped

1/2 celery stalk

2 garlic cloves, minced

1/2 cup (125mL) green cabbage, shredded

1/2 cup (125mL) zucchini, sliced

1/2 tsp (2mL) dried basil, crushed

1/2 tsp (2mL) thyme

freshly ground pepper, to taste

1 small tomato, diced

2 cups (500mL) very low-sodium chicken broth

nonfat cooking spray

1 Coat a medium saucepan with nonfat cooking spray. Add onion, carrot, celery and garlic.

2 Cook, stirring occasionally, over medium heat for 15-20 minutes, or until carrots begin to soften.

3 Stir in cabbage, zucchini, basil, thyme and pepper. Cook for 5-10 minutes longer, or until cabbage is tender.

4 Stir in tomato and broth. Bring to a boil. Reduce heat; cover and simmer for another 10 minutes, to allow flavors to meld.

5 Serve immediately.

Chicken Caldo

1 *serving*

- SERVING SIZE: 1 RECIPE
- COUNTS AS:
  1 PROTEIN
  2 VEGETABLES

☀ Ingredients

5oz (150g) boneless, skinless chicken breast

freshly ground pepper, to taste

3 green onions, chopped

1 garlic clove, minced

2 cups (500mL) water

1/2 large celery stalk, sliced

1/2 medium carrot, sliced

1/2 cup (125mL) zucchini, sliced

1/2 cup (125mL) cabbage, chopped

1/4 tsp (1mL) lite salt

1 Rinse chicken and pat dry. Cut into bite size pieces. Season with pepper, to taste.

2 Place chicken, onion and garlic in a medium saucepan.

3 Cover with water; bring to a boil.

4 Reduce heat; simmer for 30 minutes, or until chicken is tender.

5 Add remaining ingredients; simmer for another 20 minutes, or until vegetables are soft.

6 Serve immediately or refrigerate up to 24 hours.

Savory
Soups&
❖ Salads

1 *serving*

- SERVING SIZE: 1 RECIPE
- COUNTS AS:
  2 VEGETABLES

meals in minutes

Spinach Soup

☀ Ingredients

2 cups (500mL) very low-
sodium chicken bouillon

1/4 tsp (1mL) garlic powder

1 1/2 cup (375mL) fresh
spinach, coarsely chopped

1/2 cup (125mL) fresh
mushrooms, chopped

1 Tbsp (15mL) lemon juice

salt & pepper, to taste

1　In a medium saucepan combine chicken bouillon and
garlic powder. Bring to a boil.

2　Stir in spinach and mushrooms, allowing spinach to
wilt; return to boiling.

3　Reduce heat; cover and simmer for 2 minutes, or until
vegetables are tender. Stir in lemon juice.

4　Season to taste with salt and pepper.

Chicken & Lemongrass Soup

4 *servings*

- SERVING SIZE:
  1 CUP (250ML)
- COUNTS AS:
  1 PROTEIN
  1 VEGETABLE
  1 DAIRY
  1 FAT

☀ Ingredients

1 pound (450g) skinless chicken
breast filets

4 stalks lemongrass, tender inner
part only

1/2 tsp (2mL) fennel seeds,
lightly crushed

2 green onions, finely sliced

finely grated zest and juice of
1 lime

1 Tbsp (15mL) fish sauce

2-3 small fresh red or green
chilies, deseeded

3 cups (750mL) low-sodium
chicken broth

2 inch (5cm) piece fresh ginger,
peeled

1 Tbsp (15mL) fresh coriander

1 garlic clove

1 Tbsp (15mL) vegetable oil

1/2 cup (125mL) light coconut
milk

1 cup (250mL) evaporated skim
milk

freshly ground pepper, to taste

1　Cut the chicken crossways into thin slices. Place in a
non-metallic bowl.

2　Very finely slice one of the lemongrass stalks and scatter
over the chicken.

3　Add the zest and fish sauce; mix together. Marinate
chicken for 30-60 minutes.

4　Chop the remaining lemongrass and two chilies roughly
and put in a pan with the broth, half the ginger, sliced
and coriander stems (chop leaves and reserve).

5　Bring to boil, then simmer covered for 30 minutes.
Strain, reserving stock.

6　In a large sauce pan combine onion, fennel seeds, garlic
and remaining ginger, finely chopped. Cook until onion
is soft.

7　Add the strained stock and simmer for 10 minutes, then
add the coconut milk and evaporated milk.

8　When the mixture comes back to a simmer, add the
chicken with all its marinade and half the chopped
coriander leaves.

9　Simmer gently for 6-7 minutes until chicken is cooked
thoroughly.

10　Add the lime juice, season with pepper to taste.

11　Sprinkle with the rest of the coriander
and the third chili, finely sliced if desired.

Savory
Soups&
✤ Salads

Waldorf Salad

4 *servings*

- **SERVING SIZE:**
  1/4 OF RECIPE
- **COUNTS AS:**
  1 VEGETABLE
  1 FRUIT
  2 FATS

☀ Ingredients

1/4 cup (50mL) lite mayonnaise

1/4 cup (50mL) plain nonfat yogurt

1/2 tsp (2mL) sugar substitute

3 tart apples, peeled, cored and chopped

1 Tbsp (15mL) lemon juice

1 cup (250mL) seedless grapes, sliced in half

2 celery stalks, chopped

1/4 cup (50mL) chopped walnuts, toasted

1 head of iceberg lettuce, quartered

1. In a small bowl, whisk together mayonnaise, yogurt and sugar substitute to make dressing. Set aside.

2. In a large bowl, toss apples with lemon juice. Add grapes, celery, and walnuts.

3. Add dressing to apple mixture; toss to coat. Cover and refrigerate for 1 hour.

4. To serve, arrange one quarter of lettuce in a shallow bowl or plate. Divide salad evenly among plates.

Spicy Shrimp Salad

4 *servings*

- **SERVING SIZE:**
  1/4 OF RECIPE
- **COUNTS AS:**
  1 PROTEIN
  2 VEGETABLES

meals in minutes

☀ Ingredients

1 1/2 pounds (675g) small shrimp, peeled and deveined

1/4 cup (50mL) finely chopped celery

1/4 cup (50mL) finely chopped green onion

1/4 cup (50mL) whole grain mustard

1 Tbsp (15mL) fresh chopped parsley

4 tsp (20mL) olive oil

1 Tbsp (15mL) cider vinegar

2 tsp (10mL) hot sauce

8 cups (2L) salad greens (2 cups (500mL) per salad)

1. Place shrimp and enough water to cover in a 2-quart (2L) saucepan over high heat and bring to boil.

2. Boil 2 minutes until shrimp are tender.

3. Drain well and set aside to cool.

4. Combine celery, green onions, mustard, parsley, olive oil, cider vinegar and hot sauce in a bowl; toss with shrimp.

5. To serve, arrange on salad greens (2 cups) (500mL) of choice.

Savory
Soups &
✤ Salads

Sweet & Sour Cabbage

1 *serving*

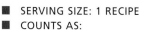

meals in minutes

- SERVING SIZE: 1 RECIPE
- COUNTS AS:
  1/2 PROTEIN
  2 VEGETABLES

☀ Ingredients

1 egg, beaten

1/2 packet of sugar substitute

1/4 cup (50mL) rice or red wine vinegar

2 Tbsp (30mL) water

1/4 tsp (1mL) lite salt

1/4 tsp (1mL) dry mustard

1 cup (250mL) cabbage, shredded

1/2 green pepper, chopped

freshly ground pepper, to taste

1. Beat egg in a small bowl until thick and lemon colored.

2. In a saucepan, heat sugar substitute, vinegar, water, salt and dry mustard to boiling, stirring constantly.

3. Temper by gradually stirring at least half of the hot mixture into the egg. Stir and pour back into the hot vinegar mixture.

4. Cook over low heat, stirring constantly, until slightly thickened.

5. Pour over cabbage and green pepper; toss to coat. Season with pepper

---

Vegetable Pasta Salad

1 *serving*

- SERVING SIZE: 1 RECIPE
- COUNTS AS:
  1 STARCH
  2 VEGETABLES
  1 FAT

☀ Ingredients

1 cup (250mL) zucchini or yellow summer squash, sliced

1/2 medium green pepper, chopped

1 garlic clove, minced

1/3 cup (75mL) cooked pasta, such as macaroni

2 Tbsp (30mL) white wine vinegar

1/4 tsp (1mL) dried dill

1/8 tsp (.5mL) lite salt

freshly ground pepper, to taste

1 small tomato, chopped

1 tsp (5mL) olive oil

1 Tbsp (15mL) grated parmesan

nonfat cooking spray

1. In a large skillet, coated with nonfat cooking spray, sauté squash, green pepper and garlic over medium heat until crisp-tender.

2. Add pasta, vinegar, dill, salt and pepper to vegetable mixture; toss to combine. Top with chopped tomato.

3. Sprinkle with parmesan cheese and mix with olive oil.

4. Refrigerate for 1 hour before serving.

Savory
Soups &
❖ Salads

Stir-Fried Chicken Salad

1 *serving*

- **SERVING SIZE: 1 RECIPE**
- **COUNTS AS:**
  1 PROTEIN
  3 VEGETABLES
  1 CONDIMENT

good source of fiber

☀ Ingredients

5oz (150g) raw chicken breast sliced thin

3 Tbsp (45mL) white wine vinegar

2 tsp (10mL) Dijon mustard

1/2 packet sugar substitute

2 tsp (10mL) lite soy sauce

1/8 tsp (.5mL) paprika

1/8 tsp (.5mL) freshly ground pepper

1 1/2 cups (375mL) fresh spinach

1 small tomato, chopped

1/4 medium carrot, shredded

nonfat cooking spray

1. Place chicken in a large zip top plastic bag.
2. In a small bowl, mix together vinegar, mustard, sugar substitute, soy sauce, paprika and pepper. Pour over chicken and close bag. Marinate chicken in refrigerator for 2-5 hours, turning bag frequently.
3. In a large bowl, combine spinach, tomato and carrot. Set aside.
4. Coat skillet or wok with nonfat cooking spray. Heat over medium flame.
5. Drain chicken, reserving marinade.
6. Stir-fry chicken for 2-3 minutes or until no longer pink. Add marinade and heat until boiling.
7. Place spinach mixture on dinner plate. Pour hot chicken mixture over salad.
8. Serve immediately.

Spaghetti Squash Salad

6 *servings*

- **SERVING SIZE:**
  1/6 OF RECIPE
- **COUNTS AS:**
  1 VEGETABLE
  1 STARCH
  1 FAT

☀ Ingredients

3 pounds (1.3kg) spaghetti squash

1/4 cup (50mL) parsley, chopped

2 Tbsp (30mL) olive oil

2 garlic cloves, minced

1/2 pound (225g) fresh mushrooms, sliced

nonfat cooking spray

1. With a knife, pierce the skin of the squash in several places, to allow steam to escape while cooking.
2. Place whole squash in the microwave and cook on high for 15 minutes, turning twice.
3. Remove from microwave, let stand for 10 minutes.
4. In a small bowl, mix parsley, olive oil and garlic, set aside.
5. Sauté mushrooms in a nonstick skillet coated with nonfat cooking spray.
6. Cut squash in half lengthwise and remove seeds with a spoon.
7. With a fork, gently pull spaghetti-like flesh away from the sides of the skin.
8. Combine squash with mushrooms. Toss to combine.
9. Pour oil mixture over; stir and serve warm or chilled.

Savory Soups & ❖ Salads

Mediterranean Tuna Salad

1 *serving*

- SERVING SIZE: 1 RECIPE
- COUNTS AS:
  - 1 PROTEIN
  - 1 VEGETABLE
  - 1 FAT

❋ Ingredients

4oz (120g) canned tuna, drained

2 tsp (10mL) lite mayonnaise

dash of lite salt

freshly ground pepper, to taste

1 Tbsp (15mL) diced red onion

1 Tbsp (15mL) diced red peppers

1 Tbsp (15mL) shredded carrot

1 celery stalk, sliced finely

3 black olives, diced

1 Combine all ingredients; mix well.

2 Cover and refrigerate at least 1 hour. Serve chilled.

Hot & Sour Salad

8 *servings*

- SERVING SIZE:
  1/2 CUP (125ML)
- COUNTS AS:
  - 1 VEGETABLE
  - 1 CONDIMENT

family fare

❋ Ingredients

3 cups (750mL) shredded bok choy

1/2 carrot, shredded

1 large red pepper, thinly sliced

5 green onions, sliced

1/4 cup (50mL) sliced mushrooms

1/2 tsp (2mL) red pepper flakes

2 garlic cloves, sliced

1 Tbsp (15mL) ginger, minced

2 tsp lite soy sauce

1 tsp (5mL) olive oil

1 packet sugar substitute or to taste

2/3 cup (150mL) rice wine vinegar

1 tsp (5mL) Dijon mustard

1 Combine bok choy, carrot, mushrooms, pepper and onion in large bowl.

2 Whisk together remaining ingredients in small bowl.

3 Pour vinegar mixture over vegetables.

4 Refrigerate 1-2 hours.

5 Mix well before serving.

Savory
Soups&
❖ Salads

Crab Salad

1 *serving*

- SERVING SIZE: 1 RECIPE
- COUNTS AS:
  1 PROTEIN
  1 VEGETABLE

✳ Ingredients

4oz (120g) crab meat, cooked

1/2 tsp (2mL) parsley

1/2 tsp (2mL) chives

1 tsp (5mL) fresh lemon juice

1/4 cucumber, peeled and diced

freshly ground pepper, to taste

1 Toss together all ingredients in a medium bowl.

2 Cover and refrigerate at least 1 hour. Serve chilled.

Glazed Chicken & Avocado Salad

5 *servings*

- SERVING SIZE: 1/4 OF RECIPE
- COUNTS AS:
  1 PROTEIN
  3 VEGETABLES
  1 FRUIT
  1 FAT
  1 CONDIMENT

✳ Ingredients

1/2 cup (125mL) sugar-free apricot preserves

1/4 cup (50mL) water

1/2 cup (125mL) red wine

1 cup (250mL) fresh squeezed orange juice

1 tsp (5mL) wasabi paste

1 1/2 pounds (675g) chicken breast, boneless and skinless, sliced into strips

1 large tomato, diced

1/4 cup (50mL) red onion, diced

2 Tbsp (30mL) fresh cilantro

juice of 2 limes

1 avocado, peeled, pitted and diced

8 cups (2L) salad greens

hot sauce, to taste (optional)

nonfat cooking spray

1 Preheat oven to 400°F (200°C).

2 In a large Dutch oven, heat apricot preserves and water together over medium high heat, stirring occasionally.

3 Remove from heat and slowly add the wine.

4 Return to heat and stir until all particles dissolve.

5 Add orange juice and wasabi paste; cook, stirring occasionally, until well combined.

6 Brush chicken strips with the glaze. Place on a baking sheet coated with nonfat cooking spray.

7 Bake until thoroughly cooked, about 20 minutes.

8 While the chicken is cooking, toss together the tomatoes, red onion, cilantro, lime juice, avocado and hot sauce (optional).

9 Arrange 2 cups (500mL) salad greens on 4 salad plates.

10 Top with 1/4 of the vegetable mixture and chicken strips; serve.

Savory
Soups &
✤ Salads

Rainbow Salad

 4 *servings*

- **SERVING SIZE:**
  1 CUP (250ML)
- **COUNTS AS:**
  2 VEGETABLE

 *good source of fiber*

☀ Ingredients

1 pound (450g) fresh spinach

1/2 yellow pepper, diced

1/2 red pepper, diced

1/2 cup (125mL) fresh broccoli florets

1/2 red onion, diced

1 yellow summer squash, diced

10 cherry tomatoes

1 carrot, shredded

1/2 cup (125mL) fresh mushrooms, sliced

1 Place spinach in a large bowl.

2 Top with peppers, broccoli, onion, yellow summer squash, tomatoes, carrots and mushrooms.

3 Serve chilled with your choice of fat-free dressings.

Cheesy Taco Salad

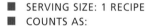 **1** *serving*

- **SERVING SIZE: 1 RECIPE**
- **COUNTS AS:**
  1 PROTEIN
  2 VEGETABLES
  1 STARCH
  1/2 DAIRY

 good source of calcium

☀ Ingredients

5 or 7oz (150 or 200g) fresh ground turkey breast

1/4 tsp (1mL) garlic powder

1/4 tsp (1mL) chili powder

1/4 tsp (1mL) lite salt

1 cup (250mL) lettuce, shredded

1 small tomato, chopped

1oz (30g) reduced-fat cheddar cheese

1 bag L A Cheese Curls

2 Tbsp (30mL) salsa

1 Cook turkey in medium sauté pan; add garlic powder, chili powder and salt to flavor.

2 Drain any excess oil or fat from turkey.

3 Assemble lettuce on plate.

4 Top lettuce with meat, tomatoes and cheese.

5 Top with L A Cheese Curls.

6 Garnish with salsa.

Savory
Soups&
❖ Salads

Garlic Tomato Salad

serving

- **SERVING SIZE: 1 RECIPE**
- **COUNTS AS:**
  - 1 VEGETABLE
  - 2 CONDIMENTS

☼ Ingredients

1 medium tomato, cut into 1-inch (2.5cm) slices

2 Tbsp (30mL) fat-free Italian salad dressing

2 Tbsp (30mL) red wine vinegar

1/8 tsp (.5mL) lite salt

dash hot pepper sauce

2 large garlic cloves, finely chopped

1 cup (250mL) salad greens, torn into bite size pieces

1 Place tomato slices in glass dish.

2 Combine dressing, vinegar, salt, pepper sauce and garlic in covered container or jar and shake, vigorously, to mix.

3 Pour mixture over tomato slices.

4 Refrigerate for 1 hour before serving.

5 Serve on a bed of salad greens.

Cucumber & Shrimp Salad

serving

- **SERVING SIZE: 1 RECIPE**
- **COUNTS AS:**
  - 1/2 PROTEIN
  - 2 VEGETABLES

☼ Ingredients

1/4 cup (50mL) vinegar

1/2 packet sugar substitute

1 tsp (5mL) low-sodium soy sauce

1/4 tsp (1mL) lite salt

2oz (60g) cooked shrimp

1/4 medium cucumber, thinly sliced

3 cups (750g) lettuce or salad greens torn into bite-size pieces

1/2 Tbsp (7.5mL) sesame seeds, toasted

1 Mix vinegar, sugar substitute, soy sauce and salt in a medium bowl.

2 Add shrimp and cucumbers; toss. Cover and refrigerate at least 1 hour.

3 Line salad plate with lettuce or salad greens.

4 Remove shrimp with slotted spoon; place on top of salad greens. Sprinkle with sesame seeds.

Savory Soups & ♣ Salads

Fruited Chicken Salad

1 *serving*

- **SERVING SIZE: 1 RECIPE**
- **COUNTS AS:**
  - 1 PROTEIN
  - 1 VEGETABLE
  - 1 FRUIT
  - 1 FAT

※ Ingredients

5oz (150g) chicken, cooked and cut into bite-size pieces

1 Tbsp (15mL) lite mayonnaise

1/2 Tbsp (7.5mL) lemon juice

1 celery stalk, thinly sliced

17 green grapes, cut in half

dash lite salt

freshly ground pepper, to taste

1/8 tsp (.5mL) dried onion flakes

1 Combine all ingredients in a large bowl; toss to mix well.

2 Cover and refrigerate at least 1 hour. Serve chilled.

Oriental-Style Shrimp Salad

family fare

4 *servings*

- **SERVING SIZE:**
  1/4 OF RECIPE
- **COUNTS AS:**
  - 1 PROTEIN
  - 1 STARCH
  - 3 VEGETABLES

※ Ingredients

1 pound (480g) large shrimp, peeled and deveined

1 garlic clove, minced

1-inch (2.5cm) piece of ginger, peeled and minced

4 Tbsp (60mL) low-sodium soy sauce, divided

6oz (180g) uncooked capellini/angel hair pasta

10oz (285g) baby spinach

1 cup (250mL) mung bean sprouts, cooked and drained

1/4 cup (50mL) mint leaves, firmLy packed

5 medium scallions, chopped

2 baby carrots, shredded

juice from 1 lime

1 Toss shrimp with garlic, ginger and 2 Tbsp (30mL) low-sodium soy sauce.

2 Cover; refrigerate and marinate for at least 30 minutes.

3 Meanwhile, cook pasta according to package directions.

4 Toss pasta with spinach, mung beans, mint, scallions and carrots.

5 Mix together lime juice and 2 Tbsp (30mL) of low-sodium soy sauce and pour over the salad.

6 Allow to sit for 15 minutes while the shrimp is cooking.

7 Grill shrimp, or sauté, in a nonstick pan.

8 Allow shrimp to cool, and then toss with the salad.

Savory
Soups &
❖ Salads

Grilled Chicken Cobb Salad

4 *servings*

- **SERVING SIZE:**
  1/4 OF RECIPE
- **COUNTS AS:**
  1 PROTEIN
  2 VEGETABLES
  1 FAT

☀ Ingredients

3 Tbsp (45mL) lemon seasoning
(see recipe on page 218)

20oz (600g) chicken breast,
boneless and skinless

6 cups (1.5L) salad greens of your
choice, torn

2oz (60g) lite feta cheese,
shredded

2 large, hard-boiled eggs, sliced

1 large tomato, chopped

2 pieces low-sodium turkey
bacon, cooked and drained,
chopped

1. Preheat grill to medium high.

2. Put lemon seasoning on a plate. Coat chicken thoroughly in seasoning.

3. Cook on grill 5 minutes; turn and cook for another 5 minutes, or until juices run clear when a fork is inserted.

4. Remove from grill; cool and cut into chunks or strips. Set aside.

5. Onto each of four salad plates, arrange salad greens. Top greens with chicken, cheese, eggs, chopped tomato and bacon. Drizzle with your favorite fat-free salad dressing.

Eggplant & Pepper Salad

6 *servings*

- **SERVING SIZE:**
  1/6 OF RECIPE
- **COUNTS AS:**
  2 VEGETABLES
  2 FATS

☀ Ingredients

4 cups (900g) eggplant,
unpeeled, large dice

2 red bell peppers

2 cloves garlic, sliced

4 Tbsp (60mL) parsley,
roughly chopped

1 tsp (5mL) dried oregano

4 leaves fresh basil,
chiffonade

2oz (60g) olive oil

3 Tbsp (45mL) lemon juice

salt and pepper, to taste

1. Toss the eggplant in half of the olive oil and roast in a 400-degree convection oven on a sheet pan lined with parchment for 15 minutes. Allow to cool.

2. Roast the peppers over an open flame until charred on all sides. Place the peppers into a plastic bag for 10 minutes to allow it to steam. Remove the peppers from the bag. Peel and seed the peppers and slice into julienne.

3. Combine the eggplant, peppers and remaining ingredients in a bowl. Toss lightly and allow to marinate for one hour before serving.

"The recipes from the L A Lite Cookbook take food items right from my menu plan!"

- Lynn K.

Savory
Soups &
❖ Salads

Sirloin Caesar Salad

1 *serving*

- SERVING SIZE: 1 RECIPE
- COUNTS AS:
  1 PROTEIN
  2 VEGETABLES
  1 STARCH
  1 CONDIMENT

meals in minutes

☀ Ingredients

4oz (120g) sirloin steak

3 tsp (15mL) parmesan cheese

2 green onions, chopped

2 Tbsp (30mL) fat-free Caesar salad dressing, divided

2 cups (500mL) romaine lettuce

12 fat-free croutons

nonfat cooking spray

1 Combine 1 Tbsp (15mL) Caesar dressing, 1 tsp (5mL) parmesan cheese and onions in medium bowl.

2 Cut beef into strips and place in bowl with marinade; toss to coat.

3 Coat skillet with nonfat cooking spray and heat over medium flame. Remove beef from marinade and place in skillet; discard marinade.

4 Sauté 5-6 minutes, or until beef is cooked to your liking.

5 Place lettuce on a serving plate. Top with beef, remaining dressing, parmesan and croutons.

Blackened Portabella Salad

4 *servings*

- SERVING SIZE:
  1/4 OF RECIPE
- COUNTS AS:
  3 VEGETABLES

family fare

☀ Ingredients

1/4 cup (50mL) red wine vinegar

1/4 cup (50mL) balsamic vinegar

1/4 cup (50mL) low-sodium tomato juice

2 tsp (10mL) Dijon mustard

2 tsp (10mL) whole grain mustard

1/4 tsp (1mL) freshly ground pepper

4 whole portabella mushrooms

1 Tbsp (15mL) cajun spice seasoning (see recipe on page 215)

8 cups (2L) romaine lettuce

1 tomato, cut into 8 wedges

1/2 cup (125mL) red onion, thinly sliced

1 Combine the first 6 ingredients in a large zip-top plastic bag.

2 Add mushrooms to bag; seal. Marinate 10 minutes, turning occasionally.

3 Remove mushrooms from bag, reserving marinade.

4 Season mushrooms with Cajun spice.

5 Over medium-high heat, grill mushrooms for 2 minutes on each side, or until tender and browned.

6 Cool; cut diagonally into thin slices.

7 Arrange 2 cups (500mL) romaine on each of 4 salad plates. Top with mushroom slices, 2 tomato wedges and onions.

8 Drizzle with the reserved marinade or use fat-free dressing of your choice.

Savory
Soups &
♣ Salads

Carrot Salad

1 *serving*

- **SERVING SIZE: 1 RECIPE**
- **COUNTS AS:**
  1 VEGETABLE
  1 FRUIT

good source of fiber

☀ Ingredients

1/2 medium carrot, shredded

1 celery stalk, thinly sliced

1 tsp (5mL) lemon zest

1 tsp (5mL) lemon juice

1/2 tsp (2mL) brown sugar substitute

2 Tbsp (30mL) raisins

dash of ground ginger

1 Mix all ingredients together in small bowl.

2 Cover and chill for at least 1 hour before serving.

"So many recipes in the cookbook I can choose something new every day."

- Amanda P.

Chicken Broccoli Pasta Salad

6 *servings*

- **SERVING SIZE:
  1/6 OF RECIPE**
- **COUNTS AS:**
  1 PROTEIN
  1 VEGETABLE
  1 STARCH
  1 FAT

☀ Ingredients

1/4 cup (50mL) lemon seasoning (see recipe on page 218), divided

8oz (225g) dry penne pasta (or pasta of choice)

2 pounds (900g) boneless chicken breast, cut into bite size pieces

2 Tbsp (30mL) olive oil

2 cups (500mL) broccoli florets

1/4 cup (50mL) very low-sodium chicken broth

3 Tbsp (45mL) parmesan cheese

5 green onions, chopped

1 cup (250mL) cherry tomatoes, halved

1 Add half of lemon seasoning to a large pot of boiling water; add pasta and cook according to package directions. Drain; set aside.

2 While pasta is cooking, heat 1 Tbsp (15mL) olive oil in a large skillet. Sauté the chicken, about 6-8 minutes per side, over medium heat.

3 Add broth, broccoli, and remaining lemon seasoning to the chicken; cover and cook for 3-5 minutes.

4 Toss pasta in a large bowl with remaining olive oil and parmesan cheese. Add chicken and broccoli, onions and toss again.

5 Chill at least 1 hour.

6 Divide among 6 plates. Garnish with cherry tomatoes.

Savory
Soups &
❖ Salads

Sweet Potato Salad

6 *servings*

- **SERVING SIZE:**
  1/2 CUP (125ML)
- **COUNTS AS:**
  1 STARCH
  1 VEGETABLE

✷ Ingredients

6 sweet potatoes, boiled, peeled and cubed

1/2 cup (125mL) chopped red pepper

1/4 cup (50mL) chopped onion

1/2 tsp (2mL) lite salt

1/4 tsp (1mL) freshly ground pepper

1/3 cup (75mL) lite mayonnaise

1/4 tsp (1mL) hot pepper sauce

1/2 tsp (2mL) paprika

1 In large bowl, combine onion, pepper and potatoes.

2 Gently fold in remaining ingredients.

3 Chill 1-2 hours before serving.

"This cookbook is fantastic. It puts variety into my meals, and at the same time helps me stick to my menu plan."

- Karen D.

Asparagus Salad

1 *serving*

- **SERVING SIZE: 1 RECIPE**
- **COUNTS AS:**
  1/2 PROTEIN
  1 VEGETABLE
  1/2 DAIRY
  2 CONDIMENTS

✷ Ingredients

4oz (125mL) nonfat plain yogurt

2 Tbsp (30mL) fat-free French dressing

1/2 cup (125mL) cooked asparagus spears, chilled

1 hard cooked egg, sliced

1 cup (250mL) salad greens, torn into bite-size pieces

1 Mix nonfat yogurt and French dressing in a small bowl.

2 Cover and refrigerate at least 1 hour.

3 Arrange chilled asparagus on salad greens; top with egg slices.

4 Spoon dressing over top.

Savory
Soups&
❖Salads

Strawberry & Melon Salad

4 *servings*

- **SERVING SIZE: 1 CUP (250ML)**
- **COUNTS AS:**
  1 VEGETABLE
  1 FRUIT
  1 FAT

☀ Ingredients

1/4 cup (50mL) freshly squeezed orange juice

1 Tbsp (15mL) olive oil

2 Tbsp (30mL) water

12oz (340g) salad greens, of your choice

1 cup (250mL) honeydew, cubed

1 cup (250mL) cantaloupe, cubed

1 cup (250mL) watermelon, cubed

1 cup (250mL) strawberries, sliced

3 Tbsp (45mL) sunflower seeds, unsalted

1 Mix juice, oil and water until blended.

2 Place salad greens, melon cubes and strawberry slices in a large bowl; toss.

3 Pour dressing over salad and sprinkle with sunflower seeds.

> "The L A Lite Cookbook recipes are so easy to follow, my boyfriend has meals made and ready to eat when I get home from work."
>
> *- Rachel P.*

Tomato Basil & Mozzarella Salad

1 *serving*

- **SERVING SIZE: 1 RECIPE**
- **COUNTS AS:**
  1 VEGETABLE
  1 FAT
  1 DAIRY

meals in minutes

☀ Ingredients

1 very ripe, small tomato

2oz (60g) lite or reduced-fat mozzarella cheese, shredded or sliced

4 basil leaves, fresh

1 tsp (5mL) olive oil

1 tsp (5mL) balsamic vinegar

freshly ground pepper, to taste

1 Cut tomato into 4 thick slices.

2 Arrange slices on a salad plate. Top tomato slices with mozzarella.

3 Thinly slice basil; sprinkle over tomato and cheese.

4 Drizzle with oil and vinegar and a dash of freshly ground pepper.

Savory
Soups &
♣ Salads

Ginger Apple Slaw

4 servings

- **SERVING SIZE:**
  1/4 CUP (50ML)
- **COUNTS AS:**
  1 FRUIT
  1 VEGETABLE
  1 FAT

good source of calcium

☀ Ingredients

1 small head napa cabbage

1 Red Delicious apple, peeled, cored and thinly sliced

1 Granny Smith apple, peeled, cored and thinly sliced

1/4 cup (50mL) carrot, shredded

1 tsp (5mL) fresh ginger, grated

2 Tbsp (30mL) parsley, rough chopped

1/3 cup (75mL) natural apple juice concentrate

1/3 cup (75mL) apple cider vinegar

2 Tbsp (30mL) canola oil

1/2 packet sugar substitute

1 tsp (5mL) lite salt

freshly ground pepper, to taste

1. Quarter the Napa cabbage, removing the core. Slice finely.

2. Place the cabbage, apples and carrot into a bowl. Add the ginger and parsley.

3. In a separate bowl, combine the apple juice, vinegar, oil, sugar substitute, salt and pepper, whisking vigorously. Pour the dressing over the cabbage mixture, mixing well. Allow to marinate for 1 hour before serving, tossing occasionally to meld the flavors.

Citrus Salad

6 servings

- **SERVING SIZE:**
  1-1/2 CUPS (375ML)
- **COUNTS AS:**
  1 VEGETABLE
  1 FRUIT
  2 FATS

☀ Ingredients

1/4 cup (50mL) red wine vinegar

1 tsp (5mL) Dijon mustard

1 tsp (5mL) fennel seeds, crushed and toasted

1/3 cup (75mL) olive oil

pinch sugar substitute

freshly ground pepper, to taste

1 ruby red grapefruit, segmented

1 blood orange, segmented

1/2 head radicchio, torn into bite-size pieces

6 cups (1.5L) baby spinach leaves

3 leaves of endive, shredded

1. Combine vinegar, mustard and fennel seeds in a medium bowl.

2. Gradually whisk in oil; add sugar substitute.

3. Season with pepper.

4. Add grapefruit segments and orange segments into the dressing and toss. Let stand about 15 minutes.

5. Toss radicchio, spinach and endive in a bowl.

6. Add greens to dressing. Toss before serving.

Savory
Soups&
❖Salads

Dilled Pasta Salad

1 *serving*

- SERVING SIZE: 1 RECIPE
- COUNTS AS:
  - 1 STARCH
  - 1 FAT
  - 1 VEGETABLE

☀ Ingredients

1/2 Tbsp (7.5mL) snipped fresh dill or 1/4 tsp (1mL) dried dill

1/4 tsp (1mL) lite salt

1/4 tsp (1mL) dry mustard

freshly ground pepper, to taste

1 Tbsp (15mL) lite mayonnaise

1/3 cup (75mL) cooked rotini pasta

1/4 cucumber, diced

1/4 medium carrot, shredded

2 green onions, diced

1 Tbsp (15mL) vinegar

1 Mix together all ingredients in a large bowl.

2 Cover and refrigerate at least 2 hours before serving.

"The L A Lite Cookbook recipes are so simple to make and so good to eat."

- Lynn K.

Cucumber & Tomato Salad

1 *serving*

- SERVING SIZE: 1 RECIPE
- COUNTS AS:
  - 3 VEGETABLES
  - 1/2 DAIRY

☀ Ingredients

1/4 medium cucumber

5 green onions, thinly sliced

1 tomato, chopped

1/4 tsp (1mL) lite salt

1/2 Tbsp (7.5mL) snipped parsley

1/8 tsp (.5mL) ground cumin

freshly ground pepper, to taste

1 garlic clove, finely chopped

1/2 cup (125mL) nonfat plain yogurt

1 Cut cucumbers in half, lengthwise. Scoop seeds from cucumber with a spoon, then chop into bite-size pieces.

2 Mix cucumber, green onion and salt. Let stand 10 minutes.

3 Add tomatoes, parsley, cumin, lite salt, pepper and garlic to cucumbers.

4 Cover and refrigerate 1 hour.

5 Just before serving, drain vegetables thoroughly in a colander or sieve. Add yogurt; mix well to combine.

Savory Soups & ❖ Salads

Sesame Ginger Chicken Salad

1 *serving*

■ SERVING SIZE: 1 RECIPE
■ COUNTS AS:
  1 PROTEIN
  3 VEGETABLES
  1 FRUIT

☀ Ingredients

1 cup (250mL) lettuce, shredded

5oz (150g) chicken, cooked and cut into bite-size pieces

1/2 medium carrot, shredded

5 green onions with tops, sliced

1/2 cup (125mL) mandarin oranges, drained

1 Tbsp (15mL) toasted sesame seeds

Ginger Dressing:

1/4 cup (50mL) white wine vinegar

1/2 to 1 packet sugar substitute

2 tsp (10mL) low-sodium soy sauce

1/4 tsp (1mL) lite salt

freshly ground pepper, to taste

1/4 tsp (1mL) ground ginger

1 Prepare dressing first. Combine vinegar, sugar substitute, soy sauce, salt, pepper and ginger. Shake all ingredients in covered container or jar. Refrigerate.

2 Toss together lettuce, chicken, carrot, green onion and ginger dressing.

3 Place mixture on plate and top with oranges. Sprinkle with sesame seeds.

May be served over brown rice. (Optional-please refer to the menu plan for serving and exchanges).

Tomato Pasta Salad

1 *serving*

■ SERVING SIZE: 1 RECIPE
■ COUNTS AS:
  1 STARCH
  1 VEGETABLE

☀ Ingredients

1 small tomato, chopped

1 garlic clove, finely chopped

1 Tbsp (15mL) snipped parsley

2 Tbsp (30mL) fat-free Italian dressing

1/4 tsp (1mL) dried basil leaves

1 tsp (5mL) parmesan cheese

1/3 cup (75mL) cooked pasta shells

1 Mix tomato, garlic, parsley, Italian dressing and basil.

2 Toss pasta shells with tomato mixture. Top with parmesan cheese.

3 Cover and refrigerate at least 2 hours.

Savory
Soups&
❖ Salads

Cantaloupe with Chicken Salad

1 *serving*

- SERVING SIZE: 1 RECIPE
- COUNTS AS:
  - 1 PROTEIN
  - 2 FRUITS
  - 1 FAT

☀ Ingredients

4oz (120g) cooked chicken breast, cubed

1/4 cup (50mL) blueberries

10 grapes

1 celery stalk, sliced

1/8 cantaloupe, cubed

Dressing

1 Tbsp (15mL) low-fat mayonnaise

1 Tbsp (15mL) fat-free sour cream

1/4 tsp (1mL) grated lemon peel

1 packet of sugar substitute

1. In a medium bowl, combine chicken, blueberries, celery and grapes.

2. In a small bowl, mix dressing ingredients whisking vigorously.

3. Pour dressing over chicken mixture and toss to coat.

4. Arrange cantaloupe on a serving plate or shallow bowl; top with chicken salad.

Spinach Tossed Salad

1 *serving*

- SERVING SIZE: 1 RECIPE
- COUNTS AS:
  - 1 STARCH
  - 2 VEGETABLES

good source of fiber

☀ Ingredients

1 cup (250mL) spinach leaves

1/2 cup (125mL) mushrooms, sliced

1 cup (250mL) bean sprouts

3 melba toast, crumbled

2 green onions, thinly sliced

freshly ground pepper, to taste

1. Tear spinach into small pieces. Toss all ingredients together.

2. Serve with freshly ground pepper and fat-free dressing of choice.

Savory
Soups&
❖ Salads

Coleslaw

1 *serving*

- SERVING SIZE: 1 RECIPE
- COUNTS AS:
  2 VEGETABLES
  1 FAT
  1/2 DAIRY

✳ Ingredients

4oz (120mL) nonfat plain yogurt

1 Tbsp (15mL) lite mayonnaise

1/2 packet sugar substitute

1/4 tsp (1mL) dry mustard

1/4 tsp (1mL) lite salt

freshly ground pepper, to taste

1 cup (250mL) cabbage, shredded

1/2 medium carrot, finely shredded

dash of paprika or dried dill

1. Mix yogurt, mayonnaise, sugar substitute, dry mustard, salt and pepper.
2. Toss with cabbage and carrot.
3. Sprinkle with paprika or dried dill.
4. Cover and refrigerate for 1-2 hours.

Grilled Chicken Caesar Salad

4 *servings*

- SERVING SIZE: 1/4 OF RECIPE
- COUNTS AS:
  1 PROTEIN
  2 VEGETABLES
  1 FAT

✳ Ingredients

Chicken

20oz (600g) chicken breasts, boneless and skinless

2 Tbsp (30mL) citrus rub (see recipe on page 224)

1 Tbsp (15mL) olive oil

Dressing

2 Tbsp (30mL) fresh lemon juice

1/2 tsp (2mL) freshly ground pepper

1/4 cup (50mL) lite mayonnaise

1 tsp (5mL) Worcestershire sauce

1 Tbsp (15mL) lemon seasoning (see recipe on page 218)

Salad

8 cups (2L) romaine lettuce, torn

1/4 cup (50mL) lite parmesan cheese, grated

1/2 cup (125mL) unseasoned fat-free croutons

1. Preheat grill or broiler to medium high.
2. Brush chicken on both sides with olive oil.
3. Season chicken with citrus rub, until well coated.
4. Grill for 5 minutes then turn and grill for 5 additional minutes or until juices run clear when pierced with a fork.
5. Remove from grill; cool and cut into strips; set aside.
6. For dressing, combine the lemon juice, mayonnaise, Worcestershire, pepper and lemon seasoning; prepare while chicken is cooking.
7. For the salad, place 2 cups (500mL) romaine on each of four salad plates. Divide chicken strips, evenly, among romaine; top with cheese, croutons and 2 Tbsp (30mL) of dressing.

♣ Shrimp or steak may be substituted for the chicken in this recipe.

Savory
Soups&
✤ Salads

Grilled Asparagus, Tomato & Carrot Salad

6 *servings*

family fare

- SERVING SIZE: 1 CUP (250ML)
- COUNTS AS:
  3 VEGETABLES
  1 FAT

❈ Ingredients

2 bunches asparagus

5 green onions

3 carrots, chopped into matchstick pieces

12 cherry tomatoes, halved

Marinade

1/4 cup (50mL) olive oil

1/4 cup (50mL) balsamic vinegar

freshly ground pepper, to taste

Vinaigrette

1/4 cup (50mL) olive oil

1/4 cup (50mL) vinegar

3 Tbsp (45mL) fat-free sour cream

1 Tbsp (15mL) chopped garlic

2 Tbsp (30mL) finely chopped savory

1/2 tsp (2mL) cumin

dash of low-sodium Worcestershire sauce

1 tsp (5mL) lime juice

freshly ground pepper, to taste

1. Snap the bottom section off asparagus stalks at their natural break point.

2. Chop the remaining asparagus into thirds.

3. Remove bottoms from green onions and place in a large mixing bowl with the asparagus pieces.

4. Add the marinade ingredients to mixing bowl and toss well.

5. Grill vegetable mixture lightly over medium high heat for 2-3 minutes, so they still have crunch.

6. Remove from the grill to cool and chop green onions into small pieces.

7. In a separate salad bowl, mix all ingredients of vinaigrette and whisk vigorously.

8. Add grilled asparagus and green onions.

9. Add carrot pieces and cherry tomatoes.

10. Mix gently by hand, tossing to coat, cover and refrigerate until serving.

Shrimp Salad

1 *serving*

- SERVING SIZE: 1 RECIPE
- COUNTS AS:
  1 PROTEIN
  1 FAT

❈ Ingredients

4oz (120g) cooked shrimp

1 Tbsp (15mL) lite mayonnaise

1/2 Tbsp (7.5mL) lemon juice

dash of lite salt

freshly ground pepper, to taste

1 celery stalk, finely sliced

1/2 tsp (2.5mL) dried onion flakes

1. Combine all ingredients; mix well.

2. Cover and refrigerate at least 1 hour.

3. Serve chilled.

Savory
Soups&
♣ Salads

Oriental Bean Salad

 1 *serving*

■ SERVING SIZE: 1 RECIPE
■ COUNTS AS:
   3 VEGETABLES
   1 FAT

good source of fiber

✳ Ingredients

1 Tbsp (15mL) lime or lemon juice

1/2 Tbsp (7.5mL) lite soy sauce

1/2 Tbsp (7.5mL) parsley

1/2 packet sugar substitute

dash of garlic powder

dash of crushed red pepper

1/2 cup (125mL) cooked wax beans

1/2 cup (125mL) cooked green beans

1/2 cup (125mL) fresh bean sprouts

1/4 medium red pepper, cut into 1/2-inch (1.3cm) pieces

1 Tbsp (15mL) toasted sesame seeds

1 In a mixing bowl, stir together lime or lemon juice, soy sauce, parsley, sugar substitute, garlic powder and crushed red pepper.

2 Add wax beans and green beans, bean sprouts and red pepper; toss to coat. Cover and refrigerate 1 hour.

3 Before serving, sprinkle with toasted sesame seeds.

Chicken Salad

 1 *serving*

■ SERVING SIZE: 1 RECIPE
■ COUNTS AS:
   1 PROTEIN
   1 FAT

✳ Ingredients

4oz (120g) cooked chicken and cut into bite-size pieces

1 Tbsp (15mL) lite mayonnaise

1 tsp (5mL) mustard

1 celery stalk, thinly sliced

freshly ground pepper, to taste

1/2 tsp (2mL) parsley

1/2 tsp (2mL) dried minced onion (optional)

1 Combine all ingredients. Cover and refrigerate, at least 1 hour.

2 Serve chilled.

Savory
Soups&
✤ Salads

Tuna Pasta Salad

- **SERVING SIZE: 1 RECIPE**
- **COUNTS AS:**
  1 PROTEIN
  1 STARCH
  1 VEGETABLE
  1 CONDIMENT

☀ Ingredients

4oz (120g) of canned tuna, drained
(choose low-sodium if available)

1 tomato, chopped

1/2 celery stalk, chopped

1 Tbsp (15mL) white onion, chopped

1/4 medium carrot, diced

1 garlic clove, crushed

1/4 tsp (1mL) dried onion flakes

1 Tbsp (15mL) snipped parsley

1/4 tsp (1mL) lite salt

1/4 tsp (1mL) dried basil leaves

1/8 tsp (.5mL) dried oregano leaves

freshly ground pepper, to taste

2 Tbsp (30mL) fat-free Italian
dressing

1/3 cup (75mL) cooked
pasta bows

1. Mix all ingredients, except pasta bows, in a large bowl.
2. Cover and refrigerate at least 1-2 hours.
3. Toss pasta with tuna mixture just before serving.

"I love leftovers, so I double up the recipe."

- Kirsten D.

Strawberry Spinach Salad

good source of fiber

- **SERVING SIZE:**
  1/3 OF RECIPE
- **COUNTS AS:**
  1 VEGETABLE
  1 FRUIT
  1 FAT

☀ Ingredients

8oz (225g) spinach leaves

1 cup (250mL) fresh
strawberries, sliced

1 kiwi, sliced

1 Tbsp (15mL) slivered almonds

Dressing

2 Tbsp (30mL) sugar-free
raspberry preserves

1 Tbsp (15mL) olive oil

1 Tbsp (15mL) rice vinegar

lite salt, to taste

1. Place salad ingredients in a large bowl.
2. For dressing, combine remaining ingredients in a small bowl; whisk vigorously.
3. Toss dressing with salad.

Savory
Soups &
❖ Salads

Fresh Vegetable Salad

 6 *servings*

- SERVING SIZE: 1 CUP (250ML)
- COUNTS AS:
  2 VEGETABLES

☀ Ingredients

1 red bell pepper, sliced

1 yellow pepper, sliced

1 green pepper, sliced

1 medium red onion, thinly sliced

1 head of broccoli, cut into bite-size pieces

1 head of cauliflower, cut into bite-size pieces

1 small zucchini, thinly sliced

1 medium carrot, shredded

Dressing

2 Tbsp (30mL) red wine vinegar

2 Tbsp (30mL) fresh lemon juice

dash of white pepper

1/4 tsp (1mL) dry mustard

1 Tbsp (15mL) olive oil

sprinkle with fresh herbs, such as tarragon, basil, chives, dill, oregano, basil or mint (optional)

1 Combine all vegetable ingredients in a large salad bowl.

2 For dressing, whisk together vinegar, lemon juice, pepper and dry mustard.

3 Slowly stream olive oil into bowl, whisking continuously, to emulsify the dressing.

4 Stir in the herbs just before adding to the salad (optional).

> "I still use this cookbook weekly even after completing and exceeding my goal. Thanks L A Weight Loss!"
>
> *- Michele G.*

Sweet & Sour Dressing

6 *servings*

- SERVING SIZE: 1 TBSP (15ML)
- COUNTS AS:
  1 CONDIMENT

☀ Ingredients

1 Tbsp (15mL) lemon juice

1 Tbsp (15mL) apple cider vinegar

1/3 cup (75mL) water

1 garlic clove, minced

1/4 tsp (1mL) lite salt

freshly ground pepper, to taste

1/2 packet sugar substitute

1 Combine all ingredients in a jar and shake to mix.

2 Store in the refrigerator for up to 1 week.

Savory
Soups&
❖ Salads

Lite Vinaigrette

8 *servings*

- **SERVING SIZE: 1 TBSP (15ML)**
- **COUNTS AS:**
  1 CONDIMENT

☀ Ingredients

1 packet sugar substitute

1/4 tsp (1mL) lite salt

2 garlic cloves, minced

1/8 tsp (.5mL) dry mustard

freshly ground pepper, to taste

1/4 cup (50mL) water

3 Tbsp (45mL) wine vinegar or
lemon juice

1 In a screw-top jar, combine sugar substitute, salt, garlic, dry mustard and pepper.

2 Add water and vinegar.

3 Cover tightly with lid and shake until well blended. Let stand 3-4 minutes. Shake again.

4 Store in the refrigerator for up to 1 week.

Chicken Salad with Orange Vinaigrette

1 *serving*

- **SERVING SIZE: 1 RECIPE**
- **COUNTS AS:**
  1 PROTEIN
  2 VEGETABLES
  1 FRUIT

☀ Ingredients

3 Tbsp (45mL) fat-free red wine
vinaigrette salad dressing

1 Tbsp (15mL) lemon pepper
seasoning blend

5oz (150g) chicken breast,
boneless and skinless

1 cup (250mL) romaine lettuce,
torn

1/2 cup (125mL) mandarin
oranges

1 cup (250mL) fresh mushroom
slices

1 Tbsp (15mL) chopped onion

1 Mix together dressing and lemon pepper seasoning blend, set aside.

2 Brush chicken with 1 Tbsp (15mL) of dressing mixture.

3 Grill chicken until done.

4 Cool slightly and then cut chicken into strips.

5 Place romaine lettuce on a large dinner plate, top with mandarin oranges, mushrooms, onion and chicken.

6 Drizzle dressing over the salad.

Savory
Soups &
❖ Salads

Poppy Seed Vinaigrette

 **16** *servings*

- **SERVING SIZE:** 1 TBSP (15ML)
- **COUNTS AS:**
  1 CONDIMENT

✳ Ingredients

1/2 cup (125mL) cold water

1/2 cup (125mL) cider vinegar

1 tsp (5mL) lemon juice

1/2 tsp (2mL) lite salt

1/2 tsp (2mL) freshly ground pepper

2 Tbsp (30mL) poppy seeds

1 packet sugar substitute

1 Combine all ingredients in a jar or container and shake well.

2 Store in the refrigerator for up to 1 week. Shake well before each use.

Yogurt-Dill Dressing

16 *servings*

- **SERVING SIZE:** 1 TBSP (15ML)
- **COUNTS AS:**
  1 CONDIMENT

✳ Ingredients

8oz (250mL) plain, nonfat yogurt

3 green onions, chopped fine

1 tsp (5mL) lemon juice

1/4 tsp (1mL) dry mustard

1/4 tsp (1mL) garlic powder

1/2 tsp (2mL) dried dill weed

1/2 tsp (2mL) lite salt

1 Mix all ingredients in a bowl; whisk thoroughly.

2 Store in the refrigerator for up to 1 week. Mix well before each use.

Savory
Soups&
❖ Salads

Appetite
♣ Delights

Appetizers are a family favorite! Appetizers can be a great combination with any soup or salad for a light meal or be a perfect choice for entertaining. We have lightened up some old favorites to use for any eating occasion. We have also provided a number of dips that can be a great complement to any vegetable snack. Enjoy!

◀ Tortilla Roll-Up recipe can be found on page 60

Let's get the party started!

Appetizers are the main ingredients to any get together or special occasion. Keep in mind you don't want to fill up before the main course, so appetizers should be simple, tasty…and of course, light. Here are some tips to remember when preparing and serving appetizers for your own gathering, or bringing a special dish to a special occasion.

■ Be sure not to offer excessive servings of appetizers. Appetizers are meant to tease the palate, not to replace a full-course meal.

■ Using colorful garnish such as a sprig of parsley or a lemon and lime wedge give that extra added festive touch on any tray of appetizers.

■ Try serving a medley of appetizers. Be sure that there is a little something for everyone – it doesn't need to be extravagant, perhaps roasted peppers for the veggie lovers and deviled eggs for those who are looking for a heartier snack.

■ When preparing a veggie platter, try to incorporate some unusual and interesting vegetables such as fresh brussel sprouts and sugar snap peas. The platter will look more interesting and appealing.

■ Spice up the dip by placing it in a brightly colored bowl. Get creative by hollowing out bread loaves, heads of cabbage or winter squash.

■ Guests should be able to eat appetizers without utensils. Most partygoers are busy mingling and would rather not think about cutting their food.

■ Keep the appetizer simple. Some guests may avoid food that looks messy to prevent the embarrassment of getting it all over their hands and faces.

♣ TIP!

If an appetizer needs to be cooled before serving, use shallow containers and leave air space around the containers to promote rapid cooling of the food.

♣ TIP!

When deciding how many appetizers to serve, estimate each guest will eat 5-6 pieces. If it's closer to mealtime, then assume they will eat 10-12 pieces. Younger guests tend to eat more and the older company will usually have less of an appetite.

Deviled Eggs

 2 *servings*

- **SERVING SIZE: 2 EGGS**
- **COUNTS AS:**
  1 PROTEIN
  1 FAT

❋ Ingredients

6 eggs, hard boiled

2 Tbsp (30mL) lite mayonnaise

dash onion powder

1 tsp (5mL) Dijon mustard, dry

1/2 tsp (2mL) paprika

1. Remove shells. Cut eggs in half, lengthwise.
2. Remove egg yolks and mash them with a fork in a small mixing bowl.
3. Add mayonnaise, onion powder and dry mustard to egg yolks.
4. Spoon mixture into egg whites. Sprinkle with paprika. Chill before serving.

Creamed Crab & Veggie Dip

 2 *servings*

good source of calcium

- **SERVING SIZE:
  1/2 OF RECIPE**
- **COUNTS AS:**
  1 PROTEIN
  1 DAIRY
  2 VEGETABLES
  1 FAT

❋ Ingredients

2oz (60g) part-skim ricotta cheese

1 Tbsp (15mL) low-fat mayonnaise

4oz (125mL) skim milk

2 cups (500mL) fresh chopped artichoke hearts

3 green onions, chopped

1/4 red pepper, chopped

1/4 tsp (1mL) garlic powder

2 garlic cloves, minced

1 cup (250mL) fresh raw spinach

1oz (30g) shredded reduced-fat cheese (recommend Monterey Jack or Mozzarella)

4oz (120g) fresh crabmeat

1/4 tsp (1mL) hot sauce

nonfat cooking spray

1. Preheat oven to 350°F (180°C).
2. Spray casserole dish with nonfat cooking spray.
3. In small bowl, combine ricotta, mayonnaise and skim milk. Stir well and set aside.
4. Spray medium skillet with nonfat cooking spray. Add artichokes, onion, pepper, garlic powder and garlic. Sauté 2 minutes. Remove from heat.
5. Add spinach, hot sauce, vegetable mixture and crabmeat to cheese mixture.
6. Stir in 3/4oz (21g) shredded cheese and place in a casserole dish.
7. Bake 15 minutes, stir mixture well and then top with remaining 1/4oz (7g) of cheese.
8. Bake 10-15 minutes, or until all cheese is melted and casserole is bubbly.

   Serve over roasted veggies or as a dip for crackers and fresh veggies. (Optional-please refer to the menu plan for serving and exchanges).

Appetite
❖ Delights

Tortilla Roll-Up Appetizer

10 *servings*

- SERVING SIZE: 4 PIECES
- COUNTS AS:
  1 STARCH

☀ Ingredients

2oz (60g) fat-free cream cheese, softened

2oz (60g) lite cream cheese, softened

5 green onions, sliced

1/4 cup (50mL) salsa

2oz (60g) lite or reduced-fat cheddar cheese, shredded

5- 8 inch (20cm) whole wheat or spinach tortillas

1/4 cup (50mL) chopped black olives

1/2 cup (125mL) iceberg lettuce, shredded

1 In a medium bowl, with a hand-mixer, blend cream cheeses, until soft.

2 Add onion, salsa and cheese. Stir until well combined.

3 Divide cream cheese mixture among tortillas. Spread a thin layer on each.

4 Sprinkle each tortilla with black olives and lettuce.

5 Roll each tortilla and refrigerate about 4-6 hours before slicing.

6 Just before serving, slice each tortilla roll into 1-inch (2.5cm) pieces.

5-Layer Dip

4 *servings*

good source of fiber

- SERVING SIZE: 1/4 RECIPE
- COUNTS AS:
  1/2 PROTEIN
  1 VEGETABLE
  1 FAT
  1/2 DAIRY
  1 STARCH
  2 CONDIMENTS

☀ Ingredients

8 green onions, chopped

4 tsp (20mL) oil

2 cups (500mL) cooked kidney beans

2 tomatoes, chopped

4oz (120g) shredded lite cheddar cheese

1/2 cup (125mL) salsa

1/4 cup (50mL) fat-free sour cream

4-4inch (10cm) whole wheat pita

1 In medium bowl, combine oil, cooked beans and 3/4 of the green onions.

2 With a fork, mash mixture to form a paste.

3 Place mixture in bottom of small bowl.

4 Top with chopped tomato.

5 Top tomato with cheese, and then follow with salsa.

6 Spread sour cream over cheese and salsa layer.

7 Sprinkle with remaining green onion.

8 Serve with 4-inch (10cm) whole wheat pita, cut into small triangles.

Appetite
❖ Delights

Eggplant Caponata

18 *servings*

- SERVING SIZE: 1/3 CUP (75ML)
- COUNTS AS:
  1 VEGETABLE

✳ Ingredients

1 Tbsp (15mL) olive oil

1 medium eggplant, peeled and diced

2 garlic cloves

1/2 cup (125mL) red onion, chopped

1/2 cup (125mL) green bell pepper, chopped

1/4 cup (50mL) water

1/4 cup (50mL) fresh parsley, chopped

3-4 Tbsp (45-60mL) black olives, pitted and chopped

2 Roma tomatoes, seeded and chopped

2 Tbsp (30mL) red wine vinegar

1/4 tsp (1mL) lite salt

1/8 tsp (.5mL) freshly ground pepper

1. Preheat oven to 350ºF (180ºC).

2. In a baking dish, combine olive oil, eggplant, garlic, onion and green pepper. Cover and bake in oven for 15 minutes.

3. Remove from oven; add water, parsley, black olives, tomatoes, vinegar, salt and pepper to baking dish. Stir to combine.

4. Return to oven and continue to bake 30 minutes, or until eggplant is soft.

5. Remove from oven and transfer to a bowl; cover and refrigerate at least 8 hours or overnight before serving.

Guacamole

 4 *servings*

- SERVING SIZE: 1/4 CUP (50ML)
- COUNTS AS:
  1 VEGETABLE
  3 FATS

✳ Ingredients

2 avocados, diced

1/2 small onion, diced

1-2 garlic cloves, minced

1 Roma tomato, seeded and diced

juice of 1 lime

1/2 tsp (2mL) lite salt

1 jalapeño, diced (optional)

1. In a large bowl, lightly mash avocado with a fork.

2. Add remaining ingredients; toss to combine.

3. Chill 30 minutes before serving.

Appetite
❖ Delights

Roasted Garlic Spread

6 *servings*

- **SERVING SIZE: 2-3 CLOVES**
- **COUNTS AS:**
  - 1 CONDIMENT

※ Ingredients

- 1 head of garlic
- 1 tsp (5mL) olive oil

1. Preheat oven to 450°F (230°C).
2. Trim 1/4-inch of top off the head of garlic. Place in the middle of a square piece of aluminum foil.
3. Drizzle with olive oil. Tightly form foil over the garlic bulb.
4. Roast in oven for approximately 1 hour.
5. Allow to cool at least 15 minutes before serving.
6. To use, squeeze cloves from bulb by applying pressure to the bottom, as if a tube of toothpaste.

With its creamy texture and sweet aroma, roasted garlic is great to use in place of butter on bread or bruschetta, as well as in dishes, such as pastas, vegetables, beef or poultry. (Optional-please refer to the menu plan for serving and exchanges.)

Balsamic Grilled Bruschetta

12 *servings*

- **SERVING SIZE: 1 SLICE**
- **COUNTS AS:**
  - 1 STARCH
  - 1 CONDIMENT

※ Ingredients

- 10 Roma tomatoes, seeded and diced
- 2-3 Tbsp (30-45mL) fresh basil, chopped
- 2-3 garlic cloves, minced
- 2 Tbsp (30mL) parmesan cheese, shredded
- 1 Tbsp (15mL) olive oil
- 1 Tbsp (15mL) balsamic vinegar
- 1/4 tsp (1mL) lite salt
- 1/8 tsp (.5mL) freshly ground pepper
- 1 loaf French bread, cut into 12 slices

1. In a bowl, toss together tomatoes, basil, garlic, cheese, oil, vinegar, and salt and pepper.
2. Cover and refrigerate for 1-2 hours, to allow flavors to meld.
3. Meanwhile, grill bread until lightly browned.
4. Divide tomato mixture evenly among sliced bread before serving. If desired, garnish with extra basil and an extra drizzle of balsamic vinegar.

Appetite
❖ Delights

Tzatziki

8 *servings*

- SERVING SIZE: 1/2 CUP (125ML)
- COUNTS AS:
  1/2 DAIRY

☀ Ingredients

2 cups (500mL) plain nonfat yogurt

2 medium cucumbers, peeled and shredded

2-3 garlic cloves, minced

1-2 Tbsp (15-30mL) lemon juice

1 Tbsp (15mL) olive oil

2 Tbsp (30mL) fresh mint, chopped

1/2 tsp (2mL) lite salt

1/4 tsp (1mL) freshly ground pepper

1 In a colander, squeeze any excess liquid out of cucumber; discard liquid.

2 In a bowl, combine all ingredients. Mix well.

3 Refrigerate, allowing flavors to combine, at least 2 hours, before serving.

   Great with fresh vegetables or pitas as a dip, or as a dressing for lamb or chicken. (Optional-please refer to the menu plan for serving and exchanges.)

Romaine Roll-up

1 *serving*

- SERVING SIZE: 1 LETTUCE ROLL
- COUNTS AS:
  1 PROTEIN
  1 FAT

☀ Ingredients

1 leaf romaine lettuce

filling of your choice
  - tuna
  - ground beef, cooked
  - fresh sliced chicken or turkey

1 Tbsp (15mL) lite mayonnaise (optional)

1 Place lettuce sideways on a plate, gently press down to flatten lettuce. Spread with mayonnaise.

2 Place filling in center of lettuce leaf and roll up.

3 Use toothpick to hold in place.

4 Cut in half and serve.

Appetite
❖ Delights

Veggies with Tarragon Dip

- **SERVING SIZE:**
  1 CUP (250ML) WITH 1 TBSP (15ML) DIP
- **COUNTS AS:**
  2 VEGETABLES
  1 FAT

✳ Ingredients

1 pound (450g) asparagus, trimmed

1 pound (450g) fresh green beans, trimmed

1/2 cup (125mL) lite mayonnaise

zest and juice of 1 lemon

1 small green onion, finely chopped

2 Tbsp (30mL) chopped fresh tarragon

2 Tbsp (30mL) chopped parsley leaves

dash of lite salt

freshly ground pepper

1. Cook asparagus and green beans in 1 inch of boiling water, covered, for 3 or 4 minutes.
2. Drain and cool the vegetables and arrange them on a serving plate.
3. Combine remaining ingredients in a small bowl.
4. Place dip on side of serving plate.

Roasted Peppers

8 *servings*

- **SERVING SIZE: 1/2 PEPPER**
- **COUNTS AS:**
  1 VEGETABLE
  [IF USING OLIVE OIL TO STORE, COUNTS AS 1 VEGETABLE, 1 FAT]

✳ Ingredients

4 large red or yellow bell peppers

olive oil (optional)

Balsamic vinegar (optional)

crushed garlic (optional)

1. Preheat oven to 500°F (260°C).
2. Place clean peppers on a baking sheet. Roast until skin begins to blister and turn black, approximately 30-45 minutes.
3. Remove peppers from oven and place in a paper bag for about 15-20 minutes, this will allow the skin to separate from the flesh using steam.
4. Once cool enough to touch, gently peel the skin from the flesh.
5. Store peppers in an air-tight container in the refrigerator; sprinkle with olive oil, balsamic vinegar and crushed garlic, if desired.

Appetite
❖ Delights

Spinach & Artichoke Dip

9 *servings*

- **SERVING SIZE:**
  1/3 CUP (75ML)
- **COUNTS AS:**
  1 VEGETABLE
  1 FAT

family fare

☀ Ingredients

1 cup (250mL /156g) frozen spinach, drained and thawed

1 cup (250mL /180g) cooked sliced artichoke hearts

1/4 cup (50mL /4g) chopped white onions

1 tsp (5mL) fat-free Italian salad dressing

2 Tbsp (30mL) red bell pepper, minced

1/2 tsp (2mL) lite salt

freshly ground pepper

1 cup (250mL) lite sour cream

2 Tbsp (30mL) dried onion

1 tsp (5mL) garlic powder

1 Tbsp (15mL) capers

3 Tbsp (45mL) grated parmesan cheese

1. In large mixing bowl combine spinach, artichokes, onion, red pepper and salad dressing. Sprinkle with salt and pepper.

2. Fold in sour cream and blend well. Add dried onion, garlic powder and capers. Mix in parmesan cheese. Chill for at least 1 hour.

Serve with veggies, crackers or toasted pita triangles. (Optional-please refer to the menu plan for serving and exchanges.)

Creamy Fruit Dip

2 *servings*

- **SERVING SIZE:**
  1/2 CUP (125ML)
- **COUNTS AS:**
  1/2 DAIRY

☀ Ingredients

8oz (250mL) lite fruited yogurt, any flavor (such as strawberry or raspberry)

2 Tbsp (30mL) fat-free whipped topping

1. Combine ingredients in a medium bowl and blend until smooth.

Serve with bite size pieces of fresh fruit.
(Optional-please refer to the menu plan for serving and exchanges.)

> "So many recipes to choose from choose something new every day."
>
> *- Sharon T.*

Appetite
❖ Delights

In-House Steak House

Are you a meat and potatoes lover? Then you'll love our variety packed In-House Steak House recipes. From easy to elaborate, our savory beef dishes are hardy and satisfying. Whether you prefer to cozy up by the fire with a delicious cup of beef stew, or throw some marinated filets on the grill, we've got the recipes that will add that extra bit of zest to each mouth-watering bite. Plus you'll learn more ways to cook, prepare and store beef than you ever thought possible.

Stuffed Peppers recipe can be found on page 74

In-House Steak House

Beef Kabobs

Beef Roast

Beef Dijon

Beef Teriyaki

London Broil

Italian-Style Beef

Beef & Broccoli

Sesame Beef

Meatloaf

Stuffed Peppers

Stuffed Cabbage

Salisbury Steak

Steak Fajitas

Herb-Crusted Steak

Beef Burgundy

Steak & Onions

Open-Faced Beef Sandwich

Italian-Style Burger

Meatball Sandwich

Mushroom & Swiss Burger

Beef Tenderloin with
   Mushroom Wine Sauce

Open-Faced Burger with
   Mustard Sauce

Beef Stroganoff

Steak Burger

Savory Beef Stew

Cheesy Beef & Broccoli

Hot Beef Sandwich

Beef and Mushroom Kabobs

Hamburger Patty

Philly Cheesesteak

BBQ Cheddar Burger

Cuts of Beef

Loin Cuts

- Porterhouse steak
- T-bone steak
- Strip steak
- Sirloin roast
- Tenderloin roast
- Tenderloin steak
- Sirloin steak

Round Cuts (Leg)

- Top round steak
- Eye round steak
- Round cube steak
- Top round roast
- Eye round roast

Rib Cuts

- Boneless rib roast
- Boneless rib eye steak

Chuck/Shoulder Cuts

- Brisket
- Chuck eye steak
- Chuck roast
- Chuck steak
- Shoulder roast
- Shoulder steak
- Stew beef chunks

Flank

- Flank steak

Plate

- Short ribs
- Skirt steak

Basic cooking methods

- **Braising** — Cooking with a moist heat, which is great for less tender cuts of beef. Meat may be browned first to seal in juices and flavor, a small amount of liquid such as broth is then added to pan. Beef is then cooked at a low heat for a lengthy period of time. This works well for round, flank, plate and chuck cuts.

- **Oven Roasting** — Dry heat method. Best used for larger quantities of meat such as a loin or round roast. Meat cooked in the oven in an uncovered pan.

- **Grilling** — Preparing food on a grill over hot coals or other direct heat source. This method is great for cooking loin cuts and steaks.

- **Stir-Frying** — Quickly cooking food in a large pan or wok over very high heat. Food needs to be constantly stirred to prevent sticking. Good cooking method for sirloin steak strips.

- **Pan-Searing** — Uses high heat to create a crust and seal in meat juices. Cooking is usually finished in the oven. Use this for loin, rib and round cuts.

TIP!

Beef is a great source of zinc, which helps keep your immune system working well.

Know what's best to buy

Sometimes it gets confusing to understand the labels of meat in the supermarket. Grades on the packages are determined mostly by marbling and age of the animal. There are three USDA grades that you should keep in mind when buying beef:

- **Prime** — Usually found in restaurants or specialty meat stores. Even though it holds one of the highest grades of meat, it's often the most marbled of the three grades and is the most flavorful steak you can find.

- **Choice** — The most common grade in the supermarket. It's your next best choice under prime cut for flavor because it has less marbling.

- **Select** — This grade has the least fat of the three grades. It's leaner and often more tender.

Look for "loin" or "round" in any grade of meat for the leanest cuts, such as "sirloin" or "top round steak." When you want the freshest, most flavorful steak in the supermarket, look for meat that is bright red and any marbling should be creamy white.

✿TIP!

Beef is packed with protein that is essential for your body's tissues, muscles and organs. So for your active lifestyle, remember beef is a good source to keep your body strong.

Food Safety

- Keep raw beef away from cooked and ready-to-eat foods.

- Use a separate cutting board for beef.

- Never defrost beef at room temperature. Thaw overnight in the refrigerator; under cold running water; or in the microwave.

- Cook ground beef to an internal temperature of 160°F (70°C).

- Cook whole cuts of beef such as roasts and steaks to an internal temperature of 145°F (60°C) (medium) to 160°F (70°C) (well done).

Beef Roasting

- Preheat oven to 450°F (230°C).

- Season meat and place on roasting rack in roasting pan.

- Roast for 15 minutes at 450°F (230°C).

- Reduce heat to 350°F (180°C) and cook:
  - Tenderloin: 8-11 minutes per pound (.5kg).
  - Sirloin, top rounds, rib roasts: 20-25 minutes per pound (.5kg).

- Check internal temperature to be sure meat is at desired doneness.

- Allow meat to rest 10-15 minutes before carving.

In-House
✿ Steak
House

Beef Kabobs

- **SERVING SIZE: 2-3 KABOBS**
- **COUNTS AS:**
  - 1 PROTEIN
  - 2 VEGETABLES
  - 1 FRUIT

☀ Ingredients

juice from 1 orange

1 Tbsp (15mL) brown sugar substitute

1/4 tsp (1mL) ground ginger

4oz (120g) sirloin steak, cut into 1 inch pieces (2.5cm)

1/4 medium green pepper, cut into 1-inch (2.5cm) squares

1 cup (250mL /113g) zucchini or yellow squash, cut into 1-inch (2.5cm) pieces

1/4 medium red onion, cut into 1-inch (2.5cm) squares

1. Mix orange juice, brown sugar substitute and ginger. Add beef and green pepper; stir to coat meat. Cover and marinate for 1 hour in refrigerator. Drain and reserve marinade.

2. On a skewer, alternate beef, pepper, zucchini or yellow squash and onion, leaving 1/4 inch (1/2cm) between pieces. Place kabobs on broiler pan. Brush with marinade.

3. Broil 4 inches from heat about 8 minutes, or until desired doneness.

Beef Roast

family fare

- **SERVING SIZE: 3OZ (90G) COOKED ROAST AND 1/4 RECIPE SAUCE**
- **COUNTS AS:**
  - 1 PROTEIN
  - 2 VEGETABLES

☀ Ingredients

1 pound (450g) eye round roast

1/2 cup (125mL) red wine

2 cups (500mL) fresh mushrooms, finely chopped

1/2 tsp (2mL) dried dill weed

1/4 tsp (1mL) lite salt

1/4 cup (50mL) green onions, thinly sliced

4oz (125mL) plain nonfat yogurt

dash white pepper

1 cup (250mL) low-sodium beef broth

2 Tbsp (30mL) flour

1/2 cup (125mL) water

1. Trim any excess, visible fat from roast. Cut 2 pockets into sides of roast, making a 3-inch (8cm) deep cut. Place roast in large, zip-top plastic bag set in bowl or baking pan. Pour wine over roast. Close the bag. Marinate for 3-6 hours, in refrigerator.

2. Combine mushrooms, water, dill weed and salt. Cook, uncovered, over medium heat until the liquid is evaporated. Stir in onion.

3. Remove roast from marinade. Place mushroom mixture into pockets.

4. Bake in preheated 325°F (160°C) oven for 1-1 1/2 hours, or until meat reaches an internal temperature of 150°F (65°C).

5. For sauce, mix together yogurt, flour and pepper in a small saucepan. Stir in broth. Cook, until sauce is thickened, over medium heat.

6. Slice roast between the 2 filled pockets. Place on dinner plate top with sauce.

In-House
❖ Steak
House

Beef Dijon

 serving

- **SERVING SIZE: 1 RECIPE**
- **COUNTS AS:**
  - 1 PROTEIN
  - 3 VEGETABLES
  - 1/2 DAIRY

☀ Ingredients

4oz (120g) beef flank steak

1 tsp (5mL) freshly ground pepper

1 cup (250mL) fresh mushrooms, sliced

5 green onions, thinly sliced

1/2 cup (125mL) water

1/2 packet low-sodium beef bouillon

1/2 cup (125mL) nonfat plain yogurt

1 Tbsp (15mL) flour

2 tsp (10mL) Dijon mustard

1 cup (250mL) fresh asparagus spears

nonfat cooking spray

1 Rub pepper on both sides of the steak.

2 Broil steak, 3 inches (8cm) from heat, for 6 minutes. Turn steak over and brown for 6-8 minutes more. Keep warm, allowing to rest 5-10 minutes before slicing.

3 Coat skillet with nonfat cooking spray. Combine mushrooms, green onion, half the water and beef bouillon; cook until mushrooms are tender.

4 Mix together the remaining water and the steak. Add to pan. Simmer for an additional 5 minutes.

5 Mix together yogurt, flour and mustard. Stir into mushroom mixture. Cool and stir until thickened.

6 Cook asparagus by microwaving or steaming.

7 Slice steak, thinly, against the grain. Arrange steak slices and asparagus on dinner plate. Serve with sauce.

Beef Teriyaki

serving

- **SERVING SIZE: 1 RECIPE**
- **COUNTS AS:**
  - 1 PROTEIN
  - 1 CONDIMENT

☀ Ingredients

4oz (120g) sirloin steak, cubed

2 Tbsp (30mL) low-sodium soy sauce

2 Tbsp (30mL) white wine

1/4 tsp (1mL) ground ginger

1 packet sugar substitute

1/2 tsp (2mL) garlic powder

1 Place beef in a bowl.

2 Combine all other ingredients in a measuring cup or small bowl; pour over beef. Cover and refrigerate, at least 1 hour.

3 Remove beef from marinade; reserve marinade.

4 Brush meat with marinade and broil 4 inches (10cm) from heat, about 5 minutes. Turn meat over; brush with marinade and broil another 5-6 minutes longer.

Serve the beef over brown rice. (Optional-please refer to the menu plan for serving and exchanges).

In-House
❖ Steak
House

London Broil

1 *serving*

- **SERVING SIZE: 1 RECIPE**
- **COUNTS AS:**
  1 PROTEIN
  1 VEGETABLE
  1 FAT

☀ Ingredients

4oz (120g) flank steak

5 green onions, thinly sliced

1/4 tsp (1mL) lite salt

1 tsp (5mL) canola oil

1 tsp (5mL) lemon juice

1/8 tsp (.5mL) freshly ground pepper

1 garlic clove, crushed

nonfat cooking spray

1. Score flank steak with a knife, diagonally, in a diamond pattern, about 1/8-inch (.3cm) deep.

2. Coat skillet with nonfat cooking spray. Sauté onion; set aside.

3. Combine in a small bowl salt, oil, lemon juice, pepper and garlic. Brush half of the mixture on one side of beef.

4. Broil 2-3 inches (5-8cm) from heat until brown, about 5 minutes; turn meat over. Brush with remaining mixture and broil another 5-7 minutes.

5. Slice beef thinly, against the grain, on a bias (an angle).

6. Serve with sautéed onions.

Italian-Style Beef

1 *serving*

- **SERVING SIZE:1 RECIPE**
- **COUNTS AS:**
  1 PROTEIN
  3 VEGETABLES

☀ Ingredients

4oz (120g) beef round steak

1/2 cup (125mL) fresh mushrooms, sliced

1/4 cup (50mL) white onion, diced

1/2 green pepper, chopped

1/2 celery stalk, chopped

1 garlic clove, minced

1/2 tomato, diced

1/4 tsp (1mL) dried basil, crushed

1/4 tsp (1mL) dried oregano, crushed

1/8 tsp (.5mL) cayenne pepper

1/2 cup (125mL) low-sodium beef broth

1 Tbsp (30mL) grated parmesan cheese

nonfat cooking spray

1. Cut meat into 2-3 pieces. Coat skillet with nonfat cooking spray. Brown meat on all sides. Remove from skillet.

2. Combine mushrooms, onion, green pepper, celery and garlic in skillet; cook until vegetables are tender. Add tomatoes, basil, oregano and cayenne pepper.

3. Place meat back in skillet, top with vegetable mixture. Add beef broth. Cover and simmer about 45-60 minutes, or until meat is tender, stirring occasionally.

4. Place meat on dinner plate, spoon vegetables over meat.

5. Top with grated parmesan cheese.

In-House
❧ Steak
House

Beef & Broccoli

1 *serving*

- **SERVING SIZE: 1 RECIPE**
- **COUNTS AS:**
  1 PROTEIN
  2 VEGETABLES

❊ Ingredients

4oz (120g) beef round steak

1 Tbsp (15mL) low-sodium soy sauce

1 Tbsp (15mL) vinegar

1 Tbsp (15mL) brown sugar substitute

1 garlic clove, minced

1/8 tsp (.5mL) cayenne pepper

1/2 medium carrot, thinly sliced

1 cup (250mL) fresh broccoli floret

1 tsp (5mL) cornstarch

1 Tbsp (15mL) cold water

nonfat cooking spray

1 Partially freeze meat. Thinly slice meat, across the grain, into bite-size strips. Set aside.

2 In a bowl, stir together soy sauce, vinegar, brown sugar substitute, garlic and cayenne pepper. Stir in meat. Cover and refrigerate for 10 minutes.

3 Coat skillet with nonfat cooking spray and heat over medium-high flame; add sauce mixture and meat. Cook until meat is no longer pink.

4 Add vegetables and cook until vegetables are tender.

5 Stir together cornstarch and water; stir into skillet and cook until thickened.

   May be served over brown rice. (Optional-please refer to the menu plan for serving and exchanges).

Sesame Beef

1 *serving*

- **SERVING SIZE: 1 RECIPE**
- **COUNTS AS:**
  1 PROTEIN
  2 FATS
  1 VEGETABLE

❊ Ingredients

4oz (120g) sirloin steak

1 packet sugar substitute

1 tsp (5mL) canola oil

1 Tbsp (15mL) low-sodium soy sauce

1 Tbsp (15mL) chopped green pepper

1/8 tsp (.5mL) freshly ground pepper

2 green onions, finely chopped

1 garlic clove, crushed

1 Tbsp (15mL) sesame seeds

nonfat cooking spray

1 Cut beef into strips.

2 Mix sugar substitute, oil, soy sauce, green pepper, freshly ground pepper, onions and garlic in non-metal bowl; stir in beef until well coated. Marinate for at least 30 minutes in refrigerator.

3 Drain beef from marinade. Coat skillet with nonfat cooking spray and stir in half sesame seeds; cook until light brown. Remove from skillet.

4 Add beef to skillet and cook until browned. Sprinkle with remaining sesame seeds and serve.

   May be served over salad greens. (Optional-please refer to the menu plan for serving and exchanges).

In-House ❖ Steak House

- SERVING SIZE: 1/4 OF LOAF
- COUNTS AS:
  1 PROTEIN
  1 STARCH

family fare

Meatloaf

☀ Ingredients

1 pound (450g) lean ground sirloin

1/2 cup (125mL) breadcrumbs (see recipe on pg 154)

1/4 cup (125mL) egg substitute

2 Tbsp (30mL) dried onion

1 tsp (5mL) low-sodium Worcestershire sauce

1 Tbsp (15mL) Dijon mustard

1/4 tsp (1mL) lite salt

1/4 tsp (1mL) freshly ground pepper

1 tsp (5mL) garlic powder

3 Tbsp (45mL) ketchup, divided

nonfat cooking spray

1 Preheat oven to 350°F (180°C).

2 Mix together all ingredients, reserving 2 Tbsp (30mL) of ketchup. Form into loaf.

3 Coat loaf pan with nonfat cooking spray. Place meatloaf in pan. Spoon remaining ketchup on top of loaf and spread evenly.

4 Bake about 45 minutes or until desired doneness. To be sure meat is fully cooked, insert thermometer and bake until internal temperature reaches 160°F (70°C).

---

2 *servings*

- SERVING SIZE: 2 PEPPER HALVES
- COUNTS AS:
  1 PROTEIN
  1 STARCH
  2 VEGETABLES
  1/2 DAIRY

good source of calcium

Stuffed Peppers

☀ Ingredients

2 whole green peppers

8oz (225g) lean ground sirloin

1/4 cup (50mL) chopped white onion

2/3 cup (150mL) cooked brown rice

1/4 tsp (1mL) lite salt

1 tsp (5mL) garlic powder

1 small tomato, chopped

1/3 cup (75mL) lite tomato sauce

2oz (60g) reduced-fat mozzarella cheese, shredded

1/4 cup (50mL) water

nonfat cooking spray

1 Preheat oven to 350°F (180°C).

2 Cut peppers in half and remove seeds. Cook peppers in boiling water for approximately 5 minutes, until just tender; drain and set aside.

3 Brown beef and onion in skillet coated with nonfat cooking spray. Add rice, salt and garlic powder to skillet and heat through.

4 Stuff each pepper half with beef mixture. Coat baking pan with nonfat cooking spray. Place peppers in baking pan. Top with chopped tomato and tomato sauce. Add water to bottom of baking pan.

5 Cover and bake for 30-45 minutes, or until peppers and tomatoes are tender.

6 Uncover; sprinkle with cheese. Place back in oven and bake until cheese is melted.

In-House
❖ Steak
House

Stuffed Cabbage

1 *serving*

■ SERVING SIZE: 3-4 ROLLS
■ COUNTS AS:
  1 PROTEIN
  1 STARCH
  2 VEGETABLES
  1 CONDIMENT

good source of fiber

☀ Ingredients

3-4 cabbage leaves

4oz (120g) lean ground sirloin

1/3 cup (75mL) cooked brown rice

1/4 cup (50mL) low-sodium beef broth

1/4 tsp (1mL) lite salt

1/8 tsp (.5mL) freshly ground pepper

1 tsp (5mL) garlic powder

1 Tbsp (15mL) dried onion

1/2 tomato, chopped

2 Tbsp (30mL) lite tomato sauce

1 Tbsp (15mL) water

nonfat cooking spray

1 Preheat oven to 350°F (180°C).

2 Steam cabbage leaves until tender.

3 Mix together beef, rice, broth, salt, pepper, garlic powder and onion. Divide meat mixture among the cabbage leaves. Roll and tuck in ends. Secure with a toothpick, if necessary.

4 Coat a 1 1/2 qt (1.5L) casserole dish with nonfat cooking spray. Place cabbage rolls in casserole dish.

5 In small bowl, combine chopped tomato, tomato sauce and water. Top rolls with tomato mixture. Cover the casserole with a lid or foil.

6 Bake for about 1 hour, or until beef has reached an internal temperature of 160°F (70°C) .

Salisbury Steak

1 *serving*

■ SERVING SIZE: 1 RECIPE
  COUNTS AS:
  1 PROTEIN
  1 STARCH
  1 VEGETABLE

☀ Ingredients

4oz (120g) lean ground sirloin

1/4 cup (50mL) breadcrumbs (see recipe on pg 154)

1/4 tsp (1mL) lite salt

1/8 tsp (.5mL) freshly ground pepper

1 Tbsp (15mL) dried onion

1 cup (250mL) low-sodium beef broth

1 cup (250mL) fresh mushrooms, sliced

1 Tbsp (15mL) water

1 tsp (5mL) cornstarch

nonfat cooking spray

1 Mix ground beef, breadcrumbs, salt, pepper and 1/4 cup (50mL) broth in a bowl; combine well. Form meat into oval patty.

2 Coat skillet with nonfat cooking spray. Heat skillet over medium heat and cook patty until brown on both sides.

3 Add onion, remaining broth and mushrooms. Heat to boiling; reduce heat and cover. Simmer until desired doneness.

4 Remove patty; keep warm. Heat remaining mixture to boiling; mix in water and cornstarch and cook until thickened. Serve sauce over patty.

75

In-House
❖ Steak
House

1 *serving*

- **SERVING SIZE: 1 RECIPE**
- **COUNTS AS:**
  1 PROTEIN
  3 VEGETABLES
  1/2 DAIRY

good source of calcium

Steak Fajitas

❊ Ingredients

4oz (120g) sirloin steak

1/4 cup (50mL) red wine vinegar

1 packet sugar substitute

1/2 tsp (2mL) oregano

1/2 tsp (2mL) chili powder

1/4 tsp (1mL) garlic powder

dash of freshly ground pepper

1/4 tsp (1mL) lite salt

1/2 cup (125mL) raw white
  onions, sliced

1/2 green pepper, sliced

1oz (30g) reduced-fat cheddar or
  monterey jack cheese, shredded

3-4 large leaves of iceberg lettuce

1 Tbsp (15mL) salsa

nonfat cooking spray

1 To make marinade, combine vinegar, sugar substitute, oregano, chili powder, garlic powder, pepper and salt.

2 Cut beef into strips and place into bowl with marinade. Refrigerate 30 minutes.

3 Coat large skillet with nonfat cooking spray and sauté green peppers and onions over high heat about 3-5 minutes, until they begin to soften.

4 Remove steak from marinade and place in skillet with vegetables. Cook 5-10 minutes, or until beef is cooked through.

5 Remove fajita mixture from skillet and place on plate. Use lettuce leaves as fajita wraps; top with cheese and salsa.

Herb-Crusted Steak

1 *serving*

- **SERVING SIZE: 1 RECIPE**
- **COUNTS AS:**
  1 PROTEIN
  1 STARCH

❊ Ingredients

4oz (120g) sirloin steak

small handful of mixed herbs
  to taste (such as thyme,
  rosemary, basil, sage, parsley)

2 garlic cloves, peeled

1 Tbsp (15mL) green onion,
  finely chopped

1 slice (1oz) white
  country style bread

freshly ground pepper, to taste

nonfat cooking spray

1 Preheat oven to 375°F (190°C).

2 Place the herbs, garlic, onion, bread and pepper in a food processor and blend.

3 Coat skillet with nonfat cooking spray.

4 Sear the steak in the skillet; top with herbed breadcrumb mixture.

5 Cook for 8-10 minutes.

In-House
❖ Steak
House

Beef Burgundy

1 *serving*

- **SERVING SIZE: 1 RECIPE**
- **COUNTS AS:**
  1 PROTEIN
  2 VEGETABLES

☀ Ingredients

4oz (120g) sirloin steak

1/4 cup (50mL) burgundy wine

1/4 cup (50mL) low-sodium
beef broth

1/4 tsp (1mL) garlic powder

1/4 tsp (1mL) freshly ground
pepper

1/4 tsp (1mL) thyme

1/4 tsp (1mL) lite salt

1/8 tsp (.5mL) oregano

1/4 tsp (1mL) dried onion

1 cup (250mL) fresh mushroom
slices

1/2 celery stalk, chopped

nonfat cooking spray

1. In a small bowl, combine garlic powder, pepper, salt, thyme, oregano and onion.

2. Rub seasoning blend into steak.

3. Coat medium skillet with nonfat cooking spray and heat over high flame.

4. Place beef in skillet, sear on each side, approximately 3 minutes, or until browned.

5. While beef is cooking, combine wine and broth in small bowl.

6. Once beef has been browned on all sides, pour wine mixture over beef. Add mushrooms and celery. Continue to cook until all liquid has evaporated. Serve hot.

Steak & Onions

4 *servings*

family fare

- **SERVING SIZE: 3OZ (90G) COOKED; AND 1/4 CUP (50ML) SAUCE**
- **COUNTS AS:**
  1 PROTEIN
  2 VEGETABLES

☀ Ingredients

1 pound (450g) beef top round,
cut into thin slices

1/3 cup (75mL) white vinegar

freshly ground pepper, to taste

10 large olives, sliced

3 garlic cloves, peeled and
chopped

1 cup (250mL) low-sodium beef
broth, divided

1 cup (250mL) green pepper,
cut into strips

2 cups (500mL) Spanish yellow
onion slices

nonfat cooking spray

1. Pound meat to tenderize. Season with freshly ground pepper.

2. Combine vinegar, and broth. Add the olives and garlic; set aside.

3. Coat skillet with nonfat cooking spray, sear the beef on all sides; remove from the pan.

4. Reheat the skillet, add onions and green peppers; saute for 1 minute.

5. Return the meat to the pan. Pour the broth and vinegar mixture over the meat.

6. Cook, partially covered, for 20 minutes or until tender.

In-House
❧ Steak
House

Open-Faced Beef Sandwich

- **SERVING SIZE: 1/4 RECIPE**
- **COUNTS AS:**
  1 PROTEIN
  1 STARCH
  2 VEGETABLES

family fare

☀ Ingredients

4 slices whole wheat bread

1 pound (450g) round steak, cubed

2 tomatoes, diced

4 garlic cloves, minced

2 cups (500mL) low-sodium beef broth

1 tsp (5mL) lite salt

1 Tbsp (15mL) hot sauce

1 green pepper, diced

5 green onions, diced

water as needed

nonfat cooking spray

1 Coat large saucepan with nonfat cooking spray. Heat over high heat.

2 Sprinkle beef with salt and sauté in skillet until brown.

3 Add onion, green pepper and garlic to skillet. Sauté 2 minutes.

4 Add tomato and hot sauce to beef mixture and cook 1-2 minutes.

5 Add beef broth to the beef mixture and bring to a boil.

6 Reduce heat and cook covered for about 1 1/2 hours, stirring occasionally. More water may be added to cover meat while cooking; add 1/4 cup (50mL) of warm water at a time.

7 Meat is done when it can be shredded with a fork. Once beef is done, drain any remaining liquid. Place beef on plate and shred.

8 Serve shredded beef over bread.

Italian-Style Burger

1 *serving*

- **SERVING SIZE: 1 BURGER**
- **COUNTS AS:**
  1 PROTEIN
  1 STARCH
  1/2 DAIRY

good source of calcium

☀ Ingredients

4oz (120g) lean ground sirloin

1/3 cup (75mL) breadcrumbs (see recipe on pg 154)

1/4 cup (50mL) low-sodium beef broth

1 Tbsp (15mL) dried onion

1 Tbsp (15mL) fresh parsley, snipped

1/8 tsp (.5mL) garlic powder

1/8 tsp (.5mL) freshly ground pepper

1 slice of tomato

1/8 tsp (.5mL) dried oregano, crushed

1oz (30g) reduced-fat mozzarella cheese, shredded

1 Mix together breadcrumbs, broth, onion, parsley, garlic powder and pepper. Add meat; mix well. Shape into patty.

2 Broil 3 inches (8cm) from heat for 6 minutes. Turn and broil 6-8 minutes longer, or until meat is no longer pink.

3 Top patty with tomato slice. Sprinkle with oregano, then mozzarella cheese. Broil another 1-2 minutes more, or until cheese is melted.

In-House
♣ Steak
House

Meatball Sandwich

4 *servings*

family fare

- SERVING SIZE: 3OZ (90G) COOKED WITH 1/2 CUP (125ML) SAUCE
- COUNTS AS:
  1 PROTEIN
  1 VEGETABLE
  1 STARCH
  1/2 DAIRY

☼ Ingredients

1 pound (450g) lean ground sirloin

1 tsp (5mL) oregano

1 tsp (5mL) basil

1 tsp (5mL) lite salt

1 tsp (5mL) freshly ground pepper

3 Tbsp (45mL) chopped onion

5 garlic cloves, minced, divided

1 cup (250mL) chopped fresh spinach

1 cup (250mL) lite tomato sauce

1/2 cup (125mL) hot water

1 tomato, seeded and diced

four 4-inch (10cm) whole wheat pitas

4oz (120g) reduced-fat mozzarella cheese

nonfat cooking spray

1. In medium bowl combine meat, oregano, basil, salt, pepper, onion and half of the minced garlic. Mix well.

2. Form small balls with meat mixture.

3. Spray medium sauce pan with nonfat cooking spray. Gently add meatballs to saucepan and sauté until brown. Remove the meatballs from the pan.

4. Add the remaining garlic to the pan; Sauté for 15 seconds.

5. Add spinach and sauté 1 minute.

6. Add tomato sauce, water, and tomato to pan. Return the meatballs to the pan. Continue to simmer, until meatballs are cooked and sauce reduces.

7. Use slotted spoon to remove meatballs. Place in pita and top with sauce and cheese.

Mushroom & Swiss Burger

1 *serving*

good source of calcium

- SERVING SIZE: 1 BURGER
- COUNTS AS:
  1 PROTEIN
  1 DAIRY
  1 CONDIMENT

☼ Ingredients

Hamburger Patty (see recipe on page 84)

1/4 cup (50mL) sliced mushrooms

1/4 tsp (1mL) garlic powder

1 green onion, sliced

2oz (60g) reduced-fat Swiss cheese

nonfat cooking spray

1. Coat small skillet with nonfat cooking spray.

2. Place mushrooms, garlic powder and onion in skillet and sauté over medium heat until mushrooms are fully cooked.

3. Place mushrooms on top of burger.

4. Place cheese on burger and place on grill or under broiler to melt cheese.

In-House
❖ Steak
House

Beef Tenderloin with Mushroom Wine Sauce

7 servings

- SERVING SIZE: 3OZ (90G) COOKED AND 1/4 CUP (50ML) SAUCE
- COUNTS AS:
  1 PROTEIN
  1 FRUIT

family fare

✳ Ingredients

1 1/2 pounds (675g) beef tenderloin

2 Tbsp (30mL) olive oil

1 cup (250mL) chopped green onion

2 garlic cloves, chopped

2 celery stalks, chopped

2 cups (500mL) shitake mushrooms, chopped

2 Tbsp (30mL) fresh thyme, chopped

1 bay leaf

1/2 tsp (2mL) freshly ground pepper

1 1/2 cups (375mL) red wine

1 Tbsp (15mL) low-sodium Worcestershire sauce

1 Tbsp (15mL) balsamic vinegar

flour

Nonfat cooking spray

1. Preheat oven to 400°F (200°C).

2. Roll tenderloin, lightly, in flour. Coat skillet with nonfat cooking spray. Sear tenderloin on all sides and remove to an ovenproof dish.

3. Place in oven for 15-20 minutes. Allow to rest 10-15 minutes; slice tenderloin thinly. Cover loosely with foil to keep warm.

4. In a pan, sauté the onion, garlic and celery in oil for about 2 minutes.

5. Add the mushrooms and continue to sauté for about 4-5 minutes.

6. Add all remaining ingredients and bring to a boil.

7. Reduce heat, cover and simmer about 20 minutes.

8. Remove bay leaf and serve over sliced beef tenderloin.

Open-Faced Burger with Mustard Sauce

1 serving

- SERVING SIZE: 1 BURGER
- COUNTS AS:
  1 PROTEIN
  1 STARCH
  1 FAT
  2 CONDIMENTS

✳ Ingredients

4oz (120g) lean ground sirloin

1/3 cup (75mL) breadcrumbs (see recipe on pg 154)

1/4 cup (50mL) low-sodium beef broth

1 Tbsp (15mL) dried onion

1 Tbsp (15mL) fresh parsley, snipped

1/8 tsp (.5mL) lite salt

2 Tbsp (30mL) fat-free sour cream

1 Tbsp (15mL) lite mayonnaise

1 tsp (5mL) Dijon mustard

1/8 tsp (.5mL) dried dill

1 lettuce leaf

1. Mix breadcrumbs, broth, onion, parsley and salt. Add meat and mix well. Shape into patty.

2. Broil patty 3 inches from the heat (8cm) for 5 minutes. Turn and broil 5-7 minutes more, or until meat is no longer pink.

3. Stir together sour cream, mayonnaise, mustard and dill. Spoon sauce over burger.

4. Arrange on lettuce leaf.

In-House
♣ Steak
House

Beef Stroganoff

10 *servings*

- SERVING SIZE: 1 CUP (250ML)
- COUNTS AS:
  - 1/2 PROTEIN
  - 1 FAT
  - 1 STARCH

family fare

Ingredients

2 pounds (1kg) lean beef tenderloin, thinly sliced

1 Tbsp (15mL) olive oil

1 tsp (5mL) freshly ground pepper

1 Tbsp (15mL) butter

1 cup (250mL) mushrooms, sliced

1/2 cup (125mL) chopped green onion

1/4 cup (50mL) white wine

2 tsp (10mL) Dijon mustard

3 cups (750mL) low-sodium beef broth

1 1/4 cups (300mL) fat-free sour cream

3 cups bow tie pasta, cooked

small can tomato paste

salt, to taste (optional)

1. In a large pot, heat oil over high heat.
2. Season beef with the pepper and sauté in small batches until browned.
3. Remove the beef from the pot and set aside, pour off any excess fat from the pot.
4. Melt the butter in the pot and sauté the mushrooms and onions for 3 minutes.
5. Add the white wine and simmer until liquid is reduced by half.
6. Stir in the tomato paste and mustard; cook for 2 minutes.
7. Add the broth and beef, bring to a boil.
8. Reduce the heat and simmer for 5 minutes.
9. Stir in the sour cream and adjust the seasoning to taste.
10. Mix with pasta and serve.

Steak Burger

1 *serving*

- SERVING SIZE: 1 BURGER
- COUNTS AS:
  - 1 PROTEIN
  - 1 CONDIMENT

Ingredients

Hamburger Patty (see recipe on page 84)

1/4 cup (50mL) sliced mushrooms

1/4 tsp (1mL) garlic powder

1 green onion, sliced

2 tsp (10mL) steak sauce

1/4 tsp (1mL) black pepper

nonfat cooking spray

1. Coat small skillet with nonfat cooking spray.
2. Place mushrooms, garlic powder, pepper and onion in skillet; sauté until vegetables are fully cooked.
3. Place vegetables on top of burger.
4. Drizzle steak sauce over burger and vegetables.

Savory Beef Stew

4 *servings*

family fare

- **SERVING SIZE: 1 CUP (250ML)**
- **COUNTS AS:**
  1 PROTEIN
  1 STARCH
  2 VEGETABLES
  1 FAT

✳ Ingredients

24oz (675g) beef top round, cut into 1-inch (2.5cm) cubes

1 green pepper, seeded and chopped

4 sweet chili peppers, seeded and chopped

1 small onion, chopped

4 garlic cloves, chopped

6 fresh cilantro leaves, chopped

2 Tbsp (30mL) vinegar

2 cups (500mL) low-sodium beef broth, divided

1 cup (250mL) hot water

1/2 tsp (2mL) dried oregano, crushed

1/2 cup (125mL) lite tomato sauce

2 bay leaves

1/2 pound (225g) carrots, peeled and chopped

1/2 pound (225g) potatoes, peeled and cubed

1/4 pound (120g) green peas

12 olives, stuffed with pimientos

1 Tbsp (15mL) capers

salt, to taste (optional)

freshly ground pepper, to taste

nonfat cooking spray

1 Coat saucepan with nonfat cooking spray.

2 Add the beef and stir constantly, until meat begins to brown.

3 Add the next 11 ingredients (through bay leaves); mix and bring to a boil. Reduce heat to low, cover and cook for 1 hour.

4 Stir in carrots.

5 Bring back to a boil, reduce heat to low, cover and cook until the meat is fork tender, approximately 1 hour.

6 Add potatoes, peas, olives and capers.

7 Mix well, bring to a boil, then reduce heat to low. Cover and cook for 20 minutes or until vegetables are tender.

8 Season to taste with salt and pepper.

In-House
✿ Steak
House

Cheesy Beef & Broccoli

4 *servings*

■ SERVING SIZE: 1/4 RECIPE
■ COUNTS AS:
  1 PROTEIN
  1 VEGETABLE
  1 DAIRY

good source of calcium

✳ Ingredients

1 pound (450g) lean ground sirloin

1/2 cup (125mL) raw white onions

4 garlic cloves, minced

2 cups (500mL /140g) raw broccoli florets

2 Tbsp (30mL) white flour

2 cups (500mL) skim milk

2 tsp (10mL) Worcestershire sauce

4oz (120g) reduced-fat sharp cheddar cheese

nonfat cooking spray

1 Coat large skillet with nonfat cooking spray and heat over high flame.

2 Add beef and sauté until beef begins to brown. Add the onions and garlic.

3 Sauté onions and garlic 1-2 minutes, or until onions begin to soften.

4 Whisk together the flour, milk and Worcestershire sauce in a small bowl. Pour over beef. Bring to simmer and cook for 5 minutes.

5 Add the broccoli florets and simmer covered for an additional 8 minutes.

6 Slowly sprinkle cheese over beef mixture and mix well. Once cheese is melted, turn off heat and allow to sit for 3 minutes before serving. Serve hot.

Hot Beef Sandwich

4 *servings*

■ SERVING SIZE: 3OZ COOKED BEEF (90G), AND 2 SLICES OF LITE BREAD
■ COUNTS AS:
  1 PROTEIN
  1 STARCH
  1 VEGETABLE
  1 CONDIMENT

family fare

✳ Ingredients

1 pound (450g) beef round steak
1/4 tsp (1mL) garlic powder
1/4 tsp (1mL) freshly ground pepper
1/4 tsp (1mL) lite salt
1/2 cup (125mL) low-sodium beef broth
1 tomato, diced
3 Tbsp (45mL) dried onion
1/2 medium carrot, chopped
2 Tbsp (30mL) low-sodium Worcestershire sauce
2 Tbsp (30mL) vinegar
2 Tbsp (30mL) brown sugar substitute
2 tsp (10mL) chili powder
1 tsp (5mL) dried oregano, crushed
2 garlic cloves, minced
1 bay leaf
8 slices lite bread
nonfat cooking spray

1 Cut meat into 5-6 pieces. Sprinkle beef with garlic powder, pepper and salt.

2 Coat Dutch oven with nonfat cooking spray. Add beef and brown on both sides.

3 Add beef broth, tomato, onion, carrot, Worcestershire sauce, vinegar, brown sugar, chili powder, oregano, garlic and bay leaf. Bring to boil; reduce heat.

4 Cover; simmer for 1 hour, or until meat is very tender.

5 Remove meat and shred with a fork. Remove bay leaf from sauce.

6 Return meat to sauce and heat through. Serve hot over bread.

In-House
❖ Steak
House

Beef & Mushroom Kabobs

1 *serving*

- **SERVING SIZE: 1 RECIPE**
- **COUNTS AS:**
  1 PROTEIN
  2 VEGETABLES

✳ Ingredients

4oz (120g) beef round steak, cubed

2 large slices white onion, 1 inch (2.5cm) chunks

1/2 green pepper, 1 inch (2.5cm) chunks

1 cup (250mL) whole fresh mushrooms

2 Tbsp (30mL) balsamic vinegar

1/4 tsp (1mL) lite salt

1/4 tsp (1mL) freshly ground pepper

1/2 tsp (2mL) onion powder

1/2 tsp (2mL) garlic powder

1/4 tsp (1mL) paprika

1/4 tsp (1mL) thyme

kabob skewers

1. Place beef, onion, pepper and mushrooms on skewers, alternating meat and vegetables.

2. Brush the kabobs with half the balsamic vinegar, set remaining vinegar aside.

3. In a small bowl, combine salt, pepper, onion powder, garlic powder, paprika and thyme.

4. Sprinkle spice mixture over kabobs.

5. Place kabobs on grill over medium heat. Cook approximately 4-5 minutes and then turn them over and cook additional 4-5 minutes. Baste with remaining vinegar halfway through cooking.

6. Serve immediately.

Hamburger Patty

4 *servings*

- **SERVING SIZE: 4OZ (120G) RAW HAMBURGER PATTY**
- **COUNTS AS:**
  1 PROTEIN

✳ Ingredients

1 pound (450g) raw hamburger

3 Tbsp (45mL) dried onion

1/4 tsp (1mL) garlic powder

1 Tbsp (15mL) water

1/2 tsp (2mL) lite salt

1/2 tsp (2mL) freshly ground pepper

1. Mix all ingredients together. Form into patties.

2. Broil 3 inches (8cm) from heat until desired doneness.

3. Place any uncooked burgers in freezer bags, seal well and freeze up to 3 months.

In-House
✤ Steak
House

Philly Cheesesteak

4 *servings*

- **SERVING SIZE:** 1 SANDWICH
- **COUNTS AS:**
  1 PROTEIN
  2 STARCHES
  1/2 DAIRY
  1 FAT

❊ Ingredients

1 pound (450g) beef sirloin

1/2 tsp (2mL) salt

1/2 tsp (2mL) freshly ground pepper

1/2 tsp (2mL) onion powder

1/2 tsp (2mL) garlic powder

1/2 tsp (2mL) dried basil

1 onion, sliced

1 green bell pepper, sliced

four 6-inch (15cm) hoagie rolls, split

4oz (120g) lite mozzarella cheese, sliced

nonfat cooking spray

1. Combine seasonings in a small bowl; rub mixture into sirloin.

2. Wrap in plastic or wax paper. Partially freeze beef sirloin for about 30-60 minutes.

3. Remove from freezer and thinly slice sirloin.

4. Coat large skillet with nonfat cooking spray. Heat skillet over medium heat. Add onion and green pepper; sauté until soft and lightly browned. Remove from pan.

5. Coat skillet again with spray. Increase heat to high; add beef and cook about 5 minutes, or until desired level of doneness.

6. Divide meat and vegetables evenly among the 4 rolls; top with cheese. If desired, place in a warm oven or under a broiler to melt the cheese before serving.

BBQ Cheddar Burger

1 *serving*

- **SERVING SIZE:** 1 BURGER
- **COUNTS AS:**
  1 PROTEIN
  1/2 DAIRY
  1 VEGETABLE
  1 CONDIMENT

❊ Ingredients

Hamburger Patty (see recipe on page 84)

1 Tbsp (15mL) barbeque sauce

2 slices red onion

1 leaf lettuce

1 slice tomato

1oz (30g) reduced-fat cheddar cheese

1. Spread barbeque sauce over burger.

2. Top burger with cheese and place on grill or under broiler to melt cheese.

3. Once cheese is melted, top with onion, lettuce and tomato; serve immediately.

In-House
❧ Steak
House

Sultry ✤
Poultry

If chicken and turkey are on the tip of your taste buds then you'll be delighted with all the sultry poultry recipes inside. Hot dishes, wraps, chili, whatever suits your mood. You'll find a simple recipe for simply delicious dishes like Baked Chicken Parmesan, Garlic Chicken, Lemon-Herb Roasted Turkey and Rolled Turkey Divan. Plus you'll learn all of the latest trends and healthiest methods for preparing, storing and cooking poultry.

Marinated Chicken Kabobs recipe can be found on page 94

Chicken Cooking Techniques

Cuts of chicken

■ **Whole Fryer** — Whole chicken with skin and bones. Recommended cooking methods include oven roasting and braising.

■ **Cut up Fryer** — Whole chicken that has been separated into parts. Still contains skin and bones. Recommended cooking methods include oven roasting, braising and grilling.

■ **Wings** — Usually still contain both skin and bones. They can be grilled, oven roasted or braised.

■ **Thighs** — Dark meat cut from the leg. Can be found with bone-in or boneless. May still have skin attached. Tastes great grilled, oven roasted or braised.

■ **Drumstick** — Dark meat cut from the leg. Usually contains both skin and bones. Recommended cooking methods include oven roasting, braising and grilling.

■ **Leg Quarters** — Contains dark meat from both thigh and drumstick. Tastes great grilled, oven roasted or braised.

■ **Split Breast** — White meat cut. Usually contains skin and bones. Recommended cooking methods include oven roasting, braising and grilling.

■ **Boneless Skinless Breast** — White meat cut. Easy to use in recipes. They can be pan seared, oven roasted or stir-fried.

■ **Tenders** — White meat slices of boneless breast meat. Convenient to use. Great in stir fries. Can also be pan seared.

■ **Chicken Cutlet** — A thin cut of meat. Often pounded to increase tenderness. Best preparation method is pan searing.

TIP!

Rubbing fresh herbs such as basil, oregano or parsley on chicken before cooking is great way to add a burst of flavor, without adding any extra calories.

Basic cooking methods

- **Braising** — Cooking with a moist heat. Great for less tender cuts of chicken. Meat may be browned first to seal in juices and flavor, a small amount of liquid such as chicken broth is then added to pan. Chicken is then cooked at a low heat for a lengthy period of time. This method produces a very tender chicken.

- **Oven Roasting** — Dry heat method. Chicken will have a well-browned exterior and a moist interior. Best used for larger quantities of meat such as a whole chicken. Chicken is cooked in the oven in an uncovered pan.

- **Grilling** — Preparing food on a grill over hot coals or other direct heat source.

- **Stir-Frying** — Quickly cooking food in a large pan or wok over very high heat. Food needs to be stirred constantly to prevent sticking.

- **Pan-Searing** — Uses high heat to create a crust and seal in meat juices. Cooking is usually finished in the oven.

TIP!

When preparing chicken, be sure to cook or freeze chicken by the "use by" date. However, chicken should remain fresh for 2-3 days after the "sell by" date.

Food Safety

It's important to know the food safety rules when preparing dishes for yourself and your family. In today's busy world we often find ourselves throwing meals together without truly preparing in a way that is healthy and safe. Here is a quick "at a glance" safe cooking guide, when cooking poultry.

- Keep raw chicken away from cooked and ready to eat foods.

- Use a separate cutting board for raw chicken. Use plastic cutting boards for raw meats and poultry.

- Never defrost chicken at room temperature. Thaw overnight in the refrigerator; under cold running water; or in the microwave.

- Cook chicken to an internal temperature of 165°F (75°C).

Roasting Times

To roast chicken, use 375°F (190°C) oven.
Cook breast-side up uncovered.

- *1/2 to 2 pounds (672 - 896g): 45-60 minutes*

- *2 to 2-1/2 pounds (896 - 1.1kg): 60-90 minutes*

- *2-1/2 to 3 pounds (1.1 - 1.3kg): 1 hour – 1-1/2 hours*

- *3 to 4 pounds (1.3 - 1.8kg): 1-1/2 – 2-1/4 hours*

- *4+ pounds (1.8kg): at least 3 hours*

Chicken is done cooking when it reaches an internal temperature of 165°F (75°C).

Sultry
Poultry

Cuts of Turkey

Whole Turkey

Whole or Half Bone-In Breast

► Medallions/Tenderloins

Turkey Breast Steaks

Turkey Breast Cutlets

Turkey Breast Chops

Ground Turkey

Ground Turkey Breast

Thighs — Boneless or Bone-In

Legs/Drumsticks

Wings

Basic Cooking Methods

- **Grilling** — Cooking on a rack directly over hot coals or other direct heat source. Grilling works well for turkey breast, tenderloins, ground turkey, turkey burgers, thighs, legs and wings.

- **Broil** — Cooking directly under heat source, usually in the oven under the top broiling element. This works well for turkey breast, tenderloins, ground turkey and turkey burgers.

- **Braising** — Cooking with a moist heat. Meat may be browned first to seal in juices and flavor, then a small amount of liquid such as broth is added to the pan. The meat is then cooked at a low heat for a lengthy period of time. This works well for turkey breast, legs and wings.

- **Oven Roasting** — Cooking uncovered on a rack in a shallow pan in the oven without adding liquids. This works well for whole turkeys, turkey breast, tenderloins, thighs, legs and wings.

- **Stir-Frying** — Cooking quickly in a large pan or wok over high heat. Food needs to be moved constantly to prevent sticking and promote even cooking. This is a great method for cooking turkey breast and tenderloins.

- **Pan-Searing** — Cooking on high heat to create a crust and seal in meat juices; cooking is usually then finished in the oven. Use this method for cooking turkey breast, tenderloins, ground turkey or thighs.

TIP!

Cranberry sauce, made with fresh cranberries, as opposed to pre-made sauce, is a great light side for turkey. You can go as light on the sugar as you'd like and keep the sauce tart and lo-cal.

Roasting Turkey
Pre-heat oven to 325°F

■ Unstuffed

Weight	Roasting Time
8 to 12 pounds (3.5 to 5.4kg)	2-3/4 hours to 3 hours
12 to 14 pounds (5.4 to 6.3kg)	3 hours to 3-3/4 hours
14 to 18 pounds (6.3 to 8kg)	3-3/4 hours to 4-1/4 hours
18 to 20 pounds (8 to 9kg)	4-1/4 to 4-1/2 hours
20 to 24 pounds (9 to 11kg)	4-1/2 hours to 5 hours
24 to 30 pounds (11 to 13.5kg)	5 hours to 5-1/4 hours

■ Stuffed

Weight	Roasting Time
8 to 12 pounds (3.5 to 5.4kg)	3 hours to 3-1/2 hours
12 to 14 pounds (5.4 to 6.3kg)	3-1/2 hours to 4 hours
14 to 18 pounds (6.3 to 8kg)	4 hours to 4-1/4 hours
18 to 20 pounds (8 to 9kg)	4-1/4 hours to 4-3/4 hours
20 to 24 pounds (9 to 11kg)	4-3/4 hours to 5-1/4 hours
24 to 30 pounds (11 to 13.5kg)	5-1/4 hours to 6-1/4 hours

TIP!

Sweet potatoes are a tasty complement to any turkey dish. When preparing sweet potatoes be sure to substitute whole milk with nonfat or low-fat milk, and try using maple syrup in place of melted butter. Your taste buds will never know the difference, but your waistline will!

Food Safety

Keep raw turkey away from cooked and ready-to-eat foods. Never defrost turkey at room temperature. Thaw overnight in the refrigerator, allowing approximately 24 hours for each 5 pounds (2.3kg); under cold running water allowing 30 minutes for each pound; or in the microwave. Cook whole turkeys to an internal temperature of 180°F (85°C) in the thigh or 170°F (80°C) in the breast.

Easy Steps for Carving

As friends and guests look on in anticipation, you can carve that picture-perfect turkey like a pro! Just follow these simple steps and you'll have a perfect plate of turkey in no time.

1. Cut band of skin holding drumsticks. Grasp end of drumstick. Place knife between drumstick/thigh and body of the turkey and cut through skin to joint. Remove entire leg by pulling out and back, using the point of the knife to disjoin it. Separate the thigh and drumstick at the joint.

2. Insert fork in upper wing to steady turkey. Make a long horizontal cut above wing joint through to body frame. Wing may be disjointed from body, if desired.

3. Slice straight down with an even stroke, beginning halfway up the breast. When knife reaches the cut above the wing joint, slice will fall free.

4. Continue to slice breast meat, starting the cut at a higher point each time.

Poof! You'll have a perfectly carved turkey that everyone will enjoy. Don't forget to save the wishbone!

Sultry
Poultry

Grilled Mexican Chicken Breast

4 *servings*

- SERVING SIZE: 1 RECIPE
- COUNTS AS:
  1 PROTEIN
  1 CONDIMENT
  2 FATS

☀ Ingredients

2 cloves garlic, minced

3 Tbsp (45mL) lime juice

3 Tbsp (45mL) orange juice

1 tsp (5mL) cumin

2 Tbsp (30mL) cilantro, minced

1/2 jalapeno chili, minced

1 tsp (5mL) lite salt

1/4 tsp (1mL) pepper

3 Tbsp (45mL) oil

4 5oz (150g) chicken breasts,
  skinless, boneless, pounded

1 Tbsp (15mL) fat-free sour cream

1. For marinade, combine the first nine ingredients in a bowl. Add the chicken breasts and toss to coat.

2. Cover and refrigerate for as little as 30 minutes or up to 4 hours.

3. Grill the chicken over medium heat until just cooked through, being careful not to overcook, as they will dry out. Serve with a squirt of lime and a dollop of fat-free sour cream.

Roast Chicken

4 *servings*

- SERVING SIZE: 4OZ (120G) COOKED
- COUNTS AS:
  1 PROTEIN

family fare

☀ Ingredients

whole chicken, skin removed

salt, to taste (optional)

freshly ground pepper, to taste

1 tsp (5mL) dried thyme

1 tsp (5mL) dried rosemary, crushed

nonfat cooking spray

1. Preheat oven to 350°F (180°C).

2. Rinse chicken, inside and out; pat dry.

3. Combine salt, freshly ground pepper, thyme and rosemary.

4. Rub chicken with herb mixture.

5. Spray roasting pan, with rack, with nonfat cooking spray. Place chicken on rack, breast side up.

6. Cook until done, or approximately 180°F (85°C), as measured by a meat thermometer when placed in the thigh.

7. Use the following roasting times:
   - 3-4 pound (1.3-1.8kg) whole chicken for 1 1/2-2 1/4 hours.
   - 5-7 pound (2.2-3.1kg) whole chicken for 3 hours.

Sultry ♣
Poultry

Chicken Marsala

1 *serving*

meals in minutes

- **SERVING SIZE: 1 RECIPE**
- **COUNTS AS:**
  1 PROTEIN
  2 VEGETABLES
  1 FRUIT

✴ Ingredients

5oz (150g) boneless, skinless chicken breast

1 cup (250mL) fresh mushrooms, diced

5 green onions, sliced

2 Tbsp (30mL) water

1/8 tsp (.5mL) lite salt

1/4 cup (50mL) dry Marsala or cooking sherry

nonfat cooking spray

1. With meat mallet, pound chicken to 1/4-inch thickness.

2. Coat skillet with nonfat cooking spray. Preheat over medium heat. Add chicken to pan and cook until tender and no longer pink.

3. Remove chicken from pan and keep warm.

4. Add mushrooms, green onions, water and salt to skillet. Cook mushrooms until tender and most of the liquid has evaporated. Add Marsala or cooking sherry to skillet. Heat through.

5. Top chicken with vegetables before serving.

Curried Stuffed Chicken Breast

1 *serving*

- **SERVING SIZE: 1 RECIPE**
- **COUNTS AS:**
  1 PROTEIN
  1 STARCH
  1 VEGETABLE
  1 FRUIT

✴ Ingredients

5oz (150g) boneless, skinless chicken breast

1 Tbsp (15mL) water

1/2 medium carrot, shredded

5 green onions, sliced

1/2 tsp (2mL) curry powder

1 slice lite bread, toasted and cubed

2 Tbsp (30mL) raisins

1/8 tsp (.5mL) lite salt

1/8 tsp (.5mL) paprika

1. Preheat oven to 350°F (180°C).

2. In a small saucepan, combine water, carrot, green onions and curry powder. Cook until vegetables are tender.

3. Remove pan from heat; add bread cubes and raisins. Toss ingredients together to combine.

4. With meat mallet, pound chicken to 1/4-inch (1/2cm) thickness. Sprinkle chicken with salt. Place chicken in a baking dish.

5. Place stuffing on one half of chicken breast; fold breast in half. Sprinkle with paprika. If needed, secure with a toothpick.

6. Bake for 20 minutes, or until chicken is no longer pink and juices run clear.

93

Sultry ✤
Poultry

Marinated Chicken Kabobs

1 *serving*

- **SERVING SIZE: 2-3 KABOBS**
- **COUNTS AS:**
  1 PROTEIN
  1 VEGETABLE

☀ Ingredients

5oz (150g) boneless, skinless chicken breast, cut into 1-inch (2.5mL) cubes

2 Tbsp (30mL) lemon juice

2 Tbsp (30mL) water

1/2 tsp (2mL) dried tarragon, crushed

1/8 tsp (.5mL) lite salt

1 clove garlic, minced

1 cup (250mL) zucchini, cut into 1-inch (2.5cm) pieces

1/2 medium green pepper, cut into 1-inch (2.5cm) pieces

kabob skewers

1. For the marinade, combine lemon juice, water, tarragon, salt and garlic in a non-metal bowl. Add chicken cubes and toss to combine.

2. Place bowl in refrigerator and marinate for approximately 20 minutes.

3. Drain chicken; reserve marinade.

4. On skewers alternate chicken, zucchini and green pepper. Place on broiler pan.

5. Broil 4-5 inches (10-13cm) from heat about 8-10 minutes or until chicken is tender and no longer pink. Brush chicken with marinade throughout cooking.

Italian-Style Chicken Tenders

2 *servings*

- **SERVING SIZE: 4OZ (120G) COOKED**
- **COUNTS AS:**
  1 PROTEIN
  1 STARCH

☀ Ingredients

1 pound (450g) boneless chicken tenders

salt and pepper

1 cup (250mL) breadcrumbs (see recipe on pg 154)

1/2 cup (125mL) egg substitute

1/2 tsp (2mL) hot sauce (optional)

1 Tbsp (15mL) water

nonfat cooking spray

1. Coat cooking sheet with nonfat cooking spray; preheat oven to 350°F (180°C).

2. In a small bowl, combine egg substitute, water and hot sauce.

3. Sprinkle 1/2 of the breadcrumbs onto a plate.

4. Season chicken with salt and pepper.

5. Dip each chicken tender in the egg mixture and then into breadcrumbs. Place on baking sheet.

6. Once all tenders have been breaded, coat them with nonfat cooking spray.

7. Bake for approximately 10 minutes.

8. Remove from oven and turn over, coat again with cooking spray.

9. Place back in the oven and bake additional 10 minutes, or until crispy.

   Serve over salad or with your favorite dipping sauce. (Optional-please refer to the menu plan for serving and exchanges.)

Sultry ❧ Poultry

Caraway Chicken

1 serving

- **SERVING SIZE: 1 CHICKEN BREAST WITH SAUCE**
- **COUNTS AS:**
  1 PROTEIN
  2 VEGETABLES
  1/2 DAIRY
  1 CONDIMENT

☀ Ingredients

5oz (150g) boneless, skinless chicken breast

1/2 cup (125mL) low-sodium chicken broth

1 green onion, thinly sliced

1/2 tsp (2mL) caraway seed, slightly crushed

freshly ground pepper, to taste

1/2 cup (125mL) skim milk

1 1/2 tsp (7.5mL) cornstarch

nonfat cooking spray

1 Coat skillet with nonfat cooking spray. Add chicken and cook 10 minutes, turning to brown evenly.

2 Add broth, green onion, caraway seed and pepper. Bring to a boil; reduce heat.

3 Cover and simmer for 20-30 minutes or till chicken is no longer pink. Remove chicken from skillet; keep warm.

4 Stir milk and cornstarch together; add to skillet.

5 Stir while cooking until thickened.

6 Top chicken with sauce before serving.

Serving suggestion: serve over 1/3 cup (75mL) cooked noodles or 1/3 cup (75mL) cooked rice, count as 1 Starch.

Oven Fried Chicken

1 serving

- **SERVING SIZE: 1 CHICKEN BREAST**
- **COUNTS AS:**
  1 PROTEIN
  1 STARCH
  1/2 DAIRY

☀ Ingredients

5oz (150g) boneless, skinless chicken breast

1/2 cup (125mL) breadcrumbs (see recipe on page 154)

1 Tbsp (15mL) snipped fresh parsley

1/2 cup (125mL) nonfat plain yogurt

1 garlic clove, minced

2 tsp (10mL) white wine or water

dash cayenne pepper

nonfat cooking spray

1 Preheat oven to 350°F (180°C).

2 Combine breadcrumbs and parsley in a shallow bowl; set aside.

3 In a separate shallow bowl, combine yogurt, garlic, wine and cayenne pepper.

4 Dip chicken into yogurt mixture, then coat with breadcrumbs.

5 Coat the chicken with nonfat cooking spray.

6 Bake for 30-45 minutes, or until chicken is no longer pink and juices run clear.

Sultry ❖ Poultry

Indian-Style Chicken

 serving

- **SERVING SIZE: 1 CHICKEN BREAST WITH RICE AND VEGETABLES**
- **COUNTS AS:**
  1 PROTEIN
  1 STARCH
  3 VEGETABLES
  1 DAIRY

☀ Ingredients

5oz (150g) boneless, skinless chicken breast

2 garlic cloves, minced

1/2 onion, chopped

1/3 cup (75mL) cooked brown rice

1 cup (250mL) plain nonfat yogurt

2 Tbsp (30mL) flour

1 tsp (5mL) ground cumin

1/4 tsp (1mL) ground ginger

1 medium green pepper, chopped

1 small tomato, seeded and chopped

nonfat cooking spray

1 Preheat oven to 350°F (180°C).

2 Coat skillet with nonfat cooking spray. Sauté onion and garlic. Stir in cooked rice.

3 Coat casserole dish with nonfat cooking spray. Spread rice mixture on bottom of casserole. Place chicken on top of rice.

4 In a bowl, mix together yogurt, flour, cumin and ginger. Stir in chopped green pepper and salt. Spoon over chicken.

5 Cover and bake for 30-40 minutes, or until chicken is cooked through and no longer pink.

6 Add tomatoes before serving.

Orange Chicken with Carrots

1 **serving**

- **SERVING SIZE: 1 CHICKEN BREAST WITH VEGETABLES AND SAUCE**
- **COUNTS AS:**
  1 PROTEIN
  1 VEGETABLE
  1 FRUIT

☀ Ingredients

5oz (150g) boneless, skinless chicken breast

juice from 1 orange

2 Tbsp (30mL) sherry

2 tsp (10mL) cornstarch

1/2 cup (125mL) low-sodium chicken broth

1/4 tsp (1mL) ground ginger

1/4 medium carrot, shredded

3 green onions, thinly sliced

1 Preheat oven to 350°F (180°C).

2 In a bowl, mix together orange juice, sherry, cornstarch, broth and ginger. Set aside.

3 In a casserole, combine carrot and green onion. Arrange chicken on top of vegetables.

4 Pour orange juice mixture over chicken and vegetables.

5 Cover and bake for 30-40 minutes, or until chicken is cooked through.

Sultry ✿
Poultry

Vegetable Chicken Bake

1 *serving*

- SERVING SIZE: 1 CHICKEN BREAST WITH VEGETABLES AND SAUCE
- COUNTS AS:
  1 PROTEIN
  1 STARCH
  1 VEGETABLE
  1/2 DAIRY

☀ Ingredients

5oz (150g) boneless, skinless chicken breast, cut into cubes

1/2 cup (125mL) low-sodium chicken broth

1/2 cup (125mL) fresh green beans, cut into bite-size pieces

1/4 medium carrot, thinly sliced

1 large celery stalk, thinly sliced

1/4 tsp (1mL) poultry seasoning

1/8 tsp (.5mL) lite salt

freshly ground pepper, to taste

2 Tbsp (30mL) cornstarch

1/2 cup (125mL) skim milk

2 Tbsp (30mL) white wine

1/3 cup (75mL) breadcrumbs (see recipe on page 154)

nonfat cooking spray

1. Preheat oven to 350°F (180°C).

2. Coat skillet with nonfat cooking spray and sauté chicken until cooked through. Set aside.

3. In a saucepan, combine broth, green beans, carrot, celery, poultry seasoning, salt and pepper.

4. Bring to a boil; reduce heat. Cover and simmer for 5 minutes.

5. In a small bowl, mix cornstarch and milk.

6. Add milk to vegetable mixture. Cook until thickened.

7. Stir cooked chicken and wine into vegetable mixture.

8. Pour into a casserole dish. Sprinkle with breadcrumbs.

9. Bake, uncovered, for 15-20 minutes, or until heated through and bubbling.

Soy-Glazed Chicken

1 *serving*

- SERVING SIZE: 1 CHICKEN BREAST
- COUNTS AS:
  1 PROTEIN
  1 CONDIMENT

☀ Ingredients

5oz (150g) boneless, skinless chicken breast

1/4 cup (50mL) white vinegar

2 Tbsp (30mL) brown sugar substitute

2 Tbsp (30mL) low-sodium soy sauce

2 garlic cloves, minced

1/4 tsp (1mL) ground ginger

1/4 tsp (1mL) onion powder

1. Preheat oven to 350°F (180°C).

2. For marinade, mix together vinegar, brown sugar substitute, soy sauce, garlic, ginger and onion powder. Add chicken and marinate in refrigerator for at least 20 minutes, but no longer than 24 hours.

3. Remove chicken and save marinade. Arrange chicken in baking dish and pour marinade over the chicken.

4. Bake, uncovered, for 20 minutes, or until chicken is cooked through.

Sultry ✤ Poultry

Lemon Chicken

1 *serving*

- **SERVING SIZE: 1 SERVING**
- **COUNTS AS:**
  - 1 PROTEIN
  - 2 CONDIMENTS

☀ Ingredients

5oz (150g) boneless, skinless chicken breast

2 lemons

2 tsp (10mL) flour

1/4 tsp (1mL) lite salt

1/4 tsp (1mL) freshly ground pepper

1/4 tsp (1mL) dried oregano

2 Tbsp (30mL) dry white wine

1 packet sugar substitute

1/4 cup (50mL) low-sodium broth

1 garlic clove, minced

nonfat cooking spray

1 Slice lemons in half. Juice 3 of the lemon halves, set aside.

2 Use the 3 lemon halves to make 1-2 tsp (5-10mL) lemon zest, depending on taste.

3 Use a meat mallet to pound out chicken until approximately 1/4-inch (1/2cm) thick.

4 Sprinkle chicken with salt, pepper, oregano and flour.

5 Coat large skillet with nonfat cooking spray.

6 Place chicken in pan, cook 1-2 minutes on each side on high heat.

7 Turn down heat to medium; add white wine, sugar substitute, lemon juice, garlic and broth.

8 Cook approx 5-10 minutes or until liquid reduces and forms thin syrup.

9 Add lemon zest. Slice remaining lemon half and use as garnish. You may squeeze juice over chicken for additional lemon flavor.

Serve over rice or roasted vegetable. (Optional-please refer to the menu plan for serving and exchanges.)

Chicken Nuggets

1 *serving*

- **SERVING SIZE: 1 CHICKEN BREAST, OR APPROXIMATELY 8 CHICKEN NUGGETS**
- **COUNTS AS:**
  - 1 PROTEIN
  - 1 STARCH
  - 1/2 DAIRY

☀ Ingredients

5oz (150g) boneless, skinless chicken breast, cut into bite-size pieces

1/2 cup (125mL) nonfat buttermilk

1/2 cup (125mL) breadcrumbs (see recipe on page 154)

dash of salt (optional)

freshly ground pepper

nonfat cooking spray

1 Preheat oven to 350°F (180°C).

2 Place chicken and buttermilk in a bowl and refrigerate for 20-30 minutes. Drain chicken and set aside.

3 Combine breadcrumbs and seasonings in a plastic, zip-top bag.

4 Add chicken to breadcrumbs and shake bag to coat chicken. Coat chicken with nonfat cooking spray.

5 Bake for 20-30 minutes, or until cooked through.

Sultry ❖ Poultry

Sweet & Sour Chicken

1 *serving*

meals in minutes

- **SERVING SIZE: RECIPE**
- **COUNTS AS:**
  - 1 PROTEIN
  - 2 VEGETABLES
  - 1 FRUIT

☀ Ingredients

5oz (150g) boneless, skinless chicken breast

3 green onions, thinly sliced

1/4 medium green pepper, cut into 1-inch (2.5cm) pieces

2 Tbsp (30mL) red wine vinegar

1 Tbsp (15mL) cornstarch

2 Tbsp (30mL) brown sugar substitute

2 Tbsp (30mL) ketchup

1/2 cup (125mL) low-sodium chicken broth

3/4 cup (175mL) fresh pineapple, cut into 1-inch (2.5cm) pieces

1/2 tomato, seeded and diced

nonfat cooking spray

1 Cut chicken into strips or 1-inch (2.5cm) pieces.

2 Coat skillet or wok with nonfat cooking spray. Add onion and green pepper; stir-fry over medium heat until vegetables are crisp-tender. Remove and set aside.

3 Coat skillet or wok again with nonfat cooking spray. Add chicken pieces and stir-fry over medium heat until chicken is cooked through.

4 Mix vinegar, cornstarch, chicken broth, brown sugar substitute and ketchup together.

5 Add sauce to skillet, or wok, with chicken. Cook, stirring constantly, until sauce thickens.

6 Return onion and green pepper to skillet or wok. Stir in pineapple chunks. Cover and cook 2 minutes, or until heated through. Stir in tomato just before serving.

Herbed Chicken Breast

1 *serving*

meals in minutes

- **SERVING SIZE: 1 CHICKEN BREAST**
- **COUNTS AS:**
  - 1 PROTEIN

☀ Ingredients

5oz (150g) boneless, skinless chicken breast

1 Tbsp (15mL) dried minced onion

1 clove garlic, crushed

1 Tbsp (15mL) water

1/2 tsp (2mL) dried thyme

1/4 tsp (1mL) lite salt

freshly ground pepper

1/4 tsp (1mL) dried rosemary

1/8 tsp (.5mL) rubbed sage

1/8 tsp (.5mL) dried marjoram

dash of hot sauce (optional)

nonfat cooking spray

1 Preheat oven to 350°F (180°C).

2 In a bowl, combine minced onion, garlic, water, thyme, salt, pepper, rosemary, sage, marjoram and hot sauce.

3 Dip chicken in sauce, coating all sides.

4 Coat baking pan with nonfat cooking spray. Place chicken in pan.

5 Bake for 20 minutes, or until chicken is cooked through.

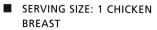

Sultry ✤ Poultry

Greek **Chicken Pita**

1 *serving*

- SERVING SIZE: 1 SERVING
- COUNTS AS:
  1/2 PROTEIN
  1 STARCH
  1/2 DAIRY

meals in minutes

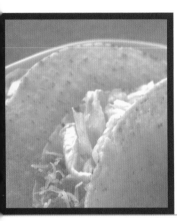

☀ Ingredients

3oz (90g) raw boneless, skinless chicken breast, cubed

2 tsp (10mL) lemon juice

dash of oregano

1/4 tsp (1mL) lite salt

freshly ground pepper, to taste

1 tsp (5mL) fat-free Italian dressing

4 inch (10cm) whole wheat pita

1oz (30g) reduced-fat or lite feta cheese

1/8 cucumber, sliced

1/2 tomato, diced

nonfat cooking spray

1 In a medium bowl, combine lemon juice, dressing, salt, pepper and oregano. Add chicken to marinade and coat well.

2 Coat skillet with nonfat cooking spray and heat over medium heat. Add chicken and cook approximately 5 minutes, or until chicken is no longer pink when cut.

3 Place chicken in pita and top with cheese, tomato and cucumber.

Creamy **Chicken Casserole**

1 *serving*

- SERVING SIZE: 1 SERVING
- COUNTS AS:
  1 PROTEIN
  1 STARCH
  1 VEGETABLE
  1 LA LITE

☀ Ingredients

5oz (150g) boneless, skinless chicken breast, diced

1 cup (250mL) raw white mushrooms, sliced

8oz (250mL) boiling water

2 green onions, sliced

1 garlic clove, minced

1/3 cup (75mL) cooked brown rice

1 packet L A Lite Cream of Chicken soup mix

nonfat cooking spray

1 Preheat oven to 375°F (190°C).

2 Coat medium skillet with nonfat cooking spray. Sauté mushrooms, onion and garlic 2-3 minutes over high heat. Set aside.

3 In a small casserole or baking dish, combine boiling water and L A Lite soup mix. Whisk together until smooth.

4 Add chicken, mushroom mixture and rice and mix well.

5 Cover casserole and bake 15 minutes. Remove cover and bake additional 5-10 minutes, or until chicken is cooked through. Serve hot.

Sultry ❧ Poultry

Almond Chicken

4 *servings*

family fare

- **SERVING SIZE:** 1/4 OF RECIPE
- **COUNTS AS:**
  1 PROTEIN
  2 VEGETABLES

✳ Ingredients

20oz (600g) boneless, skinless chicken breast, cubed

3 celery stalks, diced

1 carrot, diced

1 cup (250mL) white onion, diced

1 tsp (5mL) ground ginger

4 garlic cloves, minced

2 cups (500mL) bean sprouts

2 cups (500mL) low-sodium chicken broth

1 Tbsp (15mL) low-sodium soy sauce

2 Tbsp (30mL) almonds, chopped and toasted

nonfat cooking spray

1. Spray large skillet with nonfat cooking spray. Add onion and cook 1-2 minutes; add carrot and celery and sauté over high heat 1-2 minutes.

2. Add chicken, garlic and ginger to pan and sauté over medium high heat, until chicken is no longer pink.

3. Add broth, bean sprouts and soy sauce and bring to boil.

4. Reduce heat and simmer.

5. When liquid has evaporated and chicken is cooked through, add chopped almonds.

   Serve immediately.

BBQ Chicken Skewers

4 *servings*

family fare

- **SERVING SIZE:**
  1/4 OF RECIPE
- **COUNTS AS:**
  1 PROTEIN
  1 CONDIMENT

✳ Ingredients

20oz (600g) boneless, skinless chicken breast, cubed

1/4 cup (50mL) BBQ sauce

1-2 Tbsp (15-30mL) hot sauce

2 Tbsp (30mL) water

2 green peppers

1/2 packet brown sugar substitute

kabob skewers

1. In a small bowl, combine hot sauce, water, brown sugar substitute and half of the BBQ sauce.

2. Toss chicken in marinade to coat.

3. Cut green pepper into 1-inch (2.5cm) squares.

4. Alternate chicken and pepper on skewers; grill or cook in 400°F (200°C) preheated oven.

5. While cooking, brush remaining BBQ sauce over skewers.

6. Cook approx 10-15 minutes, or until chicken is no longer pink.

Sultry ❖ Poultry

Cheese & Apple-Stuffed Chicken

1 *serving*

- **SERVING SIZE: 1 ROLLED CHICKEN BREAST AND SLICED APPLES**
- **COUNTS AS:**
  1 PROTEIN
  1 VEGETABLE
  1 FRUIT
  1/2 DAIRY

☀ Ingredients

5oz (150g) boneless, skinless chicken breast

1 small apple, divided, peeled and cored

1oz (30g) reduced-fat mozzarella or cheddar cheese, shredded

5 green onions, sliced

1/4 cup (50mL) low-sodium chicken broth

1 tsp (5mL) cornstarch

1 tsp (5mL) cold water

1. Preheat oven to 350°F (180°C).

2. With a meat mallet, pound chicken to 1/4-inch thickness.

3. Chop one half of the apple and set aside. Slice the other half.

4. Top chicken with chopped apple and cheese.

5. Roll-up chicken, folding in sides. Secure with toothpicks or string.

6. Arrange apple slices and green onion in a baking dish. Place chicken on top.

7. Mix water and cornstarch. Add to chicken broth and pour over rolled chicken breast and sliced apple.

8. Bake for 20 minutes or until chicken is cooked through.

Chicken Caesar Wrap

1 *serving*

- **SERVING SIZE: 1 WRAP**
- **COUNTS AS:**
  1 PROTEIN
  1 STARCH
  1 VEGETABLE

☀ Ingredients

5oz (150g) boneless, skinless chicken breast, cubed

2 Tbsp (30mL) fat-free Caesar dressing

1 tsp (5mL) lemon juice

1/4 tsp (1mL) freshly ground pepper

1/2 cup (125mL) romaine lettuce

1/4 small tomato, diced

2 green onions, diced

6-inch (15cm) whole wheat flour tortilla

nonfat cooking spray

1. Preheat oven to 350°F (180°C).

2. In a small bowl, combine 1 Tbsp (15mL) Caesar dressing, pepper and lemon juice.

3. Add chicken and allow to marinate 1 hour to overnight.

4. Remove chicken from marinade and place on baking sheet that has been coated with nonfat cooking spray.

5. Bake for 15 minutes, or until chicken is cooked through.

6. Cool chicken 5 minutes.

7. To make wrap, place chicken, lettuce, tomato and onion in middle of tortilla. Drizzle with remaining dressing and roll up.

Sultry ❖ Poultry

Chicken & Greenbean Casserole

1 *serving*

- **SERVING SIZE: 1 CASSEROLE**
- **COUNTS AS:**
  1 PROTEIN
  2 VEGETABLES
  1/2 DAIRY
  1 LA LITE

❋ Ingredients

5oz (150g) boneless, skinless chicken breast

1/4 tsp (1mL) freshly ground pepper

1/4 tsp (1mL) garlic powder

1 packet L A Lite Cream of Mushroom soup mix

3/4 cup (175mL) boiling water

1 cup (250mL) fresh cut green beans

1/2 cup (125mL) fresh chopped mushrooms

3 green onions, chopped

1/2 cup (125mL) skim milk

nonfat cooking spray

1. Preheat oven to 375°F (190°C).

2. Coat small casserole dish with nonfat cooking spray.

3. Use meat mallet to pound out chicken until approximately 1/4 inch (1/2cm) thick.

4. Sprinkle chicken with pepper and garlic powder.

5. Combine boiling water and soup mix in casserole dish; mix well.

6. Add mushrooms, green beans, onions, chicken and milk to casserole dish.

7. Cover and bake for 20 minutes.

8. Uncover and bake additional 10-15 minutes, or until chicken is no longer pink. Serve hot.

Chicken Cheesesteak

1 *serving*

meals in minutes

- **SERVING SIZE: 1 SERVING**
- **COUNTS AS:**
  1 PROTEIN
  1 STARCH
  1 VEGETABLE
  1/2 DAIRY

❋ Ingredients

5oz (150g) ground white meat chicken breast

1/4 cup (125mL) raw white onions, chopped

1 Tbsp (15mL) green pepper, chopped

1/4 tsp (1mL) lite salt

1/4 tsp (1mL) onion powder

1oz (30g) reduced-fat provolone or mozzarella cheese

4 inch (10cm) whole wheat pita

nonfat cooking spray

1. Coat medium skillet with nonfat cooking spray.

2. Place onion and pepper in skillet and sauté over high heat 1 minute. Remove from pan.

3. Place chicken in same pan. Sprinkle with salt and onion powder.

4. Stir-fry the chicken until fully cooked. Return vegetables to the pan.

5. Turn off heat, push all of the chicken to one side of skillet.

6. Place cheese over chicken meat and cover loosely with foil to melt.

7. Place chicken, vegetables and cheese in pita. Serve hot.

Sultry ❀
Poultry

Buffalo Chicken Tenders

3 *servings*

- SERVING SIZE: 4OZ (120G) COOKED
- COUNTS AS:
  1 PROTEIN
  1 FAT

family fare

✲ Ingredients

1 pound (450g) boneless chicken tenders, unbreaded

3 Tbsp (45mL) lite margarine

1-2 Tbsp (15-30mL) hot sauce

1/4 tsp (1mL) garlic powder

1/8 tsp (.5mL) lemon juice

nonfat cooking spray

1 Preheat oven to 375°F (190°C).

2 Melt margarine in small sauce pan.

3 Whisk in hot sauce, lemon juice and garlic powder.

4 Place chicken tenders on baking sheet that has been coated with nonfat cooking spray.

5 Drizzle hot sauce mixture over chicken. Toss chicken to coat well.

6 Bake approx 15-20 minutes, or until chicken is cooked through.

   Serve warm over salad with celery sticks and fat-free blue cheese dressing, if desired. (Optional-please refer to the menu plan for serving and exchanges.)

Spinach & Feta Stuffed Chicken

1 *serving*

- SERVING SIZE: 1 SERVING
- COUNTS AS:
  1 PROTEIN
  1/2 DAIRY

good source of calcium

✲ Ingredients

5oz (150g) boneless, skinless chicken breast

1/4 cup (50mL) frozen chopped spinach, thawed and drained well

2 garlic cloves, minced

1oz (30g) reduced-fat feta cheese

1/4 tsp (1mL) freshly ground pepper

nonfat cooking spray

1 Use meat mallet to pound chicken breast until 1/4-inch (1/2cm) thick.

2 In small bowl combine spinach, feta and half of the garlic; mix well.

3 Place chicken on piece of aluminum foil that has been coated with nonfat cooking spray. Sprinkle chicken with pepper.

4 Place spinach mixture in middle of chicken and roll up chicken.

5 Top chicken with remaining minced garlic.

6 Roll chicken in foil to help keep it together, place in refrigerator for 1 hour to set.

7 Preheat oven to 375°F (190°C).

8 Place chicken in the foil on baking sheet and bake 20 minutes.

9 Cut open top of foil and place back in oven for 5 minutes to brown top of chicken and garlic.

   Serve hot with your favorite roasted veggies. (Optional-please refer to the menu plan for serving and exchanges.)

Sultry ❧
Poultry

Baked Chicken Parmesan

 servings

family fare

■ **SERVING SIZE: 1 CHICKEN BREAST**
■ **COUNTS AS:**
  1 PROTEIN
  1 VEGETABLE
  1/2 DAIRY

☀ Ingredients

1 pound (450g) boneless, skinless chicken breast

1/4 cup (50mL) egg substitute

1/2 cup (125mL) breadcrumbs (see recipe on pg 154)

1/4 tsp (1mL) basil

1/4 tsp (1mL) garlic powder

1/4 tsp (1mL) oregano

1 1/2 cups (375mL) lite tomato sauce

2oz (60g) part-skim mozzarella cheese, shredded

1 Preheat oven to 375°F (190°C).

2 Rinse chicken breast and dip into the egg substitute.

3 In another bowl, mix the breadcrumbs, basil, oregano and garlic powder. Place next to egg substitute. Dip chicken from egg substitute into breadcrumbs and coat well.

4 Pour 1/2 cup (125mL) tomato sauce on the bottom of a baking pan.

5 Place breaded chicken breast in pan.

6 Cover each chicken breast with remaining sauce.

7 Evenly sprinkle the shredded cheese over each chicken breast.

8 Bake for 20 minutes.

9 Remove foil and continue baking for 10-15 minutes longer to allow cheese to melt and chicken to cook through.

Serve with pasta or your favorite vegetable. (Optional-please refer to the menu plan for serving and exchanges.)

Garlic Chicken

1 serving

meals in minutes

■ **SERVING SIZE: 1 SERVING**
■ **COUNTS AS:**
  1 PROTEIN
  1 VEGETABLE
  1 CONDIMENT

☀ Ingredients

5oz (150g) boneless chicken tenders

1/2 tsp (2mL) Italian herb blend (see recipe on pg 224)

4 garlic cloves, sliced

1/2 cup (125mL) fresh mushrooms, sliced

2 green onions, sliced

1/4 tsp (1mL) garlic powder

1/4 tsp (1mL) lemon juice

1 Tbsp (15mL) dry white wine

nonfat cooking spray

1 With a fork, pierce each chicken tender to tenderize.

2 Sprinkle chicken with Italian herb blend.

3 Coat large skillet with nonfat cooking spray.

4 Place chicken, garlic, mushrooms, and onions in skillet; sauté 5 minutes or until chicken is cooked through.

5 Add lemon juice, garlic powder, and wine.

6 Continue to sauté chicken additional 5-10 minutes, or until chicken is no longer pink inside.

Serve hot over rice or roasted veggies. (Optional-please refer to the menu plan for serving and exchanges.)

Sultry ❖ Poultry

Vegetable Chicken Loaf

family fare

4 *servings*

- **SERVING SIZE: 1 SLICE**
- **COUNTS AS:**
  - 1 PROTEIN
  - 1 VEGETABLE

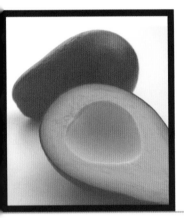

☀ Ingredients

20oz (600g) ground white meat chicken breast

1/4 cup (50mL) zucchini, finely chopped

1/4 cup (50mL) mushrooms, finely chopped

1/4 cup (50mL) chopped white onions

1/4 cup (50mL) green peppers, chopped

1/4 cup (50mL) chopped carrots

1/4 cup (50mL) parsley, chopped

1 Tbsp (15mL) fresh basil, chopped

1 tsp (5mL) garlic powder

1 tsp (5mL) fresh thyme, chopped

1/4 cup (50mL) egg substitute

1/3 cup (75mL) breadcrumbs (see recipe on pg 154)

nonfat cooking spray

1. Preheat oven to 375°F (190°C).

2. In a large mixing bowl, combine all ingredients; mix well.

3. Spread meat mixture into loaf pan coated with nonfat cooking spray.

4. Bake 35-45 minutes, or until internal temperature is 165°F (75°C).

5. Remove from oven and cool 10 minutes before slicing.

Chicken & Avocado Wrap

meals in minutes

1 *serving*

- **SERVING SIZE: 1 WRAP**
- **COUNTS AS:**
  - 1 PROTEIN
  - 1 STARCH
  - 1 FAT

☀ Ingredients

4oz (120g) plain, cooked chicken

2 Tbsp (30mL) salsa

1/8 ripe avocado, peeled, pitted and chopped

1 Tbsp (15mL) red onion, diced

1 1/2 tsp (7.5mL) pepper sauce (optional)

1 6 inch (15cm) whole wheat flour tortilla

1. In a bowl combine, chicken, salsa, avocado, red onion and pepper sauce.

2. Place chicken salad on tortilla and roll up, folding in the ends.

Sultry ♣ Poultry

White Chicken Chili

3 *servings*

- **SERVING SIZE: 1/3 RECIPE**
- **COUNTS AS:**
  1 PROTEIN
  1 STARCH
  1 VEGETABLE

✳ Ingredients

1 pound (450g) ground white meat chicken breast

5 green onions, chopped

1/2 white onion, chopped

2 small tomatoes, chopped

1 cup (250mL) fresh mushroom slices

1/2 cup (125mL) dried cooked white beans

2 1/2 cups (625mL) low-sodium chicken broth

3 garlic cloves, minced

1-2 tsp (5-10mL) chili powder, to taste

1 Tbsp (15mL) cornmeal

1/4 tsp (1mL) lite salt

1/4 tsp (1mL) ground cumin

1 tsp (5mL) cilantro

dash of hot sauce (optional)

nonfat cooking spray

1. Coat large saucepan with nonfat cooking spray.

2. Add green and white onions and mushrooms to pan; sauté 2 minutes.

3. Add chicken, tomato, garlic, chili powder, salt, cilantro and cumin to pot. Cook until chicken is browned.

4. Add broth, cornmeal and beans. Bring to a boil, cover and reduce heat.

5. Simmer 30 minutes, or until chili reaches desired consistency. You may add a dash of hot sauce if desired.

Sesame Chicken

1 *serving*

- **SERVING SIZE: 2-3 SKEWERS**
- **COUNTS AS:**
  1 PROTEIN
  1 FAT
  1 CONDIMENT

✳ Ingredients

5oz (150g) boneless, skinless chicken breast, cubed

2 Tbsp (30mL) low-sodium teriyaki sauce

1 Tbsp (15mL) water

1 garlic clove, minced

1/8 tsp (.5mL) ground ginger

1 Tbsp (15mL) sesame seeds, toasted

Kabob skewers

1. For marinade, combine teriyaki sauce, water, garlic and ginger.

2. Stir in chicken. Refrigerate and let marinate for 20 minutes.

3. Thread chicken, accordion-style, onto skewers.

4. Place on broiler pan. Broil 4-5 inches (10-13cm) from heat for 3 minutes.

5. Turn over and broil another 3-4 minutes or until chicken is no longer pink.

6. Sprinkle with toasted sesame seeds.

Sultry ❀
Poultry

4 *servings*

- **SERVING SIZE: 1/4 RECIPE**
- **COUNTS AS:**
  1 PROTEIN
  1 STARCH
  1 VEGETABLE
  1 FAT

family fare

Curry Chicken

☼ Ingredients

20oz (600g) boneless, skinless chicken breast

1 lime, juiced

1/2 cup (125mL) flour

freshly ground pepper

2 Tbsp (30mL) butter

5 green onions, chopped

1 Tbsp (15mL) curry powder

garlic powder, to taste

1 cup (250mL) low-sodium chicken broth

1 small can low-sodium stewed tomatoes

2 Tbsp (30mL) plain nonfat yogurt

salt and pepper, to taste

1 Marinate chicken in lime juice, refrigerate, for approximately 20 minutes.

2 Season flour with pepper.

3 Lightly coat each piece of chicken in flour, shaking to remove excess.

4 In a nonstick skillet, sauté chopped onions in 1 Tbsp (15mL) butter until golden. Remove and set aside.

5 Sauté chicken in remaining butter until brown.

6 Add sautéed onions, curry powder, garlic powder, broth and stewed tomatoes to pan. Bring to a boil.

7 Cover and simmer on medium-low heat for 30 minutes, or until chicken is done. Season to taste.

8 Remove chicken from pan and stir yogurt into sauce.

9 Place chicken back in sauce.

Serve with rice if desired. (Optional-please refer to the menu plan for serving and exchanges.)

---

8 *servings*

- **SERVING SIZE: 4OZ (120G) COOKED**
- **COUNTS AS:**
  1 PROTEIN

family fare

Honey Mustard Glazed Chicken

☼ Ingredients

2 1/2 pounds (1.3-1.6kg) boneless skinless, chicken breast

2 lemons

1/3 cup (75mL) chipotle pepper sauce

1/4 cup (50mL) honey mustard, fat-free or lite

1 packet sugar substitute

1 Zest the rind from one of the lemons and set aside.

2 Juice the lemons. In a glass bowl or zip-top bag, combine the lemon juice, chipolte pepper sauce and chicken.

3 Marinate for at least 1 hour or up to 2 hours in refrigerator.

4 Remove chicken from marinade; discard the marinade.

5 Make the glaze from remaining chipotle pepper sauce, sugar substitute, honey mustard and lemon zest.

6 Grill over medium high heat, about 8 minutes per side, brushing with glaze towards the end of cooking.

Sultry ❖ Poultry

Jerk Chicken

4 *servings*

family fare

- **SERVING SIZE: 4OZ (120G) COOKED CHICKEN**
- **COUNTS AS:**
  1 PROTEIN
  2 FATS

❋ Ingredients

4 boneless, skinless chicken breasts, 5oz (150g) each

5 green onions, chopped

4 garlic cloves, chopped

2 fresh Scotch bonnet or Habanero chilies, seeded and chopped

2 Tbsp (30mL) fresh lime juice

2 Tbsp (30mL) fresh lemon juice

3 Tbsp (45mL) olive oil

2 Tbsp (30mL) low-sodium soy sauce

1 Tbsp (15mL) brown sugar

1 Tbsp (15mL) fresh thyme leaves

2 tsp (10mL) ground allspice

2 tsp (10mL) freshly ground pepper

3/4 tsp (4mL) freshly grated nutmeg

1/8 tsp (.5mL) cinnamon

1. Place onion and garlic into a blender. Add chilies.

2. Squeeze in fresh lime juice, lemon juice, soy sauce, olive oil, brown sugar, thyme, allspice, pepper, nutmeg and cinnamon. Blend until marinade is smooth.

3. Using 2 separate zip-top plastic bags, pour in marinade, dividing evenly among the bags.

4. Divide the chicken between the bags and seal, pressing out any excess air.

5. Place bags into a shallow pan and into the refrigerator and marinate for 24 hours. Turn bags occasionally to evenly coat chicken with marinade.

6. Let chicken stand at room temperature for 10 minutes before cooking.

7. Preheat grill to medium temperature. Grill and cook chicken until browned on all sides. Then, lower the heat and cover until chicken is cooked through.

Chicken with Broccoli & Ziti

1 *serving*

- **SERVING SIZE: 4OZ (120G) COOKED**
- **COUNTS AS:**
  1 PROTEIN
  1 FRUIT
  1 CONDIMENT

❋ Ingredients

5oz (150g) boneless, skinless chicken breast, cubed

garlic powder

1/3 cup (75mL) cooked pasta

1 cup (250mL) cooked broccoli

1 tsp (5mL) olive oil

1oz (30g) part-skim shredded mozzarella

nonfat cooking spray

salt and pepper, to taste

1. Coat skillet with nonfat cooking spray. Season chicken with garlic powder.

2. Sauté chicken until cooked through.

3. Once chicken has been cooked, add broccoli and pasta. Season to taste with salt and pepper.

4. Toss with oil and top with cheese before serving.

Sultry ❖ Poultry

Chicken Normandy

■ SERVING SIZE: 1/4 RECIPE
■ COUNTS AS:
  1 PROTEIN
  1 FRUIT
  1 CONDIMENT

family fare

✳ Ingredients

4 boneless, skinless chicken breasts, 5oz (150g) each

freshly ground pepper, to taste

2 medium Granny Smith apples, sliced

5 green onions and tops, sliced

2/3 cups (150mL) unsweetened apple juice

2 tsp (10mL) low-sodium chicken bouillon crystals

1 1/2 tsp (7.5mL) dried sage leaves

2/3 cup (150mL) fat-free half & half

1/2 packet (50mL) sugar substitute

nonfat cooking spray

1 Coat large skillet with nonfat cooking spray; heat over medium-high heat. Sauté chicken breast until brown, 3-5 minutes on each side.

2 Season to taste with pepper.

3 Add apples, onions, apple juice, bouillon and sage to skillet; heat to boiling.

4 Reduce heat and simmer, covered, until chicken is tender, 10-12 minutes. Remove chicken and apples to serving platter. Cover loosely to keep warm.

5 Continue simmering juice mixture until reduced and almost completely evaporated.

6 Combine half & half and sugar substitute in glass measuring cup; pour into skillet.

7 Heat to boiling; boil, stirring constantly, until thickened, about 1 minute.

8 Pour over chicken and apples.

Chicken Patties

3 *servings*

■ SERVING SIZE: 1 PATTY
■ COUNTS AS:
  1 PROTEIN

✳ Ingredients

1 pound (450g) ground white meat chicken breast

1 Granny Smith apple, chopped

5 green onions, chopped

1/3 cup (75mL) breadcrumbs (see recipe on pg 154)

1 tsp (5mL) fresh mint, chopped

2 Tbsp (30mL) fresh thyme, chopped

freshly ground pepper

1 Combine all the ingredients in large mixing bowl. Form into 3 patties.

2 For best results and taste, place patties in the refrigerator for about 30 minutes.

3 Cook in a skillet, over medium heat, 5 minutes per side.

Sultry ✿
Poultry

Broccoli & Cheddar Stuffed Chicken

1 *serving*

- **SERVING SIZE: 1 SERVING**
- **COUNTS AS:**
  1 PROTEIN
  1/2 DAIRY

✳ Ingredients

5oz (150g) boneless, skinless chicken breast

1/4 cup (50mL) frozen chopped broccoli, thawed and drained well

1 Tbsp (15mL) chopped red pepper

2 garlic cloves, minced

1oz (30g) reduced-fat cheddar cheese

1/4 tsp (1mL) freshly ground pepper

nonfat cooking spray

1. Use meat mallet to pound chicken breast until 1/4-inch (1/2cm) thick.
2. In a small bowl, combine broccoli, red pepper, cheddar cheese and half of the garlic. Mix well.
3. Place chicken on piece of aluminum foil that has been coated with nonfat cooking spray.
4. Sprinkle chicken with pepper.
5. Place broccoli mixture in middle of chicken and roll up chicken.
6. Top chicken with remaining clove of minced garlic.
7. Roll chicken in foil to help keep it together, place in refrigerator for 1 hour to set.
8. Pre-heat oven to 375°F (190°C).
9. Place chicken inside the foil on baking sheet and bake 20 minutes.
10. Cut a slit in the top of foil packet and place back in oven for 5 minutes to brown top of chicken and garlic.

    Serve hot with your favorite roasted veggies. (Optional- please refer to the menu plan for serving and exchanges.)

Lemon-Herbed Marinated Chicken

1 *serving*

- **SERVING SIZE: 1 SERVING**
- **COUNTS AS:**
  1 PROTEIN
  1 FAT

✳ Ingredients

5oz (150g) boneless, skinless chicken breast

1 Tbsp (15mL) canola oil

1 Tbsp (15mL) lemon juice

1/2 tsp (2mL) rosemary

1/2 tsp (2mL) lite salt

1/4 tsp (1mL) freshly ground pepper

3 lemon slices

1. Mix oil, lemon juice, rosemary, pepper and salt.
2. Pour over chicken.
3. Allow to sit 30 minutes in refrigerator.
4. Remove chicken from marinade.
5. Grill or broil until done.
6. Serve hot, garnish with fresh lemon slices.

Sultry ✤ Poultry

Ginger Chicken & Apricots

family fare

- SERVING SIZE: 4OZ (120G) COOKED, AND 1/4 CUP (50ML) SAUCE
- COUNTS AS:
  1 PROTEIN
  1 FAT
  1 FRUIT

☀ Ingredients

2 1/2 pounds (1.4-1.7kg) boneless, skinless chicken breast

1 tsp (5mL) ground ginger

1 1/2 cups (375mL) dried apricots

1 1/2 cups (375mL) boiling water

1 Tbsp (15mL) olive oil

1 Tbsp (15mL) butter

5 green onions, finely chopped

1 1/2 tsp (7.5mL) sugar substitute

2 Tbsp (30mL) finely grated ginger

1 cinnamon stick, roughly separated

1/2 tsp (2.5 mL) cardamom, lightly crushed

1/4 tsp (1mL) ground cloves

1/4 tsp (1mL) freshly ground pepper

1 1/2 cups (375mL) low-sodium tomato juice

1/3 cup (75mL) finely chopped fresh cilantro

1 Place chicken breast in a bowl; sprinkle ginger over chicken, rubbing well to coat pieces evenly.

2 Cover and refrigerate for 1-12 hours.

3 Meanwhile cover apricots with boiling water; let stand for 30 minutes.

4 In a large, deep skillet, heat oil over medium-high heat. Brown chicken on all sides; transfer to a plate.

5 Drain off any fat; reduce heat to medium.

6 Melt butter; stir in onions, sugar substitute, ginger, cinnamon stick, cardamom, cloves and pepper. Cook, stirring often, until tender and golden, about 8 minutes.

7 Stir in tomato juice and apricots with their soaking water.

8 Bring to boil over high heat, stirring up brown bits; boil for 5 minutes or until tomatoes melt into the liquid.

9 Add the cilantro.

10 Return chicken to pan and reduce heat to medium-low; cover and simmer, turning chicken once, until juices run clear when chicken is pierced, about 20 minutes.

Chicken Sun-dried Tomato Pesto

4 *servings*

- SERVING SIZE: 1/4 RECIPE
- COUNTS AS:
  1 PROTEIN
  4 VEGETABLES

☀ Ingredients

4 skinless, boneless chicken breast halves, 5oz (150g) each

salt, to taste (optional)

freshly ground pepper, to taste

2 tsp (10mL) olive oil

1 (14.5oz) can diced tomatoes with green peppers and onions

1/4 cup (50mL) sun-dried tomato pesto

1 (14oz) can artichoke hearts in water, drained and quartered

1 Season both sides of chicken breasts with salt and pepper.

2 Heat oil in a large skillet over medium-high heat.

3 Place chicken in skillet; cook, turning once to brown each side. Remove chicken from pan, and set aside.

4 Pour tomatoes into pan; cook for 1 minute, stirring constantly.

5 Stir in pesto and artichokes, and return chicken to pan. Cover, and reduce heat to medium.

6 Simmer for 5-10 minutes, or until chicken is cooked through.

Sultry ♣ Poultry

Turkey Kielbasa

6 *servings*

- SERVING SIZE: 1/6 OF RECIPE
- COUNTS AS:
  1 PROTEIN
  1 STARCH
  1 VEGETABLE

❋ Ingredients

1 bottle (12oz) dark beer or ale

2 Tbsp (30mL) Dijon-style mustard

1/2 tsp (2mL) caraway seeds

6 cup (1.5L) coarsely shredded cabbage

1 pound (450g) turkey kielbasa or turkey sausage, cut on the diagonal into 2-inch (5cm) pieces

1 Granny Smith apple (or Braeburn or Winesap), cut into 1/4-inch (1/2cm) wedges

1 can (16oz) sweet potatoes, drained, cut into 1-1/2-inch (4cm) cubes

1. In a large deep skillet over high heat, combine beer, mustard and caraway seeds. Bring to boil.

2. Add cabbage, reduce heat to medium-low and cover. Simmer 5 to 8 minutes or until cabbage is crisp-tender.

3. Add turkey kielbasa, apple and sweet potatoes.

4. Increase heat to high and bring mixture to boil.

5. Reduce heat to medium-low, cover and simmer 3 to 5 minutes or until apple is crisp-tender and all ingredients are hot.

   Optional: Serve with whole grain mustard on the side.

Turkey Waldorf Sandwich

1 *serving*

- SERVING SIZE: 1 RECIPE
- COUNTS AS:
  1 PROTEIN
  2 STARCHES
  1 FAT

❋ Ingredients

4oz (120g) cooked turkey breast, cubed

1/8 cup (25mL) diced celery

1/4 small tart red apple, cored and cut into small cubes

1/2 Tbsp (7.5mL) walnuts, chopped

1/4 Tbsp (4mL) reduced-calorie mayonnaise

1/4 Tbsp (4mL) nonfat yogurt, plain or vanilla

pinch of freshly grated nutmeg

pinch of ground cinnamon

1 lettuce leaf, washed, cleaned and crisp

2 slices reduced-calorie raisin bread

1. In medium bowl combine turkey, celery, apple, walnuts, mayonnaise, yogurt, nutmeg and cinnamon. Blend well.

2. Cover and refrigerate at least 1 hour to allow flavors to blend.

3. To serve, arrange a lettuce leaf on a bread slice. Spoon turkey mixture over lettuce leaf and top with another slice of bread.

Sultry ❖
Poultry

Lemon-Herb Roasted Turkey

 10 *servings*

family fare

- SERVING SIZE: 4OZ (120G) COOKED SKINLESS TURKEY
- COUNTS AS:
  1 PROTEIN
  1 FAT

Can make 10-20 servings (depending on size of turkey)

☀ Ingredients

1 12-14 pound (5-6kg) fresh or frozen turkey thawed

1/3 cup (75mL) chopped fresh sage

1/3 cup (75mL) chopped fresh rosemary

1/3 cup (75mL) chopped fresh parsley

1 Tbsp (15mL) lemon zest

3 Tbsp (45mL) olive oil

1/2 cup (125mL) low-sodium chicken broth

1 tsp (5mL) lite salt

3 Tbsp (45mL) lemon juice

2 Tbsp (30mL) honey

2 lemons, quartered

nonfat cooking spray

1. Preheat oven to 325°F (160°C).

2. To prepare turkey, remove and discard giblets; rinse turkey inside and out with cold water, and pat dry.

3. Trim away any excess fat from the body. Starting around the neck, use your fingertips to loosen the skin of the bird from the flesh. Tuck wings under the body of the bird.

4. Place turkey on a broiler pan (or roasting pan with rack) coated with nonfat cooking spray. Combine sage, parsley, rosemary, lemon zest, olive oil and salt in a small bowl. Rub the herb mixture under the skin of the bird and along the cavity. Combine broth, 2 Tbsp (30mL) lemon juice and honey; pour half of mixture over the turkey. Stuff cavity of bird with lemon pieces.

5. Insert an oven-safe meat thermometer into the meaty part of the thigh, making sure not to touch the bone. Roast in oven for approximately 3 hours or until thermometer registers 180°F (80°C).

6. Halfway through roasting pour remaining lemon juice mixture over turkey. Remove turkey from oven, cover loosely with foil and let stand 15-20 minutes, before carving.

Turkey Meatballs

8 *servings*

family fare

- SERVING SIZE:
  2 MEATBALLS
- COUNTS AS:
  1 PROTEIN

☀ Ingredients

1 pound (450g) raw ground turkey breast

1/4 cup (50mL) breadcrumbs (see recipe on page 154)

2 Tbsp (30mL) egg substitute

2 tsp (10mL) low-sodium Worcestershire sauce

1 cup (250mL) low-sodium chicken broth

3 green onions, sliced

2 tsp (10mL) garlic powder

nonfat cooking spray

1. In a bowl, combine breadcrumbs, garlic powder, onions and Worcestershire sauce. Add turkey and egg substitute; mix well to combine all ingredients. Shape into 16 meatballs.

2. Coat baking dish with nonfat cooking spray. Arrange meatballs in a baking dish. Pour broth over meatballs. Bake in 350°F (180°C) oven until no longer pink. Drain off any excess fat.

   Serve meatballs over pasta. (Optional-please refer to the menu plan for serving and exchanges.)

Sultry ✤ Poultry

Rolled Turkey Divan

 1 *serving*

- **SERVING SIZE: 1 RECIPE**
- **COUNTS AS:**
  - 1 PROTEIN
  - 3 VEGETABLES
  - 1/2 DAIRY
  - 1 STARCH
  - 1 CONDIMENT

☀ Ingredients

5oz (150g) turkey breast tenderloin

1/2 cup (125mL) low-sodium chicken broth

1 cup (250mL) fresh mushrooms, sliced

1/2 cup (125mL) skim milk

2 Tbsp (30mL) dry sherry

1/8 tsp (.5mL) ground nutmeg

dash of red pepper

4 broccoli spears, cooked and drained

1 Tbsp (15mL) cornstarch

1 Tbsp (15mL) cold water

1 Tbsp (15mL) parmesan cheese

nonfat cooking spray

1. Cut turkey into 2-4 equal portions. Place piece of turkey between 2 pieces of wax paper or plastic wrap. Working from center to the edges, pound the turkey lightly with a meat mallet until the tenderloin is 1/4 inch (1/2cm) thick. Repeat with remaining turkey.

2. For sauce, whisk together chicken broth, milk, sherry, nutmeg, red pepper, cold water and cornstarch in a bowl; set aside.

3. Coat large skillet with nonfat cooking spray. Sauté mushrooms over medium heat until tender. Add to sauce mixture.

4. Divide broccoli among turkey slices, placing spears crosswise near one end of each slice.

5. Spoon about 1 Tbsp (15mL) of the sauce over each portion of broccoli. Roll turkey over broccoli and sauce. Secure with a toothpick, if necessary.

6. Coat baking dish with nonfat cooking spray. Arrange turkey rolls, seam side down, in baking dish. Pour remaining sauce over turkey rolls. Sprinkle with Parmesan cheese.

7. Bake, uncovered, in a 350°F (180°C).oven for 30 minutes, or until turkey is no longer pink.

Turkey with Barbeque Sauce

1 *servings*

- **SERVING SIZE: 1 RECIPE**
- **COUNTS AS:**
  - 1 PROTEIN
  - 2 CONDIMENTS

☀ Ingredients

5oz (150g) turkey breast tenderloin

2 Tbsp (30mL) barbeque sauce

1 Tbsp (15mL) water

1/2 packet sugar substitute

1/2 tsp (2mL) lemon juice

dash of garlic powder

1/8 tsp (.5mL) dried thyme, crushed

1. Preheat oven to 350°F (180°C).

2. Combine barbeque sauce, water, lemon juice, sugar substitute, garlic powder and thyme.

3. Place turkey breast in baking pan. Pour mixture over turkey.

4. Bake turkey approximately 20 minutes or until cooked through.

Sultry ❧ Poultry

Spinach Stuffed Turkey

4 *servings*

- **SERVING SIZE: 1/4 OF RECIPE**
- **COUNTS AS:**
  1 PROTEIN
  1 VEGETABLE
  1/2 DAIRY

❋ Ingredients

20oz (600g) turkey breast cutlets

2 garlic cloves, minced

1/2 cup (125mL) chopped onions

1 cup (250mL) button mushrooms, sliced

1 bag (10oz / 300g) baby spinach leaves

4oz (120g) reduced-fat shredded cheddar cheese, divided

freshly ground pepper, to taste

1 Tbsp (15mL) flour

1/2 cup (125mL) low-sodium chicken broth

nonfat cooking spray

1. Preheat oven to 350°F (180°C).

2. Coat skillet with nonfat cooking spray. Heat over medium heat. Add garlic and onions; sauté 1-2 minutes, until tender.

3. Add mushrooms, tossing with other ingredients to combine; cook until mushrooms soften.

4. Add spinach and broth to pan; toss ingredients together to allow spinach to wilt and cook down. Remove from heat and allow to cool to room temperature. Stir in flour.

5. Rinse off turkey cutlets and pat dry. Season with salt and pepper.

6. Divide spinach mixture evenly among turkey cutlets, forming a mound in the center of each cutlet. Sprinkle half of cheese over turkey. Gently roll turkey over spinach, securing with butcher's string or toothpicks, as needed.

7. Transfer stuffed turkey breasts to an oven-safe skillet or sauté pan that has been sprayed with nonfat cooking spray.

8. Bake for approximately 15 minutes. Top with remaining cheese and cook until all cheese is melted.

Turkey á la King

1 *serving*

meals in minutes

- **SERVING SIZE: 1 RECIPE**
- **COUNTS AS:**
  1 PROTEIN
  1 VEGETABLE
  1 LA LITE

❋ Ingredients

5oz (150g) fresh turkey tenderloins

1/4 cup (50mL) frozen peas, thawed

1/2 cup (125mL) fresh mushrooms, sliced

1 green onion, sliced

1 packet L A Lite Cream of Mushroom soup mix

3/4 cup (175mL) boiling water

nonfat cooking spray

1. Chop turkey into 1-inch (2.5cm) pieces.

2. Spray medium skillet with nonfat cooking spray.

3. Add onion, mushrooms and turkey to skillet. Sauté 5 minutes.

4. Add peas and reduce heat to low, continue to sauté until turkey is cooked through.

5. While turkey is cooking, combine boiling water and soup mix. Whisk together with a fork until smooth to make a gravy.

6. Turn off heat and pour gravy over turkey, stir to combine.

   Serve over rice or vegetables. (Optional-please refer to the menu plan for serving and exchanges.)

Sultry ❖ Poultry

Raspberry Turkey Delite

meals in minutes

1 *serving*

- SERVING SIZE: 1 RECIPE
- COUNTS AS:
  1 PROTEIN
  2 VEGETABLES
  1 CONDIMENT
  1 FRUIT (optional)

❋ Ingredients

5oz (150 or 196g) ground white meat turkey breast, formed into patty

1 cup (250mL) fresh mushroom slices

1/2 medium green pepper, chopped

5 whole green onions

3oz (90g) white zinfandel wine (optional)

1 Tbsp (15mL) fat-free raspberry vinaigrette

nonfat cooking spray

1. Coat pan with nonfat cooking spray.

2. Sauté mushrooms, green peppers and whole green onions; remove from pan and set aside.

3. Place turkey patty in skillet and brown on each side.

4. Return vegetables to pan.

5. Pour wine into pan, simmer another 5 minutes, or until turkey is cooked through.

6. Serve hot, drizzle with raspberry vinaigrette, before serving.

Sloppy Joe

family fare

4 *servings*

- SERVING SIZE: 1/4 OF RECIPE
- COUNTS AS:
  1 PROTEIN
  1 STARCH
  1 VEGETABLE

❋ Ingredients

20oz (450g) ground white meat turkey breast

1/2 cup (125mL) diced white onion

1/2 cup (125mL) diced green pepper

2 small tomatoes, diced

2 Tbsp (30mL) ketchup

1/2 tsp (2mL) garlic powder

1/4 tsp (1mL) paprika

2 tsp (10mL) vinegar

1 packet sugar substitute

1 tsp (5mL) Worcestershire sauce

dash of hot sauce

dash of oregano

dash of red pepper flakes

4 slices lite bread

nonfat cooking spray

1. Coat Dutch oven with nonfat cooking spray. Brown ground turkey, onions and peppers. Add remaining ingredients, except lite bread.

2. Cook over low heat 10-15 minutes.

3. Serve over lite bread.

"So many recipes to choose from, something new every day."

- Morgan D.

117

Sultry ♣ Poultry

Vegetable Stuffed Turkey Roll

1 serving

- SERVING SIZE: 1 RECIPE
- COUNTS AS:
  1 PROTEIN
  1 STARCH
  1 VEGETABLE

good source of fiber

❄ Ingredients

5oz (150g) turkey breast tenderloin

1/2 cup (125mL) mushrooms, sliced

1/4 medium carrot, shredded

1 stalk celery, thinly sliced

2 Tbsp (30mL) diced white onions

1/2 tsp (2mL) dried thyme, crushed

1/2 tsp (2mL) dried sage

freshly ground pepper, to taste

1 slice whole wheat bread, toasted and cubed

1-2 Tbsp (15-30mL) water

nonfat cooking spray

1. Preheat oven to 350°F (180°C)

2. Rinse turkey; pat dry. Place between 2 pieces of clear plastic wrap or waxed paper. With a meat mallet, pound turkey to 1/2 inch (1cm) thickness.

3. Coat skillet with nonfat cooking spray. Add mushrooms, carrot, celery, onion, thyme, sage, salt and pepper; cook over medium heat until tender.

4. Add bread cubes and toss lightly to mix. Stir in enough of water to moisten. Spoon stuffing over pounded turkey.

5. Roll turkey over stuffing, tucking ends under; secure with string or a toothpick. Place on a rack in a shallow baking pan.

6. Bake, covered loosely with foil, for 20-30 minutes. Remove foil. Bake 5-10 minutes more. Remove string. Let stand 10 minutes before slicing.

Open-Faced Turkey Sandwich

1 serving

- SERVING SIZE: 1 SANDWICH
- COUNTS AS:
  1 PROTEIN
  1 STARCH
  1 VEGETABLE
  1 LA LITE

❄ Ingredients

5oz (150g) fresh turkey tenderloins

1/4 tsp (1mL) lite salt

1/4 tsp (1mL) freshly ground pepper

1/4 tsp (1mL) onion powder

1/4 tsp (1mL) garlic powder

1 slice whole wheat bread

1 packet L A Lite Cream of Chicken soup mix

3/4 cup (175mL) boiling water

1/2 cup (125mL) green beans, cooked

nonfat cooking spray

1. Preheat oven to 375°F (190°C).

2. Coat large baking sheet with nonfat cooking spray.

3. Place turkey on sheet, sprinkle with onion powder, pepper, salt and garlic powder.

4. Bake approximately 25 minutes, or until turkey is cooked through.

5. While turkey is cooking, combine boiling water and soup mix. Whisk together with a fork until smooth to make a gravy.

6. Remove turkey from oven and place on top of bread. Serve green beans on the side.

7. Top turkey and green beans with gravy.

Sultry ♣ Poultry

Turkey Chili

4 *servings*

family fare

- **SERVING SIZE: 1 1/2 CUPS (375ML)**
- **COUNTS AS:**
  1 PROTEIN
  1 VEGETABLE

❉ Ingredients

20oz (600g) ground white meat turkey breast

2 garlic cloves

1/2 cup (125mL) water

1 cup (250mL) low-sodium chicken broth

6 tomatoes, seeded and chopped

1/2 cup (125mL) raw white onions, chopped

1/2 cup (125mL) canned kidney beans, drained and rinsed

1/2 Tbsp (7.5mL) chili powder

1/2 tsp (2mL) cumin

1/2 tsp (2mL) paprika

1/2 tsp (2mL) lite salt

1/2 tsp (2mL) freshly ground pepper

nonfat cooking spray

1 Coat a pot with nonfat cooking spray and heat over medium heat.

2 Add garlic and cook until golden brown.

3 Add turkey breast and water.

4 Add in chopped vegetables, broth, beans and spices.

5 Simmer over medium-low heat for 45 minutes.

"The chili recipe is my favorite... so tasty. Thought I would never be able to eat it again but L A Weight Loss proved me wrong."

- Gina H.

Basic Turkey Burger

1 *serving*

- **SERVING SIZE: 1 BURGER**
- **COUNTS AS:**
  1 PROTEIN

❉ Ingredients

5oz (150g) ground white meat turkey breast

freshly ground pepper, to taste

dash of onion powder

1/8 tsp (.5mL) sage

nonfat cooking spray

1/4 tsp (1mL) lite salt

1 Combine turkey and spices and shape into a patty.

2 Coat skillet with nonfat cooking spray. Brown both sides of the patty; turn down heat to low and finish cooking until juices run clear.

This burger is also great on the grill!

Sultry ❖ Poultry

Pineapple-Sauced Duck Breast

6 *servings*

- SERVING SIZE: 3OZ (90G) COOKED DUCK WITH 2-3 TBSP (30-45ML) SAUCE
- COUNTS AS:
  1 PROTEIN

☀ Ingredients

24oz (675g) duck breast, skinned

2 cups (500mL) canned, crushed pineapple, with juice

1/4 cup (50mL) water

2oz (60g) dried cherries

1-2 packets sugar substitute

2 Tbsp (30mL) red onion, minced

2 Tbsp (30mL) red bell pepper, diced

1 Tbsp (15mL) minced fresh ginger

1-2 garlic cloves, minced

1/2 jalapeño, seeded and minced

1/2 tsp (2mL) lite salt

1/2 tsp (2mL) freshly ground pepper

2 green onions, sliced

2 Tbsp (30mL) cilantro, chopped

nonfat cooking spray

1. In a small saucepan, combine pineapple in juice and next eight ingredients. Bring to a boil over medium-high heat. Reduce heat and simmer, uncovered, approximately 10-15 minutes, until slightly thickened and syrupy. Remove from heat and cool to room temperature.

2. Rinse duck breast and pat dry. Season with salt and pepper. Coat skillet with nonfat cooking spray; heat over medium heat.

3. Cook duck in skillet, about 4-6 minutes per side, or until cooked through. Remove from pan and let stand about 5 minutes to allow juices to redistribute throughout the meat. Slice each breast into strips, or as desired.

4. Just before serving, add green onions and cilantro to pineapple sauce; stir to combine. Spoon sauce over duck slices.

California Turkey Burger

1 *serving*

- SERVING SIZE: 1 BURGER
- COUNTS AS:
  1 PROTEIN
  1 VEGETABLE
  1 FAT

☀ Ingredients

cooked turkey burger (see recipe on page 119)

2 Tbsp (30mL) mashed avocado

1 Tbsp (15mL) chopped green pepper

1 leaf lettuce

2 slices onion

1/8 cucumber, sliced

1. Spread avocado over turkey burger.

2. Sprinkle with chopped green pepper.

3. Top with lettuce, cucumber and onion.

Sultry ♣ Poultry

Turkey - Broccoli Bake

1 *serving*

- SERVING SIZE: 1 RECIPE
- COUNTS AS:
  1 PROTEIN
  1 STARCH
  1 VEGETABLE
  1 FAT
  1/2 DAIRY

good source of fiber

❋ Ingredients

5oz (150g) turkey tenderloins, cubed

1 cup (250mL) frozen chopped broccoli, thawed and drained

1 Tbsp (15mL) margarine, melted

1 tsp (5mL) garlic powder

1oz (30g) reduced-fat shredded cheddar cheese

3 Melba toasts

nonfat cooking spray

1 Preheat oven to 375°F (190°C).

2 Coat small casserole dish with nonfat cooking spray.

3 Combine turkey, melted margarine, and broccoli in casserole dish and sprinkle with garlic powder.

4 Bake 25-30 minutes, or until turkey is just opaque.

5 While turkey is baking, crumble Melba toasts into small bowl. Add cheese to Melba mixture and toss well to combine.

6 Remove turkey from oven, sprinkle Melba mixture over casserole.

7 Place back in oven and bake another 10-15 minutes, or until turkey is cooked through and cheese has melted.

8 Serve immediately.

Turkey Melt

1 *serving*

- SERVING SIZE: 1 SANDWICH
- COUNTS AS:
  1 PROTEIN
  2 STARCHES
  1/2 DAIRY

good source of calcium

❋ Ingredients

4oz (120g) cooked turkey breast

2 slices bread

1 Tbsp (15mL) Dijon mustard

1 slice tomato

1oz (30g) reduced-fat swiss cheese

nonfat cooking spray

1 Spread mustard over bread.

2 Place turkey, tomato, and cheese on one piece of bread. Top with other slice.

3 Coat small skillet with nonfat cooking spray.

4 Place sandwich in skillet over medium heat, cook 2 minutes, or until cheese begins to melt.

5 Flip sandwich over and cook on second side until cheese melts.

6 Serve immediately.

Sultry ❋
Poultry

Roast Turkey with Cider

8 *servings*

- SERVING SIZE: 4OZ (120G) COOKED TURKEY BREAST, SKIN REMOVED, 2 TBSP (30ML) GRAVY, AND 1/4 CUP (50ML) OF STUFFING
- COUNTS AS:
  1 PROTEIN
  1 FRUIT
  1/2 FAT

❄ Ingredients

12 pound (5.4kg) oven-ready turkey

freshly ground pepper, to taste

5 yellow onions, cut into wedges

4 garlic cloves

1 1/2 cups (375mL) apple cider

1 Tbsp (15mL) softened tub margarine

1 Tbsp (15mL) flour

3 Tbsp (45mL) fat-free half & half

lite salt, to taste

Stuffing

1 Tbsp (15mL) olive oil

10 green onions, chopped

2 garlic cloves, crushed

1 cooking apple, peeled, cored and chopped

1/2 cup (125mL) fresh breadcrumbs (see recipe on pg 154)

3oz (90g) dried prunes, chopped

2 Tbsp (30mL) freshly chopped mint

1/4 cup (50mL) egg substitute

1 Preheat the oven to 375°F (190°C).

2 Rinse turkey inside and out; pat dry. Season the body cavity with pepper.

3 To make stuffing, heat olive oil in a pan over medium heat. Sauté the onion and garlic for 5 minutes or until softened.

4 Stir in the apple. Remove from the heat and add remaining stuffing ingredients, with seasoning to taste. Mix well to form a stiff consistency.

5 Stuff the neck cavity with prepared stuffing then fold the neck flap over and secure with skewers or trussing needle and twine.

6 Place the onion wedges and whole garlic cloves in the body cavity.

7 Weigh the turkey and calculate the cooking time allowing 18 minutes per pound (450g).

8 Place breast side down in the roasting pan; pour 1/2 cup (125mL) of the cider on top of the turkey. Insert an oven-safe meat thermometer into the meaty part of the thigh, making sure not to touch the bone. Place in the oven and roast for the calculated cooking time.

9 Twenty minutes before the end of the cooking time, turn the turkey over, pour over 1/2 cup (125mL) of the cider over the turkey and continue to cook, loosely covered with aluminum foil.

10 Cook the turkey to an internal temperature of 180°F (80°C)

11 Remove from the oven, place turkey on a serving plate, loosely cover with aluminum foil and stand for 20 minutes before carving.

Gravy

1 Strain 1 cup (250mL) of the juices from the roasting pan into a saucepan and stir in the remaining cider, bring to a boil.

2 Cream the margarine with the flour, then gradually whisk into the cider mixture.

3 Cook for 2 minutes, adjust seasoning and stir in the fat-free half & half.

4 Heat gently for 1 minute; serve with the cooked turkey.

Sultry ❧ Poultry

servings

- SERVING SIZE: 3OZ (90G) COOKED DUCK WITH 2-3 TBSP (30-45ML) SAUCE
- COUNTS AS:
  1 PROTEIN
  1 FRUIT

Raspberry Glazed Duck

☀ Ingredients

1 pound (450g) duck breast, skinned

1 tsp (5mL) lite salt

2 tsp (10mL) cinnamon

1/4 tsp (1mL) ground ginger

2 packets sugar substitute

1 Tbsp (15mL) sugar

1/2 cup (125mL) red wine

3 Tbsp (45mL) sugar-free raspberry jam

1 cup (250mL) raspberries

nonfat cooking spray

1 Preheat broiler.

2 Coat large skillet with nonfat cooking spray and heat over medium-high heat.

3 Cook one side of duck breast until browned, about 5-10 minutes.

4 Meanwhile, combine sugar substitute, sugar, salt, ginger and cinnamon in small bowl.

5 Turn breasts over and cook other side until browned.

6 Remove duck from skillet. Sprinkle one side of duck with cinnamon mixture then set aside.

7 Combine red wine and jam in skillet and heat over medium heat, bring up to a low simmer and cook for 3 minutes. Add raspberries and cook 1 minute. Remove sauce from heat.

8 Place duck breasts in broiler pan and broil for about 2 minutes, or until cinnamon mixture begins to brown.

9 Remove duck from broiler and allow to rest 2-3 minutes. Slice thinly and top with sauce.

---

1 **serving**

good source of calcium

- SERVING SIZE: 1 BURGER
- COUNTS AS:
  1 PROTEIN
  1 VEGETABLE
  1/2 DAIRY

Spanish-Style Turkey Burger

☀ Ingredients

cooked turkey burger (see recipe on page 119)

1/4 cup (50mL) chopped onions

1/4 cup (50mL) green peppers, chopped

1/2 tsp (2mL) hot sauce

1 Tbsp (15mL) salsa

1oz (30g) reduced-fat cheddar cheese

nonfat cooking spray

1 Spray small skillet with nonfat cooking spray.

2 Sauté onion, pepper and hot sauce, until vegetables are cooked.

3 Spread salsa over cooked turkey burger.

4 Top burger with vegetable mixture.

5 Place cheese over burger and melt under broiler.

6 Serve hot.

Sultry ❖
Poultry

Sassy Sides

A diverse collection of starches and side dishes can make the difference between a bland meal and a gourmet meal. You'll find plenty of ways in this section to spruce up favorite sides such as potatoes, rice and mixed vegetables. Spicy Broccoli, Herbed Eggplant and Pineapple Stuffing are among the many fabulous recipes inside!

◄ Stuffed Summer Squash recipe can be found on page 148

Storage Tips

■ Root vegetables such as squashes and potatoes should be stored in a cool, well-ventilated place at 50-60°F (10-15°C).

■ Corn and peas should be stored in a ventilated container.

■ Store dry ingredients such as rice and flours in a dry, cool storage area and in airtight containers once original packaging is opened.

Potatoes

■ **Russet potatoes** — Also known as the Idaho potato, the russet is long and slightly rounded. The skin is brown and rough and has many eyes. These are best for baked potatoes and French fries because of their low moisture content and high starch content.

■ **Round red potatoes** — These are also called boiling potatoes. They have a waxy flesh with less starch and more moisture than the russet, making them a good choice for boiling. These are also good for roasting, frying and mashing.

■ **Yukon gold potatoes** — These have a golden skin and the flesh ranges from buttery yellow to golden brown. These boiling potatoes have a moist texture. Yukon gold potatoes are great for making mashed potatoes.

■ **New potatoes** — These are young potatoes of any variety. Because they are younger than most potatoes, they have not converted all of their sugar into starch. This gives them a crisp and waxy texture and a very thin skin. They are small enough to be cooked whole; new potatoes can be oven roasted or boiled. New potatoes are also popular when making potato salad because they retain their shape better than an older potato.

■ **Sweet potatoes** — This large edible root is not actually a potato; the texture is often moister than a regular potato and the flavor is sweeter. There are many varieties of sweet potatoes, each with their own distinctive flavor.

■ **Yams** — Yams are not the same as a sweet potato, although canned sweet potatoes are commonly referred to as yams. They are similar in size and shape to sweet potatoes, but have more natural sugars and higher moisture content. Yams can be substituted for sweet potatoes in most recipes.

TIP!

Steam vegetables in steaming rack or basket over 1-inch boiling water. Depending on size of vegetables, steam for 2 minutes or longer. Vegetables are best when they are still slightly crunchy.

Rice

- **Arborio rice** — This is an Italian grown grain with a high starch content. The grains are shorter and fatter than other types of short-grain rice. It is typically used in risotto due to its increased starch content, which provides a creamy texture.

- **Basmati rice** — Basmati is a long-grained rice with a very fine texture. It has a nut-like flavor and aroma because it is aged to decrease the moisture content. It is often found in Indian and Middle Eastern markets and cooking.

- **Brown rice** — This rice refers to the entire grain of rice with only the inedible husk removed. The bran coating gives it a light brown color, nutty flavor and chewy texture, and provides a higher fiber content than white rice. Brown rice takes longer to cook than white rice, although some quick cooking brown rices have recently become available in the market.

- **Long-grain rice** — This rice has a length that is four to five times that of its width. Both white and brown rice come in long-grain varieties. When cooked, long-grain rice produces a light product that separates easily.

- **Medium-grain rice** — This rice is shorter and moister than long-grain and not as starchy as short-grain. Medium-grain rice is fluffy immediately after cooking, but clumps once it cools.

- **Short-grain rice** — This rice has a fat, almost round grain. The grains have high starch content and, when cooked, it is moist and sticky. This variety is sometimes called glutinous rice (although it is gluten free) and is often seen in Asian cooking.

- **White rice** — This variety has had the husk, bran and germ removed. It is lower in fiber than brown rice, which still has the bran and germ.

Vegetables

Fresh vegetables provide the diet with a variety of vitamins and minerals; they are low in fat and provide fiber. Many vegetables also contain antioxidants, which may protect against certain types of cancers and other disease. Portion sizes are, unless noted, 1/2 cup (125mL) cooked or 1 cup (250mL) raw. Water loss during cooking is due to heat breaking down the cell membranes, leaving a more concentrated food item; this is why cooked vegetables have a smaller portion size than raw vegetables.

Basic Cooking Methods

- **Steaming** — Cooking vegetables over boiling water. Steaming is a preferred cooking method for vegetables as it will help retain flavor and color. Steaming also helps vegetables to retain many nutrients that may be lost when vegetables are boiled.

- **Sautéing** — Cooking vegetables quickly in a small amount of fat in a skillet over direct heat. This works well for fast cooking vegetables such as spinach and other greens.

- **Boiling** — Cooking in boiling water or other liquid.

- **Grilling** — Cooking over hot coals or other direct heat source. This works best for larger chunks of vegetables such as eggplant, zucchini, onions and sweet peppers.

- **Blanching** — To place vegetables into boiling water briefly, then place in cold water to stop the cooking process; this method is used to set color and flavor while keeping vegetables crisp.

- **Roasting** — This is a dry heat method most often done in the oven in an uncovered pan; vegetables are cooked at extremely high temperatures to develop the natural sweetness and flavors.

Sassy Sides

Cabbage with Apples

1 *serving*

- **SERVING SIZE: 1 RECIPE**
- **COUNTS AS:**
  2 VEGETABLES
  1 FRUIT

good source of fiber

❋ Ingredients

1 cup (250mL) cabbage, shredded

5 green onions, thinly sliced

1/4 cup (50mL) water

1 Tbsp (15mL) lemon juice

1/4 cup (50mL) low-sodium chicken broth

1/4 tsp (1mL) caraway seeds

1 small apple, cored and cut into bite-size pieces

salt and pepper to taste

1 In a saucepan, combine cabbage, onion, water, lemon juice, broth and caraway seeds.

2 Bring mixture to boiling; reduce heat. Cover and simmer for 7-8 minutes, or until cabbage is nearly tender.

3 Stir in apple. Cook for 2-3 minutes more, or until apple is tender. Season to taste with salt and pepper.

Garlic & Pepper Stir-Fry

2 *servings*

- **SERVING SIZE: 1/2 OF RECIPE**
- **COUNTS AS:**
  2 VEGETABLES

❋ Ingredients

2 garlic cloves, minced

1/2 medium carrot, thinly sliced

1/2 medium green pepper, sliced

1/2 medium red pepper, sliced

1/2 medium yellow or orange pepper, sliced

5 green onions, sliced

1 cup (250mL) fresh mushrooms, sliced

1 Tbsp (15mL) lite soy sauce

nonfat cooking spray

1 Preheat a wok or skillet over medium heat; coat with nonfat cooking spray. Add garlic and stir-fry for 20 seconds.

2 Add carrot slices and stir-fry for 2 minutes. Add pepper strips and onion; stir-fry for another 2 minutes.

3 Add mushrooms and soy sauce; stir-fry about 2 minutes more or until vegetables are crisp-tender.

"I never really cooked until I bought the L A Weight Loss cookbook. Now I love getting creative in the kitchen."

- B. Garvett

Sassy
❖ Sides

Breaded Zucchini Sticks

2 *servings*

- **SERVING SIZE: 1/2 OF RECIPE**
- **COUNTS AS:**
  1 STARCH
  1 VEGETABLE

☀ Ingredients

2 cups (500mL) zucchini, cut into sticks

2/3 cup (150mL) breadcrumbs (see recipe on page 154)

freshly ground pepper

dash of seasoning blend

nonfat cooking spray

1. Preheat oven to 375°F (190°C).

2. Combine breadcrumbs, pepper, salt and seasoning blend in small bowl.

3. Rinse off zucchini sticks in water and shake off excess water.

4. Roll in crumbs and place on a cookie sheet coated with nonfat cooking spray. Coat zucchini sticks with spray.

5. Bake for 20 minutes until lightly browned.

Twice-Baked Potatoes

8 *servings*

- **SERVING SIZE: 1/2 POTATO**
- **COUNTS AS:**
  1 STARCH

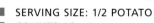

family fare

☀ Ingredients

4 small potatoes, baked

4oz (120g) reduced-fat cheddar cheese, shredded

2 Tbsp (30mL) skim milk

2 Tbsp (30mL) low-fat sour cream

2 tsp (10mL) garlic powder

1 Tbsp (15mL) chives, diced

nonfat cooking spray

1. Preheat oven to 325°F (160°C).

2. Slice a small hole on the top of each baked potato.

3. Using a spoon, remove the flesh of the potato and place into a medium mixing bowl.

4. Add milk, sour cream, garlic powder and chives to potato mixture.

5. Stir until well blended and smooth.

6. Add cheese and combine.

7. Spoon potato mixture back into the potato skins.

8. Place stuffed potatoes on a baking sheet that has been coated with nonfat cooking spray.

9. Bake 12-15 minutes, or until top of potato filling starts to brown.

Sassy
❖Sides

Pineapple Stuffing

family fare

4 *servings*

- SERVING SIZE: 1/4 PAN
- COUNTS AS:
  1 STARCH
  1 FRUIT
  1 FAT

❊ Ingredients

8 slices of lite bread

2 cups (500mL) canned, crushed pineapple, drained

1/4 cup (50mL) egg substitute

1/2 tsp (2mL) cinnamon

1/4 tsp (1mL) ginger

1/4 cup (50mL) lite margarine

nonfat cooking spray

1. Preheat oven to 350°F (180°C)
2. Dice bread into 1-inch (2.5cm) cubes.
3. In medium bowl, mix bread and pineapple.
4. Add egg to moisten bread.
5. Mix in cinnamon and ginger.
6. Melt margarine in small microwave-safe bowl.
7. Pour half of the melted margarine over bread mixture and mix well.
8. Coat 8-inch (20cm) square baking pan with nonfat cooking spray.
9. Spread bread mixture evenly in the pan.
10. Pour remaining margarine over stuffing.
11. Bake 15 minutes; center of the dish will be firm when done.

Spaghetti Squash Parmesan

1 *serving*

- SERVING SIZE: 1 RECIPE
- COUNTS AS:
  1 CONDIMENT
  1 VEGETABLE

❊ Ingredients

1/2 cup (125mL) cooked spaghetti squash

2 Tbsp (30mL) lite tomato sauce

1 Tbsp (15mL) parmesan cheese

1. Place squash on microwave-safe plate.
2. Top with sauce and cheese.
3. Heat 1-2 minutes until sauce is hot.
4. Serve hot.

"I'm eating healthier, feeling energized and loving it!"

- Paula R.

Sassy
❖ Sides

Garlic Grits

6 *servings*

- **SERVING SIZE:**
  1/3 CUP (75ML) COOKED
- **COUNTS AS:**
  1 STARCH
  1 CONDIMENT

※ Ingredients

3 1/2 cups (875mL) water

1/2 cup (125mL) skim milk

1/2 tsp (2mL) lite salt

1 cup (250mL) quick cooking
  grits (not instant!)

1 tsp (5mL) garlic powder

2 cloves roasted garlic, chopped

2 Tbsp (30mL) lite margarine

1/4 cup (50mL) water

1 Combine water, milk, and salt in medium pot.
   Bring to a boil.

2 Stir in grits slowly. Bring back to a boil, stirring for
   1 minute.

3 Reduce heat to low. Add garlic powder, stir.

4 Cook, stirring occasionally, about 5-10 minutes.

5 Grits should have a thick, yet creamy texture.

6 More water may need to be added during cooking if
   grits appear too thick; try adding 1/4 cup (50mL) of
   water at a time.

7 Stir in margarine and roasted garlic just before serving.

Turnip Casserole

good source of fiber

4 *servings*

- **SERVING SIZE:**
  1/2 CUP (125ML)
- **COUNTS AS:**
  1 VEGETABLE
  1 CONDIMENT

※ Ingredients

2 cups (500mL) raw turnips

1 Tbsp (15mL) lite margarine

1 tsp (5mL) flour

1/4 cup (50mL) skim milk

1 tsp (5mL) fat-free cream cheese

nonfat cooking spray

1 Preheat oven to 350°F (180°C).

2 Peel and chop turnips; boil in water until tender.
   Drain and set aside.

3 Coat small casserole dish with nonfat cooking spray.

4 In small saucepan, combine margarine, flour and skim
   milk. Cook, stirring constantly, until smooth, over
   medium heat.

5 Place turnips in casserole dish.

6 Place pieces of fat-free cream cheese over turnips.

7 Pour sauce over casserole.

8 Bake for about 30-35 minutes or until browned.

Sassy
❖ Sides

Whole Wheat Rigatoni

3 *servings*

- **SERVING SIZE:**
  2/3 CUP (150ML)
- **COUNTS AS:**
  1 VEGETABLE
  1 STARCH
  1 FAT

good source of fiber

☀ Ingredients

1 cup (250mL /140g) cooked whole wheat rigatoni

1 Tbsp (15mL) lite margarine

2 garlic cloves, minced

1 cup (250mL) raw spinach

1/2 cup (125mL) cooked sliced artichoke hearts

1 Tbsp (15mL) fat-free Italian dressing

2 Tbsp (30mL) pine nuts, toasted

1 Tbsp (15mL) parmesan cheese

1 Melt margarine in small saucepan. Add garlic and spinach; stir over low heat until spinach is wilted down.

2 Add artichokes, pasta and dressing. Mix well.

3 Sprinkle with pine nuts and cheese. Serve immediately.

Croutons

2 *servings*

- **SERVING SIZE: 1/2 OF RECIPE**
- **COUNTS AS:**
  1 STARCH

☀ Ingredients

4 slices lite bread

nonfat cooking spray

garlic powder, to taste

1/4 tsp (1mL) lite salt

onion powder to taste

oregano to taste

1 Dice bread into 1-inch (2.5cm) cubes.

2 Coat baking sheet with nonfat cooking spray. Place bread cubes on sheet.

3 Coat the bread cubes with cooking spray. Sprinkle with garlic powder, onion powder, oregano and salt.

4 Bake in 375°F (190°C) oven for 6-8 minutes, or until bread is lightly browned and crisp.

Sassy
❖Sides

Curried Rice

1 *serving*

- **SERVING SIZE: 1/3 CUP (75ML)**
- **COUNTS AS:**
  1 STARCH
  1 FAT

☀ Ingredients

1/3 cup (75mL) cooked brown or white rice

1 tsp (5mL) dried minced onion

1/2 tsp (2mL) curry powder

freshly ground pepper

1 Tbsp (15mL) slivered almonds, toasted, chopped

2 pimiento-stuffed olives or ripe olives, chopped (optional)

nonfat cooking spray

1. Coat small saucepan with nonfat cooking spray; add onion and sauté until soft.

2. Add curry powder and pepper; cook, stirring, for 30 seconds.

3. Stir in hot rice and almonds. Sprinkle with olives, if desired.

Egg Noodles with Mushrooms

1 *serving*

- **SERVING SIZE: 1 RECIPE**
- **COUNTS AS:**
  1 STARCH
  1 VEGETABLE
  1/2 DAIRY

☀ Ingredients

1/3 cup (75mL) cooked egg noodles

1 cup (250mL) fresh mushrooms, sliced

1 Tbsp (15mL) flour

1 Tbsp (15mL) lemon juice

1 tsp (5mL) lemon zest

1/2 cup (125mL) skim milk

pinch of dried thyme

1 Tbsp (15mL) parsley, chopped

nonfat cooking spray

salt and pepper to taste

1. Coat skillet with nonfat cooking spray; add mushrooms and sauté until tender.

2. Stir in flour, lemon juice and lemon zest.

3. Gradually add milk and thyme. Heat to boiling, stirring constantly.

4. Cook approximately 5 minutes until slightly thickened.

5. Stir in noodles and parsley. Season to taste with salt and pepper.

Sassy
❖ Sides

Cornbread

servings

- **SERVING SIZE: 1/12th OF BREAD**
- **COUNTS AS:**
  1 STARCH

☀ Ingredients

1 cup (250mL) cornmeal

1/2 cup (125mL) all-purpose flour

2 tsp (10mL) baking powder

2 tsp (10mL) sugar

1 cup (250mL) skim milk

1/4 cup (50mL) egg substitute

3 Tbsp (45mL) canola oil

nonfat cooking spray

1. Preheat oven to 425°F (220°C).
2. Coat 8-inch baking dish with nonfat cooking spray.
3. In medium bowl, combine cornmeal, flour, baking powder and sugar.
4. In separate bowl, combine milk, egg substitute and oil.
5. Add wet ingredients to dry ingredients, stirring, until just moistened.
6. Pour batter into prepared dish. Allow to rest 5 minutes before baking.
7. Bake about 15 minutes, or until lightly browned, and when a tooth pick is inserted into center comes out clean.
8. Cut into 12 squares.

Zucchini-Tomato Bake

serving

- **SERVING SIZE: 1 RECIPE**
- **COUNTS AS:**
  2 VEGETABLES
  1/2 DAIRY

☀ Ingredients

2 cups (500mL) zucchini, sliced

1/4 tsp (1mL) lite salt

1 tsp (5mL) Italian seasoning

1 small tomato, sliced

1 Tbsp (15mL) water

1oz (30g) part-skim mozzarella cheese

nonfat cooking spray

1. Preheat oven to 350°F (180°C).
2. Coat baking dish with nonfat cooking spray. Place zucchini slices in baking dish; sprinkle with salt and Italian seasoning.
3. Place tomato slices on top of zucchini. Sprinkle with water.
4. Cover and bake for 10-15 minutes, or until tender.
5. Remove from oven and sprinkle with cheese. Bake uncovered 5-10 minutes, or until cheese is melted.

Sassy
❖ Sides

Ratatouille

 2 *servings*

- **SERVING SIZE: 1/2 OF RECIPE**
- **COUNTS AS:**
  2 VEGETABLES
  2 FATS

☀ Ingredients

2 Tbsp (30mL) lite olive oil

1 garlic clove, crushed

1 cup (250mL) diced eggplant

1 cup (250mL) sliced zucchini

1/2 medium green pepper, chopped

1 small tomato, chopped

1/4 tsp (1mL) lite salt

1/4 tsp (1mL) freshly ground pepper

1/4 tsp (1mL) dried oregano

1/2 tsp (2mL) dried basil

1/2 bay leaf

1. Pour olive oil in a large skillet.

2. Add garlic and sauté until tender.

3. Add remaining ingredients.

4. Cover and cook over medium heat, stirring occasionally, about 10 minutes.

Dilled Cucumbers

4 *servings*

- **SERVING SIZE: 1/2 CUCUMBER**
- **COUNTS AS:**
  1 VEGETABLE

☀ Ingredients

2 medium cucumbers, sliced or quartered

1/2 cup (125mL) water

1/2 cup (125mL) vinegar

1/2 tsp (2mL) dill

dash garlic powder

1 tsp (5mL) lite salt

1. Combine cucumbers, water and vinegar in a sealable container.

2. Add dill, garlic powder and salt. Toss to coat.

3. Let stand at least 2 hours before serving.

"My husband uses the cookbook more than I do. He actually started losing weight without even trying."

- Rosie M.

 Sassy ❖ Sides

Stir Fried Oriental Style Vegetables

2 *servings*

- **SERVING SIZE: 1/2 OF RECIPE**
- **COUNTS AS:**
  2 VEGETABLES
  1 CONDIMENT

❊ Ingredients

1 Tbsp (15mL) brown sugar substitute

1 Tbsp (15mL) reduced-sodium soy sauce

1 Tbsp (15mL) vinegar

2 tsp (10mL) cornstarch

1 tsp (5mL) grated fresh ginger

2 green onions, sliced

1 tsp (5mL) minced garlic

1/2 cup (125mL) fresh mushrooms, sliced

1 cup (250mL) cabbage, shredded

1/2 medium green pepper, sliced

1/2 medium red pepper, sliced

1/2 cup (125mL) fresh bean sprouts

nonfat cooking spray

1 To make sauce, stir together sugar substitute, soy sauce, corn starch and vinegar. Set aside.

2 Coat a wok or skillet with nonfat cooking spray. Preheat skillet over medium-high heat. Stir fry ginger for 30 seconds.

3 Add onions and garlic and stir fry for 1 minute. Add mushrooms, cabbage and stir fry for 2 minutes. Add peppers and bean sprouts; stir fry for another minute, or until vegetables are crisp-tender.

4 Pour sauce over vegetables and toss to coat all vegetables.

Cauliflower with Cheese

1 *serving*

- **SERVING SIZE:**
  1/2 CUP (125ML) COOKED
- **COUNTS AS:**
  1 VEGETABLE
  1 DAIRY

good source of calcium

❊ Ingredients

1 cup (250mL) raw cauliflower florets

1/4 cup (50mL) water

1oz (30g) low-fat cheddar cheese, shredded

1/2 cup (125mL) skim milk

1 drop red pepper sauce, if desired

1 Place cauliflower in a microwave-safe dish. Pour water over cauliflower. Heat on high for 3-5 minutes or until tender. Drain and set aside.

2 In saucepan, heat remaining ingredients over medium heat, stirring frequently, until cheese is melted and mixture is smooth.

3 Pour over cauliflower before serving.

Sassy
❖ Sides

Sherried Mushrooms

1 *serving*

- **SERVING SIZE: 1 RECIPE**
- **COUNTS AS:**
  2 VEGETABLES

☀ Ingredients

1 cup (250mL) fresh whole mushrooms

1 green onion, chopped

1/4 cup (50mL) low-sodium broth

pinch dried tarragon, crushed

1 Tbsp (15mL) dry sherry

1 tsp (5mL) cornstarch

salt and black pepper, to taste

1 Gently clean mushrooms with a damp paper towel or soft brush.

2 In a medium skillet, combine mushrooms, onion, broth and tarragon. Bring to boil; reduce heat and cover. Simmer for 10-12 minutes, or until mushrooms are just tender.

3 In a small bowl, whisk together sherry and cornstarch until smooth; stir into skillet.

4 Add salt and pepper to taste.

5 Cook, stirring, until slightly thickened and bubbly. Continue to cook another 2 minutes before serving.

Zucchini & Peppers

1 *serving*

- **SERVING SIZE: 1 RECIPE**
- **COUNTS AS:**
  2 VEGETABLES
  1 FAT

☀ Ingredients

1 cup (250mL) zucchini, sliced

1/2 medium yellow pepper, chopped

1 garlic clove, crushed

1/4 tsp (1mL) lite salt

1/8 tsp (.5mL) freshly ground pepper

1 tomato, cut into wedges

1 Tbsp (15mL) lite margarine

nonfat cooking spray

1 Coat large skillet with nonfat cooking spray. Add zucchini, pepper, garlic, salt and pepper.

2 Cover and cook over medium heat, stirring occasionally, until vegetables are crisp-tender, about 5 minutes.

3 Add tomato. Cover again and cook over low heat just until tomato is heated through, about 3 minutes. Add margarine and heat until melted.

Sassy
❖ Sides

Stewed Tomatoes

4 *servings*

- SERVING SIZE: 1/4 OF RECIPE
- COUNTS AS:
  1 VEGETABLE

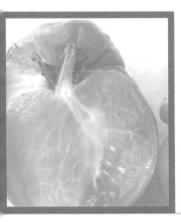

☀ Ingredients

4 tomatoes, chopped

5 green onions, finely chopped

1/2 medium green pepper, chopped

1 packet sugar substitute

1/2 tsp (2mL) lite salt

freshly ground pepper

1 tsp (5mL) garlic powder

1/4 tsp (1mL) oregano

2 Tbsp (30mL) of water

1. Combine all ingredients in medium saucepan.
2. Cover and heat to boiling; reduce heat.
3. Simmer, uncovered, 10-15 minutes.

Corn O'Brien

2 *servings*

- SERVING SIZE: 1/2 OF RECIPE
- COUNTS AS:
  1 STARCH

☀ Ingredients

1 cup (250mL) frozen, whole kernel corn

1 green onion, chopped

1 large celery stalk, diced

1/4 tsp (1mL) crushed red pepper

1/2 medium red pepper, diced

nonfat cooking spray

salt and pepper to taste

1. Cook corn by steaming or microwaving. Set aside.
2. Coat skillet with nonfat cooking spray. Add celery, green onion, crushed red pepper and red pepper; sauté until tender.
3. Add corn. Season with salt and pepper to taste. Cook over low heat, stirring occasionally, until corn is heated through.

Sassy
❖ Sides

Classic Mashed Potatoes

6 *servings*

- **SERVING SIZE:** 1/2 CUP (125ML)
- **COUNTS AS:**
  1 STARCH

☀ Ingredients

3 small potatoes, cooked

1/4 cup (50mL) milk, hot

2 Tbsp (30mL) lite margarine, melted

1/2 tsp (2mL) lite salt

1/2 tsp (2mL) garlic powder

freshly ground pepper

1. While hot, remove the skin from the potatoes.

2. Chop potatoes into a large dice and place in large mixing bowl.

3. Add milk, melted margarine, salt, garlic powder and pepper.
   For creamy potatoes: Mix using electric mixer 1-2 minutes.
   For chunky potatoes: Use a masher to soften potatoes, mix well until all ingredients are combined.

Peas & Mushrooms

2 *servings*

good source of fiber

- **SERVING SIZE:** 1/2 OF RECIPE
- **COUNTS AS:**
  1 STARCH

☀ Ingredients

1 cup (250mL) mushrooms, sliced

2 green onions, chopped

1/4 tsp (1mL) lite salt

1/2 tsp (2mL) garlic powder

1/8 tsp (.5mL) freshly ground pepper

1 cup (250mL) frozen peas, thawed

nonfat cooking spray

hot pepper sauce (optional)

1. Coat skillet with nonfat cooking spray and heat over medium flame. Add mushrooms, onions, garlic powder, salt and pepper. Sauté until mushrooms are tender.

2. Add peas to skillet and heat through.

3. Season with hot pepper sauce (optional).

"With 'No-Fuss' foods, I'm eating healthier and liking it!"

- Paula R.

Sassy ❖ Sides

Garlic 'n Herb Pita Chips

2 *servings*

- SERVING SIZE: 8 CHIPS EACH
- COUNTS AS:
  1 STARCH

meals in minutes

☀ Ingredients

6-inch (15cm) whole wheat pita

nonfat cooking spray

1 tsp (5mL) garlic powder

1/4 tsp (1mL) lite salt

oregano or thyme, sprinkle to taste

1 Preheat oven to 375°F (190°C).

2 Cut pita into 8 small pieces; separate layers into 16 wedges.

3 Spray cookie sheet with nonfat cooking spray, place pitas on sheet.

4 Spray pieces with nonfat cooking spray.

5 Sprinkle with garlic powder, salt and herbs, as desired.

6 Bake for 5 minutes, or until lightly browned.

Serve with dip or salsa. (Optional-please refer to the menu plan for serving and exchanges).

Grilled Corn on the Cob

12 *servings*

- SERVING SIZE: 1/2 LARGE EAR OF CORN
- COUNTS AS:
  1 STARCH

family fare

☀ Ingredients

6 large ears of corn

2 Tbsp (30mL) lite margarine

salt to taste (optional)

freshly ground pepper

1 Peel corn, remove silk, wash well and pat dry.

2 Preheat grill to medium.

3 Place each piece of corn on individual piece of aluminum foil.

4 Spread 1 tsp (5mL) of softened lite margarine over each piece of corn.

5 Sprinkle lightly with salt and pepper.

6 Wrap each piece of corn tightly in aluminum foil.

7 Place on grill; cook approximately 25 minutes, turning occasionally until corn is tender.

Sassy
❖ Sides

Italian-Style Beans

1 *serving*

■ SERVING SIZE: 1 RECIPE
■ COUNTS AS:
   2 VEGETABLES
   1 CONDIMENT

good source of fiber

✳ Ingredients

1 cup (250mL) fresh green beans

2 Tbsp (30mL) fat-free Italian dressing

1/2 tomato, chopped

1 Tbsp (15mL) grated parmesan cheese

1 Place green beans in 1qt (1L) boiling water.

2 Boil the beans for 4 minutes or until crisp-tender. Drain.

3 Toss hot beans with tomato, dressing and cheese.

Broccoli with Cheese

1 *serving*

■ SERVING SIZE: 1 RECIPE
■ COUNTS AS:
   1 VEGETABLE
   1 DAIRY

good source of calcium

✳ Ingredients

1 cup (250mL) raw broccoli florets

1/4 cup (50mL) water

1oz (30g) low-fat cheddar cheese, shredded

1/2 cup (125mL) skim milk

1 drop red pepper sauce, if desired

1 Place broccoli in microwave-safe dish. Pour water over broccoli. Heat on high for 3-5 minutes or until tender. Drain and set aside.

2 In saucepan, heat remaining ingredients over medium heat, stirring frequently, until cheese is melted and mixture is smooth.

3 Pour over broccoli. Serve immediately.

Sassy
❖Sides

Creamy Cucumbers

2 *servings*

- **SERVING SIZE:**
  1/2 OF RECIPE
- **COUNTS AS:**
  2 VEGETABLES
  1/2 DAIRY

good source of calcium

❋ Ingredients

1 medium cucumber, sliced

1 Tbsp (15mL) chopped onion

1 tsp (5mL) lite salt

1 tomato, chopped

2 Tbsp (30mL) cilantro

1 tsp (5mL) ground cumin

1 cup (250mL) plain nonfat yogurt

1 Mix cucumber, onion, and salt in a small bowl.

2 Allow mixture to sit for five minutes.

3 Remove excess water from cucumbers.

4 Transfer to a dry bowl.

5 Add tomato and cilantro to cucumber mixture.

6 Stir in yogurt and cumin.

7 Cover and refrigerate 1 hour before serving.

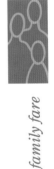

Spanish Rice

5 *servings*

- **SERVING SIZE:**
  1/5 OF RECIPE
- **COUNTS AS:**
  1 STARCH
  1 VEGETABLE

family fare

❋ Ingredients

1 1/3 cup (325mL) water

1/2 medium green pepper, diced

1/2 cup (125mL) white or yellow onion, diced

1/2 celery stalk, diced

1/4 tsp (1mL) of lite salt

2 small tomatoes, chopped

2/3 cup (150mL) uncooked brown or white rice

1/4 tsp (1mL) chili powder

freshly ground pepper

dash of hot sauce

1 In a medium saucepan, combine water, green pepper, onion, celery and salt. Bring to a boil. Reduce heat and cover; simmer for 5 minutes.

2 Stir in tomatoes, rice, chili powder, pepper and hot sauce. Return to boil. Reduce heat to low; cover and simmer approximately 20 minutes, or until liquid is absorbed.

> "This is a fantastic side dish with a turkey burger. Better than instant rice."
>
> *- Michele G.*

Sassy
❦ Sides

Balsamic-Glazed Vegetables

9 *servings*

- **SERVING SIZE:**
  1/2 CUP (125ML) COOKED
- **COUNTS AS:**
  1 VEGETABLE
  1 CONDIMENT

❋ Ingredients

1 1/2 pounds (675g) of your choice yellow squash, broccoli, cauliflower, zucchini, sliced

1/2 cup (125mL) water

1/2 cup (125mL) balsamic vinegar

1 tsp (5mL) garlic or onion powder

1 Tbsp (15mL) butter

freshly ground pepper

chopped parsley leaves, for garnish

1. Place vegetables in a pan with water, garlic or onion powder and vinegar.

2. Bring to a boil and cover. Reduce heat to medium and cook 10 minutes. Remove lid and bring back to boil.

3. Allow the water to boil away and the vinegar to reduce and glaze the vegetables, about 5 minutes.

4. When the vegetables are glazed to a rich brown color, add the butter to the pan.

5. Turn vegetables to coat lightly with butter.

6. Season with black pepper. Garnish with parsley.

Creamed Spinach

4 *servings*

- **SERVING SIZE:**
  1/2 CUP (125ML)
- **COUNTS AS:**
  1 VEGETABLE
  1/2 FAT
  1 CONDIMENT

good source of fiber

❋ Ingredients

8 cups (2L) fresh baby spinach

1 Tbsp (30mL) lite margarine

2 tsp (10mL) flour

3/4 cup (175mL) skim milk

1/4 tsp (1mL) freshly ground pepper

dash of nutmeg

1. Cut and discard tough stems from spinach. Rinse and lightly pat dry.

2. Bring 2 quarts (2L) water to boil.

3. Add the spinach and cook exactly 3 minutes.

4. Drain in colander; press spinach with hands to remove any excess moisture.

5. Chop spinach fine.

6. Melt margarine in a saucepan, add flour and cook, stirring, until a light golden brown.

7. Slowly add milk, stirring with a wire whisk, until mixture thickens.

8. Add spinach, pepper and nutmeg; toss together and serve.

Sassy ❖ Sides

Ginger Carrots

SERVING SIZE: 1/2 CUP (125ML)
COUNTS AS:
1 VEGETABLE
1 CONDIMENT

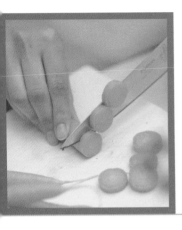

✳ Ingredients

3 cups (675g) carrot, peeled, sliced on an angle

1 Tbsp (15mL) lite margarine

2 packets (30mL) sugar substitute

2 Tbsp (30mL) fresh squeezed orange juice

2 Tbsp (30mL) grated ginger

1 1/2 Tbsp (23mL) honey

1. In a pot of water, bring carrots to a boil and cook for approximately 5 minutes, or until fork tender. Drain.

2. In a sauté pan, over low heat, add margarine and sugar substitute and honey.

3. Stir for approximately 2 minutes, or until sugar substitute begins to brown.

4. Add orange juice, ginger and carrots.

5. Simmer for approximately 5 minutes, or until liquid slightly thickens.

6. Serve immediately.

Lemon Green Beans

4 *servings*

SERVING SIZE:
1/2 CUP (125ML)
COUNTS AS:
2 VEGETABLES

good source of fiber

✳ Ingredients

1 pound (450g) fresh green beans, cleaned and trimmed

1/4 cup (50mL) green or yellow peppers, chopped

2 Tbsp (30mL) fresh dill

1 fresh green onion, sliced, thinly

1 tsp (5mL) fresh garlic, ground

2 tsp (10mL) olive oil

2 Tbsp (30mL) lemon juice

1. Place beans in 4 quarts (4L) of boiling water.

2. Cook green beans for 4-5 minutes in boiling water.

3. Drain beans and run cold water over them to stop cooking process.

4. Place green beans in a bowl; add the peppers, dill, onion, garlic, olive oil and lemon juice.

5. Toss together until coated and serve.

Sassy
Sides

Spicy Broccoli

 2 *servings*

- **SERVING SIZE:**
  1/2 CUP (125ML)
- **COUNTS AS:**
  1 VEGETABLE
  1 FAT

good source of fiber

☀ Ingredients

2 cups (500mL) raw broccoli florets

2 tsp (10mL) oil

1 tsp (5mL) crushed red pepper flakes

4 garlic cloves, chopped

1/4 tsp (1mL) lite salt

1 Simmer broccoli, covered, in 1-inch (2.5cm) of water for 5-7 minutes, until tender. Drain.

2 Heat skillet over high flame.

3 Add oil, crushed pepper and garlic.

4 Add broccoli to spiced oil and toss to combine. Add salt.

5 Serve immediately.

Green Beans with Mushrooms

 7 *servings*

- **SERVING SIZE: 1/2 CUP (125ML)**
- **COUNTS AS:**
  2 VEGETABLES

☀ Ingredients

1 1/4 pounds (570g) green beans, trimmed and halved

1 tsp (5mL) olive oil

1 Tbsp (15mL) lite margarine

1 green onion, chopped

1 cup (250mL) Portobello mushroom caps, sliced

1/2 cup (125mL) dry sherry

freshly ground pepper

1 Simmer green beans in water for about 5 minutes, until crisp-tender. Drain.

2 Heat in skillet over medium heat.

3 Add oil and margarine to the pan.

4 Add onions and sauté 2-3 minutes.

5 Add mushrooms and season with black pepper.

6 Sauté mushrooms with onions, about 3-5 minutes; add green beans back to the skillet.

7 Heat green beans through and add sherry.

8 Cook for 1-2 minutes.

Sassy ❖ Sides

Peppers & Mushrooms

3 *servings*

- **SERVING SIZE:**
  1/3 RECIPE
- **COUNTS AS:**
  2 VEGETABLES

☀ Ingredients

3 Tbsp (45mL) low-sodium vegetable broth

1 onion, cut into wedges

2 garlic cloves, crushed

1 green bell pepper, cut into 1/4 inch (1/2cm) strips

1 sweet red pepper, cut into 1/4 inch strips (1/2cm)

1/2 pound (225g) mushrooms, sliced

3 sweet chili peppers, chopped

6 cilantro leaves, chopped

freshly ground pepper

1 Tbsp (15mL) fresh parsley, chopped

1 Heat broth in a skillet; add onion and garlic and sauté until onion is translucent.

2 Add peppers, mushrooms and cilantro.

3 Stir-fry until peppers are tender.

4 Add freshly ground pepper and cook 1 minute.

5 Sprinkle with parsley and serve.

Herbed Eggplant

4 *servings*

- **SERVING SIZE:**
  1/2 CUP (125ML)
  2 VEGETABLES

☀ Ingredients

1 medium eggplant

3 tomatoes, chopped

1/4 cup (50mL) chopped onion

2 tsp (10mL) parsley

1 Tbsp (15mL) fresh cilantro

nonfat cooking spray

1 Cut eggplant in half and bake at 325°F (160°C).for 20 minutes, or until soft. Remove eggplant from oven.

2 Mash eggplant with fork or potato masher.

3 Coat medium skillet with nonfat cooking spray and heat over medium flame.

4 Sauté onions until translucent.

5 Stir in tomato; cook 1-2 minutes.

6 Stir in eggplant. Cook 4-5 minutes or until all liquid has evaporated.

7 Remove from heat and sprinkle with cilantro and parsley.

Sassy
❖ Sides

Vegetables in Peanut Sauce

2 *servings*

- **SERVING SIZE: 1/2 OF RECIPE**
- **COUNTS AS:**
  1/2 PROTEIN
  2 VEGETABLES

☀ Ingredients

1/4 pound (120g) bean sprouts

1/4 head cabbage, shredded

1/4 pound (120g) fresh spinach

1/4 cup (50mL) water

1 tsp (5mL) skim milk or plain, enriched soymilk

1/4 tsp (1mL) red pepper flakes or chili powder

2 packets brown sugar substitute

2 Tbsp (30mL) peanut butter

freshly ground pepper

1 Bring a large pot of water to a boil; add cabbage and cook 1 minute.

2 Then add spinach, cook 1 minute. Add bean sprouts and cook another minute.

3 Drain vegetables.

4 To make sauce, bring another 1/4 cup (50mL) water to a boil in small sauce pan.

5 Add milk, red pepper flakes, sugar substitute and peanut butter.

6 Mix well until ingredients form a smooth sauce.

7 Bring to a boil and remove from heat.

8 Place vegetables on platter, top with sauce and freshly ground pepper.

Sweet Cole Slaw

1 *serving*

- **SERVING SIZE: 1 RECIPE**
- **COUNTS AS:**
  2 VEGETABLES

☀ Ingredients

1 cup (250mL) shredded cabbage

1/2 cup (125mL) shredded carrots

1 Tbsp (15mL) chopped sweet pepper

1 Tbsp (15mL) rice vinegar

1 packet sugar substitute

1/2 tsp (2mL) low-sodium soy sauce

freshly ground pepper

1 Combine all ingredients in a bowl.

2 Toss together to mix well.

3 Chill at least 30-60 minutes before serving.

"The cookbook is great because it gives you the food exchange for every recipe."

- F. Grove

Sassy
❖Sides

Grilled Tomatoes & Eggplant

④ servings

- **SERVING SIZE:**
  2 TOMATO HALVES,
  1/2 CUP (125ML) COOKED EGGPLANT
- **COUNTS AS:**
  2 VEGETABLES
  1 FAT

✳ Ingredients

1 pound (450g) eggplant, trimmed
  and cut crosswise into 1-inch
  (2.5cm) slices

1 pound (450g) tomatoes, sliced

freshly ground pepper

3 Tbsp (45mL) chopped parsley

1 Tbsp (15mL) olive oil

1 large garlic clove, pressed

3 Tbsp (45mL) shredded lite or
  reduced-fat Romano cheese

nonfat cooking spray,
  olive oil flavored

1. Spray both sides of eggplant and tomato slices with nonfat cooking spray.
2. Sprinkle with freshly ground pepper to taste.
3. Grill eggplant slices until brown and tomato halves are charred.
4. Combine parsley, olive oil and garlic in a small bowl; pour over eggplant and tomatoes.
5. Top with grated cheese.

Stuffed Summer Squash

family fare

⑧ servings

- **SERVING SIZE:**
  1/4 OF A ZUCCHINI
  1/4 OF A SQUASH
- **COUNTS AS:**
  2 VEGETABLES

✳ Ingredients

2 large yellow summer squash

2 large zucchini

2 heads radicchio, roughly
  chopped

8oz (225g) baby spinach

1 Tbsp (15mL) balsamic vinegar

1 Tbsp (15mL) olive oil

1 tsp (5mL) minced garlic

freshly ground pepper

nonfat cooking spray

1. In a medium bowl, whisk together the oil, vinegar, garlic and freshly ground pepper. Set aside.
2. Cut summer squash and zucchini in half lengthwise.
3. With a melon-baller or small spoon, scoop out center of each section, leaving only the skins. Reserve the flesh for another use.
4. Coat large saucepan with nonfat cooking spray. Heat over medium flame and add radicchio.
5. Stir and cook for 30 seconds; next add baby spinach, cover and turn off heat.
6. Allow to steam for 1 minute, or until just wilted.
7. Season with pepper, to taste.
8. Drizzle inside of squash and zucchini shells with marinade, then stuff with radicchio and baby spinach.
9. Prepare grill and preheat to medium high.
10. Placed stuffed shells on grill and cook for 2-3 minutes or until bottoms are crisp-tender and slightly charred and filling is heated through.

Sassy
❖ Sides

Buttermilk Biscuits

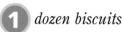
1 *dozen biscuits*

- **SERVING SIZE: 1 BISCUIT**
- **COUNTS AS:**
  1 STARCH
  1 FAT

family fare

☀ Ingredients

2 1/2 cups (625mL) all-purpose flour

1 Tbsp (15mL) sugar

1 Tbsp (15mL) sugar substitute

1/2 tsp (2mL) baking powder

1/2 tsp (2mL) salt

4 Tbsp (60mL) cold butter, cubed

4 Tbsp (60mL) cold lite margarine, cubed

1/4 cup (50mL) warm water

1 package active dry yeast

3/4 cup (175mL) warm low-fat buttermilk

nonfat cooking spray

1 In large bowl, combine flour, sugar, sugar substitute, baking powder and salt.

2 Add butter and margarine to flour mixture, stir until mixture resembles coarse crumbs, set aside.

3 Place warm water in a small bowl; sprinkle in yeast and stir until dissolved.

4 Add yeast mixture and warm buttermilk to flour mixture, stir until blended well.

5 Turn out dough onto a floured surface. Knead dough until smooth. Form into a ball.

6 With a rolling pin, roll out dough to 3/4 to 1 inch (2-2.5cm) thickness.

7 Cut biscuits with a 2 or 2 1/2 inch (5-6cm) biscuit cutter.

8 Place biscuits onto a baking sheet coated with nonstick cooking spray. Cover biscuits and let rest until doubled in size, about 30-45 minutes.

9 Meanwhile, preheat oven to 400°F (200°C).

10 Bake in oven for approximately 15 minutes or until lightly browned.

Orange Glazed Carrots

4 *servings*

- **SERVING SIZE: 6 CARROTS**
- **COUNTS AS:**
  1 VEGETABLE
  1 FAT

family fare

☀ Ingredients

24 cooked baby carrots

2 packets sugar substitute

1 Tbsp (15mL) grated orange peel

1 Tbsp (15mL) orange juice

4 Tbsp (60mL) lite margarine

dash of cinnamon

1 Melt margarine in small saucepan. Add orange peel and juice.

2 Add carrots and sugar substitute; cook over low heat, stirring occasionally, until carrots are glazed and heated through.

3 Sprinkle with cinnamon.

Sassy ✤ Sides

Cauliflower & Potatoes

serving

- **SERVING SIZE: 1 RECIPE**
- **COUNTS AS:**
  - 1 STARCH
  - 2 VEGETABLES

✷ Ingredients

1 cup (250mL) raw cauliflower, diced

1/2 potato, peeled, diced

1/4 tsp (1mL) cumin seeds

1/4 tsp (1mL) ginger, minced

1 garlic clove, minced

1/4 cup (50mL) water

1/4 tsp (1mL) turmeric

1/4 tsp (1mL) red chili powder

1 tomato, diced

1/2 tsp (2mL) garam masala
 (Recipe on page 215)

1/2 tsp (2mL) coriander powder

1/2 tsp (2mL) parsley

nonfat cooking spray

1. Heat a medium sauté pan coated with nonfat cooking spray.
2. Sauté cumin seeds for 1 minute.
3. Add ginger, garlic and diced potato.
4. Cook 1-2 minutes, stirring continuously, over medium-high heat.
5. Add water, remaining spices and tomato.
6. Simmer for 5 minutes while stirring.
7. Add cauliflower and continue to cook 1 minute on medium high. Lower heat and cover.
8. Allow to simmer 10-15 minutes, or until cauliflower and potatoes are tender.
9. Garnish with parsley.
10. Serve hot.

Rosemary Rigatoni

3 *servings*

- **SERVING SIZE:**
  1/3 CUP (75ML)
- **COUNTS AS:**
  - 1 STARCH
  - 1 FAT

✷ Ingredients

1 cup (250mL) cooked rigatoni

3 Tbsp (45mL) lite margarine

2 Tbsp (30mL) fresh rosemary, chopped

1 Tbsp (15mL) lemon zest

1 tsp (5mL) lemon juice

1/4 tsp (1mL) lite salt

1. Melt margarine in small saucepan. Add lemon zest, lemon juice, and rosemary; mix well.
2. Add pasta and stir until coated with margarine.
3. Sprinkle with salt.

Sassy
❖ Sides

Caribbean Rice & Peas

6 *servings*

- **SERVING SIZE:**
  3/4 CUP (175ML)
- **COUNTS AS:**
  1/2 PROTEIN
  1 STARCH

☼ Ingredients

1 Tbsp (15mL) olive or canola oil

1oz (30g) low-sodium Canadian bacon, diced

1/2 cup (125mL) onion, diced

1/2 medium green pepper, diced

1 celery stalk, diced

2 garlic cloves, minced

1/4 tsp (1mL) thyme

3 cups (750mL) cooked black-eyed peas

1 cup (250mL) cooked rice

1/4 tsp (1mL) lite salt

1/8 tsp (.5mL) freshly ground pepper

1/4 tsp (1mL) allspice

1/8 tsp (.5mL) cayenne pepper

1. Heat 1 tbsp (15mL) oil in a Dutch oven over medium-high heat. Add Canadian bacon and cook for approximately 2-3 minutes or until lightly browned.

2. Add onion, green pepper, celery, garlic and thyme. Cook, stirring, until just tender.

3. Add black-eyed peas, rice and seasonings; toss to combine.

4. Reduce heat to medium, and cook until heated through. Add a small amount of water if the mixture becomes too dry or starts to burn.

Stir-Fried Asparagus

1 *serving*

good source of fiber

- **SERVING SIZE:**
  1 CUP (250ML) COOKED
- **COUNTS AS:**
  2 VEGETABLES

☼ Ingredients

1 1/2 cups (375mL) fresh asparagus

1 tsp (5mL) cornstarch

2 tsp (10mL) cold water

1/4 cup (50mL) low-sodium chicken broth

1/2 cup (125mL) fresh mushrooms, sliced

1 tsp (5mL) garlic powder

nonfat cooking spray

1. Cut asparagus on an angle 1/2-inch (2.5cm) pieces.

2. Mix cornstarch and cold water; reserve.

3. Coat skillet with nonfat cooking spray. Heat skillet over medium-high heat.

4. Add asparagus and mushrooms; sprinkle with garlic powder. Stir-fry until asparagus is crisp-tender, about 3 minutes.

5. Stir in broth; heat to boiling.

6. Stir in cornstarch mixture; cook and stir until thickened, about 10 seconds.

Sassy
❖ Sides

Succotash

8 *servings*

- **SERVING SIZE:**
  1/2 CUP (125ML)
- **COUNTS AS:**
  1 STARCHES
  2 FAT

good source of fiber

✳ Ingredients

1 package (16oz / 450g) frozen lima beans

1 package (16oz / 450g) frozen whole kernel corn

1/4 tsp (1mL) lite salt

1 cup (250mL) water

1 tomato, diced

1/2 cup (125mL) diced white onion

2 Tbsp (30mL) lite margarine

1. In medium saucepan, combine corn, lima beans, salt and water.

2. Bring to a boil and reduce heat.

3. Add tomato and onion to mixture; simmer 5 minutes until all vegetables are tender. Drain and toss in margarine.

"Easy-Appetizing-Flavorful"
— *Paula R.*

Lemon Pilaf

3 *servings*

- **SERVING SIZE:**
  1/3 CUP (75ML)
- **COUNTS AS:**
  1 STARCH
  1 CONDIMENT

family fare

✳ Ingredients

2 tsp (10mL) dried minced onion

1-2 garlic cloves, finely chopped

1/2 cup (125mL) uncooked brown or white rice

1 cup (250mL) low-sodium chicken broth

1 tsp (5mL) lemon zest, minced

nonfat cooking spray

1. Coat saucepan with nonfat cooking spray. Sauté onion and garlic until soft.

2. Add remaining ingredients. Heat to boiling, stirring once or twice. Reduce heat to low and cover tightly.

3. Simmer approximately 20 minutes, or until all liquid is absorbed.

4. Remove from heat; fluff with fork and serve.

Sassy
❖ Sides

Braised Cabbage

good source of fiber

① *serving*

- **SERVING SIZE: 1 RECIPE**
- **COUNTS AS:**
  3 VEGETABLES

☀ Ingredients

2 cups (500mL) cabbage, shredded

5 green onions, chopped

1/4 tsp (1mL) onion powder

1/8 tsp (.5mL) lemon pepper

1/4 tsp (1mL) lite salt

nonfat cooking spray

1 Tbsp (15mL) water

1/4 cup (50mL) vegetable broth

1. Coat skillet with nonfat cooking spray; heat over low heat.

2. Add cabbage, onions, onion powder, lemon pepper, salt and water to skillet and sauté for 2 minutes.

3. Add vegetable broth.

4. Cover and cook over low until all vegetables are tender.

5. Serve hot.

Asparagus with Dijon Sauce

④ *servings*

- **SERVING SIZE: 1/2 CUP (125ML)**
- **COUNTS AS:**
  1 VEGETABLE
  1 CONDIMENT

☀ Ingredients

1 pound (450g) frozen asparagus spears, thawed

1 cup (250mL) low-sodium chicken broth

2 Tbsp (30mL) Dijon mustard

2 Tbsp (30mL) grated reduced-fat romano cheese

nonfat cooking spray

black pepper to taste

1. Coat large skillet with nonfat cooking spray. Heat over high heat.

2. Add asparagus to pan. Pour broth over asparagus and reduce heat; cover and steam over medium heat until crisp-tender, about 4 minutes.

3. Remove asparagus to serving plate with slotted spoon; keep warm.

4. Add mustard to skillet; bring to a boil, stirring constantly.

5. Pour over asparagus; sprinkle with cheese and black pepper to taste.

Sassy
❖ Sides

Breadcrumbs

 **3** *servings*

- SERVING SIZE: 1/3 RECIPE
- COUNTS AS:
  1 STARCH

☀ Ingredients

6 slices lite bread

1/4 tsp (1mL) lite salt

1/2 tsp (2mL) onion powder

1/2 tsp (2mL) garlic powder

1/4 tsp (1mL) oregano

1/4 tsp (1mL) basil

1. Toast bread lightly to remove any moisture.

2. Allow toast to cool.

3. Crumble toast into crumbs over large plate.

4. Mix salt, onion powder, oregano, basil and garlic powder into crumb mixture.

5. Adjust seasonings to taste.

Pad Thai Noodles

family fare

8 *servings*

- SERVING SIZE:
  1/2 CUP (125ML) COOKED
- COUNTS AS:
  1 STARCH
  1 VEGETABLE

☀ Ingredients

1 package (6.75oz / 190g) dry rice noodles

1 cup (250mL) raw bean sprouts

1 Tbsp (15mL) chopped red bell pepper

5 green onions, chopped

1 tsp (5mL) lemon juice

1 Tbsp (15mL) low-sodium soy sauce

1 tsp (5mL) rice wine vinegar

1/4 tsp (1mL) sugar

1 clove minced garlic

2 Tbsp (30mL) chopped peanuts

1 egg

nonfat cooking spray

1. Soak noodles in hot water for 15-20 minutes, or until soft. Drain and set aside.

2. Coat wok with nonfat cooking spray. Heat over medium-high heat.

3. Add red pepper and garlic; sauté for 1 minute. Remove from wok and set aside.

4. Place egg in wok and scramble. Add garlic and pepper mixture back to wok. Add noodles, bean sprouts, soy sauce and vinegar. Heat through.

5. Add green onion, lemon juice, sugar and peanuts. Mix well.

Sassy ✤ Sides

Tandoori Cauliflower

6 *skewers*

- **SERVING SIZE: 1 SKEWER**
- **COUNTS AS:**
  1 VEGETABLE
  1 FAT
  1/2 DAIRY

family fare

❋ Ingredients

2 cups (500mL) plain nonfat yogurt

1 1/2 pounds (675g) cauliflower

3 garlic cloves, minced

1 1/2 Tbsp (23mL) ginger, freshly grated

2 Tbsp (30mL) olive oil

1 tsp (5mL) cayenne pepper

1/2 tsp (2mL) freshly ground pepper

1 tsp (5mL) cumin, ground

1/2 tsp (2mL) coriander, ground

2 tsp (10mL) fresh lemon juice

2 Tbsp (30mL) whole wheat flour

bamboo skewers

1. Wrap the yogurt in cheesecloth, twist and suspend from a wooden spoon over a bowl.

2. Leave suspended in the refrigerator for 24 hours to drain the excess liquid from the yogurt.

3. Using a small grinder, reduce the garlic, ginger and oil to a paste. Place this mixture into a bowl.

4. Add cayenne, pepper, coriander, cumin, yogurt, lemon juice and flour. Mix well.

5. Separate the cauliflower into florets. Using a fork, prick florets in several places.

6. Place cauliflower into a plastic bag and pour the yogurt marinade overtop. Refrigerate for a minimum of 2 hours.

7. Soak some bamboo skewers in water for a minimum of 30 minutes.

8. Preheat the grill to medium high.

9. Remove the cauliflower and divide them among the skewers. Place the skewers on the middle burner and cook using indirect heat for 25 minutes with the lid closed.

10. Lift the lid and turn the heat up to high.

11. Move florets over to sit directly over the heat. This will crisp the outside of the florets.

12. Remove from heat once crisp and serve hot.

Corn with Basil

4 *servings*

- **SERVING SIZE:**
  1/2 CUP (125ML) COOKED
- **COUNTS AS:**
  1 STARCH

❋ Ingredients

1 (10oz / 300g) package frozen, whole kernel corn

5 green onions, chopped

1 large celery stalk, thinly sliced

1 garlic clove, minced

1 tsp (5mL) fresh basil, chopped, or 1/4 tsp (1mL) dried basil leaves

nonfat cooking spray

1. Cook corn by steaming or microwaving.

2. Coat skillet with nonfat cooking spray. Add corn, onion, celery and garlic, over low heat, until onion is tender, about 10 minutes.

3. Stir in basil; reduce heat.

4. Cover and cook until corn is tender, 3 minutes.

Sassy
❖ Sides

Marinated Cucumbers

1 *serving*

- SERVING SIZE: 1 RECIPE
- COUNTS AS:
  1 VEGETABLE

❋ Ingredients

1 Tbsp (15mL) apple cider vinegar

1 Tbsp (15mL) water

1/2 packet sugar substitute

1/4 tsp (1mL) freshly ground pepper

1/4 tsp (1mL) dill, minced

1 cup (250mL) cucumber, peeled and thinly sliced

dash lite salt

freshly ground pepper

1. Stir together vinegar, water, sugar substitute and pepper until dissolved.

2. Stir in dill. Add cucumbers to marinade.

3. Toss and chill before serving. Sprinkle with salt and pepper to taste.

Green Onions & Carrots

1 *serving*

- SERVING SIZE: 1 RECIPE
- COUNTS AS:
  2 VEGETABLES

❋ Ingredients

5 green onions, chopped

2 thin slices fresh ginger, finely chopped

1 garlic clove, finely chopped

1/2 medium carrot, shredded

1/4 tsp (1mL) lite salt

1/8 tsp (.5mL) fresh ground pepper

nonfat cooking spray

1. Coat pan with nonfat cooking spray; add onion, ginger and garlic; stir fry for approximately 2 minutes, or until onions are crisp-tender.

2. Stir in carrots and sprinkle with salt and pepper.

"The recipes taste as good as it looks in the picture!"

- Sandy S.

Sassy
❖ Sides

Peas & Onions

2 *servings*

- **SERVING SIZE:**
  1/2 OF RECIPE
- **COUNTS AS:**
  1 STARCH
  1 FAT

good source of fiber

☀ Ingredients

1/2 cup (125mL) water

1/2 tsp (2mL) lite salt

1 cup (250mL) frozen peas, thawed

1/2 cup (125mL) sliced white onion

1/4 tsp (1mL) dried thyme leaves

2 tsp margarine

1 In small saucepan, bring water and salt to a boil.

2 Add peas, onions and thyme.

3 Heat to boiling; reduce heat. Cook, uncovered, 5 minutes or until onions are tender.

4 Drain and toss with margarine. Serve hot.

Apple Chutney

6 *servings*

- **SERVING SIZE: 1/6 OF RECIPE**
- **COUNTS AS:**
  1 FRUIT

☀ Ingredients

2 tart apples, peeled, cored and finely chopped

1/8 yellow onion, quartered

1/2 (1 inch / 2.5cm) piece fresh ginger root, peeled

2 Tbsp (30mL) and 1/4 tsp (1mL) white wine vinegar

2 packets of sugar substitute

1/8 tsp (.5mL) cinnamon

1/8 tsp (.5mL) white pepper

1/8 tsp (.5mL) ground allspice

1/8 tsp (.5mL) ground nutmeg

1 In a saucepan, mix the apples, onion, ginger, vinegar, sugar substitute, cinnamon, white pepper, allspice and nutmeg.

2 Bring to a boil, reduce heat and cover.

3 Simmer 30 minutes, stirring frequently, until the apples are tender. Mix in some water if necessary to keep the ingredients moist.

4 Discard the onion and ginger, and store in the refrigerator until ready to serve.

Sassy
❖ Sides

Veal ✿ Deal Plus

From delectable Veal Involtini and Tangy Glazed Pork Chops to Stuffed Lamb and Buffalo Burgers, this unique section truly has something for everyone. No matter what your favorite dish, you'll find many new and easy ways to create delightful meals that will keep the whole family coming back for seconds every time.

Mediterranean Veal Chops recipe can be found on page 169

Cuts of Veal

Veal is a term used to describe a young calf or cow that is approximately 1-3 months old. When shopping for veal, choose a piece that has a somewhat pale pink flesh; veal that is turning red means that the calf was likely older than 3 months. The texture should be firm, finely grained and smooth.

- **Roast** — A large cut of meat that is large enough to serve multiple people. Popular roasts include loin, shoulder, rib, breast and crown roasts.

- **Breast** — Cuts from the breast region of a young calf, such as a boneless breast roast.

- **Shanks** — Cuts from the front leg of the calf. It is a very flavorful cut, but because of large amounts of connective tissue, it can be a tough cut of meat. Moist heat methods such as braising or stewing are used to prepare shank cuts. Osso buco is a popular dish made with veal shanks.

- **Round** — Cuts of meat from the leg. Popular cuts from the leg include cutlets, round steaks, rump roasts and round roasts.

- **Chops** — Cuts of meat usually from the rib section and may also include part of the rib. Chops may also come from the loin.

- **Ground Veal** — This can come from various parts of the calf, so the fat content will vary depending on which cuts are ground. Ground veal is often used in conjunction with other ground meats to make dishes such as meatballs or meatloaves.

- **Loin** — A tender cut that comes from either side of the backbone. The loin may be cut into steaks, chops or roasts.

Basic Veal Roast

Place roast (4-5 pounds) (1.8 - 2.2kg) into shallow pan and roast at 325°F (160°C), until internal temperature reads 150°F (65°C). Remove from oven and allow to rest for 10 minutes to allow juices to redistribute throughout the roast. Slice and serve.

TIP!

For more tender cuts of veal, choose loin roast, rib roast, rump roast and loin chop.

The less tender cuts, great for marinating, are shanks, shoulder roasts, breasts and riblets.

Lamb

Lamb is the meat from a sheep that is less than 1 year old. Meat from an animal that is older than 2 years is called mutton; mutton has a stronger flavor, but is less tender than lamb. Lamb is traditionally tender, with the exception of leg cuts. Baby lamb, which is from an animal younger than 8 weeks, should be pale pink when raw; other lamb cuts should be reddish-pink.

Lamb is a staple in many cultures, especially in Greece, Turkey, the Middle East, North Africa, India and beyond. Common flavors and spices you may see in lamb recipes include rosemary, lemon, garlic, mint and thyme, as well as cumin, coriander, cinnamon and turmeric.

Cuts

- **Roast** — A large cut of meat that is large enough to serve multiple people. Popular roasts include shoulder, shank leg, loin, loin eye and crown roasts.

- **Chops** — Cut of meat usually from the rib section; it may also include part of the rib. Chops may also come from the shoulder, rib or loin.

- **Ground Lamb** — Ground lamb can come from various parts of the lamb; therefore, the fat content will vary depending on which cuts are ground.

- **Legs** — Any cut of meat from the leg area. Leg cuts, such as a shank, are flavorful cuts of meat, but may be very tough. These are best suited for moist cooking methods, such as braising.

- **Loin** — A tender cut that comes from either side of the backbone. The loin may be cut into chops or roasts.

- **Rib** — A cut of meat from the rib section. It is a tender cut that may be available as chops or roasts.

Fresh Pork Cuts

- **Chops** — Cut of meat from the rib section and will usually also include part of the rib.

- **Ground Pork** — Ground pork can come from various parts of a pig, so the fat content will vary depending on which cuts are used. Ground pork is often used in conjunction with other ground meats to make meatballs and meatloaves.

- **Loin** — Cut from either side of the backbone, from the shoulder to the leg, of the pig. This is a tender cut of meat that can be cut into chops, tenderloin or roasts.

- **Ribs** — A cut of meat that is long and narrow, taken from the lower portion of the loin. This cut is usually a fatty cut of pork. These include "baby-back" ribs, spare ribs and country style ribs.

- **Roast** — A large cut of meat that is large enough to serve multiple people. Popular roasts include loin roasts, crown roasts and rib roasts.

Fresh Pork Cuts

Place roast (4-5 pounds) (1.8-2.2kg) into shallow pan and roast at 325°F (160°C) until internal temperature reads 150°F (65°C). Remove from oven and allow to rest for 10 minutes to allow juices to redistribute throughout the roast. Slice and serve.

TIP!

Cooking in a small amount of fat in a skillet over direct heat works well for pork cutlets and chops.

Pork and Pineapple Stir-Fry

1 *serving*

- **SERVING SIZE: 1 RECIPE**
- **COUNTS AS:**
  - 1 PROTEIN
  - 3 VEGETABLES
  - 1 FRUIT

good source of fiber

☀ Ingredients

4oz (120g) pork tenderloin

2 tsp (10mL) cornstarch

2 tsp (10mL) low-sodium soy sauce

1 cup (250mL) low-sodium chicken broth

1/8 tsp (.5mL) ground cumin

3 green onions, diced

1 cup (250mL) bean sprouts

3/4 cup (175mL) fresh pineapple, cut into bite-size chunks

1/2 small tomato, diced

1 cup (250mL) shredded romaine

nonfat cooking spray

1. Partially freeze meat. Thinly slice across the grain into bite-size strips. Set aside.

2. Mix chicken broth, cornstarch, soy sauce and cumin. Set aside.

3. Coat skillet or wok with nonfat cooking spray. Add pork and stir fry on medium heat until no longer pink; set aside.

4. Over high heat, add green onion and stir fry 1 minute. Add bean sprouts and stir fry another minute, or until vegetables are tender.

5. Add pork to vegetable mixture. Stir soy sauce mixture into pork and vegetables. Cook and stir until thickened.

6. Add tomato and pineapple. Toss to coat with sauce. Heat through.

7. Serve over shredded romaine lettuce.

BBQ Pulled Pork

8 *servings*

- **SERVING SIZE: 3OZ (90G) COOKED**
- **COUNTS AS:**
  - 1 PROTEIN
  - 1 VEGETABLE

family fare

☀ Ingredients

2 pounds (900g) pork loin, diced

1 can (16oz / 900g) low-sodium stewed tomatoes

2/3 cup (150mL) barbeque sauce

1/2 cup (125mL) water

1 onion, diced

2 Tbsp (30mL) vinegar

1/2 green pepper, diced

3 packets artificial sweetener

4 garlic cloves, minced

1/3 cup (75mL) hot water

1. Preheat oven to 375°F (190°C).

2. In a large casserole dish, combine all ingredients.

3. Bake 3-4 hours, or until pork is tender enough to be shredded with a fork.

4. Stir casserole every 30 minutes, if liquid evaporates, add additional hot water, 1/3 cup (75mL) at a time.

5. Once pork is tender, remove from oven. Use 2 large forks to shred all pork.

Veal ♣
Deal Plus

Veal Swiss Steak

- SERVING SIZE: 1 VEAL CUTLET WITH VEGETABLES
- COUNTS AS:
  1 PROTEIN
  1 STARCH
  2 VEGETABLES

meals in minutes

☀ Ingredients

4oz (120g) veal cutlet, unbreaded

1 Tbsp (15mL) flour

1/2 tsp (2mL) dry mustard

1/4 tsp (1mL) lite salt

1/2 small tomato, diced

1/4 tsp (1mL) garlic powder

1/2 cup (125mL) low-sodium chicken broth

1/2 medium green pepper, sliced into strips

5 green onions, thinly sliced

nonfat cooking spray

1 If necessary, pound veal 1/4-inch (1/2cm) thick, with a meat mallet.

2 In a small dish, combine flour, dry mustard, and salt.

3 Coat each side of the veal with flour mixture.

4 Coat skillet with nonfat cooking spray. Cook veal over medium-high heat until browned; remove from pan and keep warm.

5 Add tomatoes, onion, green pepper, garlic powder and chicken broth. Bring to a boil; reduce heat.

6 Cover and simmer until vegetables are tender.

7 Return veal to pan to heat through before serving.

Pork & Sauerkraut

8 *servings*

- SERVING SIZE: 3OZ (90G) COOKED PORK WITH 1/2 CUP (125ML) SAUERKRAUT
- COUNTS AS:
  1 PROTEIN
  1 VEGETABLE

☀ Ingredients

1 pork loin (2 pounds / 900g)

2 large cans sauerkraut, low-sodium if available

2 apples, peeled, cored and chopped

2 garlic cloves, minced

1/4 cup (50mL) apple juice

1/2 tsp (2mL) caraway seeds (optional)

nonfat cooking spray

1 Preheat oven to 300°F (150°C).

2 Spray casserole dish with nonfat cooking spray.

3 Cut pork loin into large chunks and combine in casserole dish with sauerkraut, apples, juice, garlic and caraway if desired.

4 Cover dish and bake for approximately 1 hour.

5 After 1 hour, stir, bake an additional 30 minutes.

6 Remove cover, turn up heat to 350°F (180°C), and bake 30-45 minutes or until pork is cooked.

Veal ✣
Deal Plus

Pork Tenderloin & Peppers

2 *servings*

- SERVING SIZE: 1/2 OF RECIPE
- COUNTS AS:
  1 PROTEIN
  2 VEGETABLES

☀ Ingredients

8oz (225g) pork tenderloin

1/2 tsp (2mL) dried thyme leaves

2 garlic cloves, crushed

1/3 cup (75mL) water

1/2 medium red pepper, cut into 1/4-inch (1/2cm) strips

1/2 medium green pepper, cut into 1/4-inch (1/2cm) strips

1/2 medium yellow pepper, cut into 1/4-inch (1/2cm) strips

3 green onions, thinly sliced

1/4 tsp (1mL) lite salt

1 Tbsp (15mL) cold water

2 tsp (10mL) cornstarch

nonfat cooking spray

1 Mix together thyme and garlic; rub over pork.

2 Coat large skillet with nonfat cooking spray. Add pork to skillet and cook until no longer pink.

3 Remove pork and cover loosely with foil to keep warm.

4 Add water, peppers, onion and salt to skillet; cover and simmer, until vegetables are tender.

5 Mix cold water and cornstarch; stir into pepper mixture. Cook, stirring, until slightly thickened.

6 Cut pork into strips and add back to vegetable mixture. Heat through and serve.

Roast Pork with Rosemary

6 *servings*

family fare

- SERVING SIZE: 3OZ (90G) COOKED PORK
- COUNTS AS:
  1 PROTEIN

☀ Ingredients

1 1/2 pounds (675g) pork loin roast

1 tsp (5mL) lite salt

1 tsp (5mL) freshly ground pepper

2 Tbsp (30mL) dried rosemary leaves, crushed or 4 Tbsp (60mL) fresh

3 garlic cloves, crushed

1 Preheat oven to 325°F (180°C).

2 Sprinkle meat with salt and pepper; rub with rosemary and garlic.

3 Place pork roast in roasting pan. Roast, uncovered until internal temperature of 160°F (70°C), about 30 minutes per pound.

Veal ♣
Deal Plus

Pork Piccata

serving

meals in minutes

- **SERVING SIZE: 1 RECIPE**
- **COUNTS AS:**
  1 PROTEIN
  1 STARCH
  1 FAT

☀ Ingredients

4oz (120g) pork tenderloin

1/3 cup (75mL) breadcrumbs (see recipe on pg 154)

1/4 tsp (1mL) lite salt

freshly ground pepper

1 tsp (5mL) garlic powder

1 Tbsp (15mL) lite margarine

1 Tbsp (15mL) lemon juice

1 Tbsp (15mL) capers

1 Tbsp (15mL) dry white wine

nonfat cooking spray

1. With a meat mallet, pound tenderloin to 1/4 inch (1/2cm) thickness.

2. Mix together breadcrumbs, salt, pepper and garlic powder. Dampen meat lightly with water, then coat with breadcrumb mixture.

3. Coat skillet with nonfat cooking spray. Heat skillet over medium heat. Add pork to skillet and cook, turning once, until done, about 7-8 minutes.

4. Remove pork from skillet; add lemon juice, margarine, capers and wine into skillet; heat to boil and serve over pork.

❖ Veal or chicken could be substituted for pork.

Italian Pork Chops

serving

- **SERVING SIZE: 1 COOKED PORK CHOP**
- **COUNTS AS:**
  1 PROTEIN

☀ Ingredients

4oz (120g) boneless pork loin chop

2 Tbsp (30mL) fat-free Italian dressing

1/8 tsp (.5mL) oregano

1/2 clove garlic, crushed

1 Tbsp (15mL) parmesan cheese

1 Tbsp (15mL) hot water

nonfat cooking spray

1. Use fork to pierce holes in pork chop to tenderize.

2. Place pork chop in plastic sandwich bag and pour salad dressing over chop. Add oregano and garlic. Place in refrigerator and allow to marinate 1 hour.

3. Coat medium skillet with nonfat cooking spray.

4. Over high heat, brown both sides of pork chop.

5. Turn down heat and continue to cook approximately 10 minutes, turning occasionally.

6. Add hot water to prevent pork from sticking to pan.

7. Sprinkle with cheese just before serving.

Veal ❖ Deal Plus

Roast Lamb

1 *serving*

- SERVING SIZE: 1 LOIN
- COUNTS AS:
  1 PROTEIN

good source of fiber

☀ Ingredients

4oz (120g) lamb loin

One of the following rubs:

Rosemary Garlic Rub

2 tsp (10mL) dried rosemary, crushed

1 garlic clove, minced

1/8 tsp (.5mL) lite salt

freshly ground pepper

OR

Lemon Thyme Rub

2 tsp (10mL) dried thyme

1 tsp (5mL) lemon zest

1 Tbsp (15mL) lemon juice

1/8 tsp (.5mL) lite salt

nonfat cooking spray

1. Preheat broiler.

2. Rinse lamb; pat dry. Combine ingredients for one of the herbal rubs in a small bowl.

3. Liberally apply the herbs to the loin, pressing the rub into the surface. Allow to rest 5-10 minutes.

4. Spray a broiler pan with nonfat cooking spray; place loin on pan.

5. Cook until desired doneness, approximately 7-11 minutes for medium rare or 15-19 minutes for medium; or to a temperature of 145°F (60°C) for medium rare or 160°F (70°C) for medium.

Pork a l'Orange

1 *serving*

- SERVING SIZE: 1 RECIPE
- COUNTS AS:
  1 PROTEIN

☀ Ingredients

4oz (120g) pork tenderloin

1 Tbsp (15mL) water

1/3 cup (75mL) orange juice

1/2 tsp (2mL) orange zest

1 tsp (5mL) cornstarch

1 tsp (5mL) low-sodium soy sauce

1/4 tsp (1mL) ground ginger

2 tsp (10mL) dried onion

nonfat cooking spray

1. Mix water, orange juice, orange zest, cornstarch, soy sauce, ginger and onion in saucepan. Cook sauce over medium heat until thickened. Set aside.

2. Coat skillet with nonfat cooking spray. Add pork; cook until pork is no longer pink. Add sauce to pan, heat through.

Veal ✤
Deal Plus

Stuffed Lamb

4 *servings*

family fare

- SERVING SIZE: 3OZ (90G) LAMB WITH 1-2 TBSP (15-30ML) SAUCE
- COUNTS AS:
  1 PROTEIN
  1 VEGETABLE

✳ Ingredients

1 pound (450g) lamb roast, untied

1/4 tsp (1mL) lite salt

1/8 tsp (.5mL) freshly ground pepper

2 medium carrots, diced

2 large celery stalks, diced

1/2 cup (125mL) yellow onion, diced

3 Tbsp (45mL) fresh mint, chopped

3 Tbsp (45mL) lemon juice

1/2 cup (125mL) low-sodium chicken broth

1 Tbsp (15mL) cornstarch

1 Tbsp (15mL) cold water

nonfat cooking spray

1. Preheat oven to 325°F (160°C).
2. Season lamb with salt and pepper.
3. Spray skillet with nonfat cooking spray. Add carrots, celery and onion; cook, stirring often, until vegetables are tender. Stir in mint and lemon juice.
4. Spread vegetable mixture evenly over lamb. Roll lamb over stuffing; secure with butchers string.
5. Place lamb in roasting pan with rack, sprayed with nonfat cooking spray.
6. Bake, uncovered, for approximately 40-45 minutes for medium, or until desired doneness.
7. Remove meat from pan; cover loosely with foil to keep warm.
8. Place roasting pan on stovetop. Add 1/2 cup (125 mL) chicken broth to pan; heat to a boil.
9. In a small bowl, mix cornstarch and cold water; add to roasting pan and heat until thickened.
10. To serve, slice meat and top with sauce.

Tangy Glazed Pork Chops

1 *serving*

- SERVING SIZE: 1 RECIPE
- COUNTS AS:
  1 PROTEIN
  1 VEGETABLE
  1 CONDIMENT

✳ Ingredients

4oz (120g) pork chop (bone and fat removed)

1 cup (250mL) zucchini, sliced

1 Tbsp (15mL) ketchup

2 tsp (10mL) low-sodium soy sauce

1 Tbsp (15mL) water

1/8 tsp (.5mL) ground ginger

dash garlic powder

nonfat cooking spray

1. Coat skillet with nonfat cooking spray. Cook pork chop over medium heat, about 10 minutes, or until meat is tender and no longer pink.
2. Meanwhile, steam zucchini for 5-6 minutes, or until crisp-tender.
3. Mix ketchup, soy sauce, water, ginger and garlic powder. Pour over pork chops in skillet; cover and heat through.

Veal ✤ Deal Plus

Lamb Kabobs

1 *serving*

- **SERVING SIZE: 1 RECIPE**
- **COUNTS AS:**
  - 1 PROTEIN
  - 2 VEGETABLES

☀ Ingredients

4oz (120g) boneless lamb, cut into 1-inch (2.5cm) cubes

1/4 cup (50mL) lemon juice

1/2 tsp (2mL) dried oregano leaves

1/8 tsp (.5mL) pepper

1/2 medium green pepper, cut into 1-inch (2.5cm) pieces

5 green onions

1 cup (250mL) eggplant, cut into 1-inch (2.5cm) pieces

1. Place lamb cubes into non-metal bowl.

2. In a separate bowl, mix lemon juice, oregano and pepper; add to lamb cubes and toss.

3. Cover and refrigerate lamb for 30 minutes to 2 hours. Reserve marinade.

4. Preheat broiler.

5. Thread lamb cubes onto long metal skewer(s), leaving space between each. Broil 3-inches (8cm) from heat and cook until desired level of doneness. Turn and brush with reserved marinade while cooking.

6. Meanwhile, prepare vegetables onto 2 or 3 more skewers, alternating the green pepper, onion and eggplant, leaving space between each piece. Broil until vegetables are crisp-tender; brush with marinade while cooking.

Veal & Mushrooms

1 *serving*

meals in minutes

- **SERVING SIZE: 1 RECIPE**
- **COUNTS AS:**
  - 1 PROTEIN
  - 1 VEGETABLE

☀ Ingredients

4oz (120g) veal cutlet, unbreaded

1 cup (250mL) fresh mushrooms, sliced

1 garlic clove, minced

1 Tbsp (15mL) low-sodium chicken broth

1 tsp (5mL) flour

1/8 tsp (.5mL) lite salt

freshly ground pepper

1 Tbsp (15mL) fresh parsley, chopped

2 Tbsp (30mL) dry white wine

nonfat cooking spray

1. Pound veal to 1/4-inch (1/2cm) thickness.

2. In skillet coated with nonfat cooking spray, sauté garlic and mushrooms until tender.

3. Add veal to skillet and cook through. Remove veal and vegetables; keep warm.

4. In a small bowl, mix chicken broth and flour, until dissolved.

5. Add flour mixture, salt and pepper to meat juices in skillet and stir until thickened.

6. Add parsley and wine; heat through.

7. Before serving, drizzle veal and mushrooms with sauce.

Veal ✦ Deal Plus

Mediterranean Veal Chops

4 *servings*

family fare

- SERVING SIZE: 1 CHOP AND APPROXIMATELY 1/2 CUP (125ML) SAUCE
- COUNTS AS:
  1 PROTEIN
  1 VEGETABLE

☀ Ingredients

4 boneless veal chops, 5oz (150g) each

1/4 tsp (1mL) lite salt

1/8 tsp (.5mL) freshly ground pepper

2 tsp (10mL) olive oil

1 garlic clove, minced

1 cup (250mL) baby spinach

1/4 cup (50mL) white wine

1 cup (250mL) grape tomatoes, halved

1 cup (250mL) artichoke hearts, roughly chopped

1 Tbsp (15mL) capers, rinsed

2 Tbsp (30mL) lemon juice

nonfat cooking spray

1. Preheat oven to 350°F (180°C).
2. Trim any excess fat from chops. Season with salt and pepper.
3. Coat a large oven-proof skillet with nonfat cooking spray. Heat over a medium-high flame.
4. Add chops to pan; sear chops on each side until lightly browned, about 3-4 minutes per side. Remove from pan; set aside.
5. Add olive oil and garlic to skillet; heat over a medium flame. Cook for 1 minute — do not allow garlic to burn.
6. Add spinach to pan; pour wine over spinach leaves. Toss together to wilt spinach.
7. Add tomatoes, artichokes, and capers. Cook until heated through, about 3 minutes.
8. Return veal chops to pan; spoon spinach-artichoke sauce over chops.
9. Cover pan loosely with foil and place in the oven for approximately 25 minutes.
10. Remove from oven, allow to rest 5-10 minutes. Sprinkle each chop with lemon juice just before serving.

Honey Mustard Pork Tenderloin

4 *servings*

- SERVING SIZE: 3OZ (90G)
- COUNTS AS:
  1 PROTEIN
  1 STARCH

☀ Ingredients

1 pound (450g) pork tenderloin, trimmed

2 Tbsp (30mL) honey

1 Tbsp (15mL) Dijon mustard

2 Tbsp (30mL) sugar substitute

2 Tbsp (30mL) cider vinegar

1. Preheat oven to 375°F (190°C).
2. Whisk honey, mustard, sugar substitute, and cider vinegar in a small bowl.
3. Brush pork with mixture, covering well.
4. Roast pork for 25-30 minutes or until an instant-read thermometer registers 160°F (70°C).

Veal
Deal Plu

1 *serving*

- **SERVING SIZE: 1 CUTLET WITH VEGETABLES AND CHEESE**
- **COUNTS AS:**
  1 PROTEIN
  4 VEGETABLES
  1/2 DAIRY

meals in minutes

Italian-Style Veal

❋ Ingredients

4oz (120g) veal cutlet, unbreaded

1/2 cup (125mL) fresh mushrooms, sliced

1/2 cup (125mL) white onion, finely chopped

1/2 medium red pepper, chopped

1/2 large celery stalk, finely chopped

1 garlic clove, minced

1 small tomato, seeded and diced

1/4 tsp (1mL) dried basil, crushed

1/4 tsp (1mL) dried oregano

1/8 tsp (.5mL) crushed red pepper (optional)

1oz (30g) reduced-fat mozzarella cheese, shredded

nonfat cooking spray

1 Coat oven-safe skillet with nonfat cooking spray. Brown both sides of veal over medium high heat. Remove from pan and keep warm.

2 Add mushrooms, onion, red pepper, celery and garlic to pan. Cook until tender.

3 Add tomatoes, basil, oregano and crushed red pepper (optional); toss to combine. Preheat the broiler.

4 Return veal to pan. Simmer until meat is heated through.

5 Top veal and vegetables with cheese. Broil, 3 inches (8cm) from heat, until cheese is melted.

---

1 *serving*

- **SERVING SIZE: 1 RECIPE**
- **COUNTS AS:**
  1 PROTEIN
  3 VEGETABLES

meals in minutes

Dijon Lamb Chops

❋ Ingredients

4oz (120g) boneless lamb chop

1 Tbsp (15mL) Dijon mustard

1/2 tsp (2mL) dried thyme

1/4 tsp (1mL) lite salt

1/2 medium carrot, sliced into thin strips

1 cup (250mL) zucchini, sliced into thin strips

1 cup (250mL) cauliflower florets

nonfat cooking spray

1 Preheat broiler.

2 In a small bowl, mix mustard, thyme and salt.

3 Place lamb chop on broiler pan, coated with nonfat cooking spray. Brush lamb chop with half of the marinade.

4 Broil chop, 3-inches (8cm) from heat, about 6 minutes. Turn chop over and brush with remaining marinade. Broil another 5-8 minutes.

5 Meanwhile, steam vegetables lightly until tender. Season to taste.

6 Serve vegetables with lamb chop.

Veal ✤
Deal Plus

4 *servings*

Veal Involtini

family fare

- **SERVING SIZE:** 1/4 OF THE RECIPE OR 1 INVOLTINI
- **COUNTS AS:**
  1 PROTEIN
  1 FAT
  1/2 DAIRY
  1 CONDIMENT

❊ Ingredients

1 1/4 pounds (570g) veal scallopini

1/8 tsp (.5mL) lite salt

1/8 tsp (.5mL) freshly ground pepper

1 cup (250mL) baby spinach leaves, rinsed

4oz (120g) lite mozzarella cheese, sliced thin

4 tsp (20mL) olive oil

2-3 garlic cloves, crushed

1/3 cup (75mL) white wine

2/3 cup (150mL) low-sodium chicken broth

1. Preheat oven to 350°F (180°C).
2. Rinse veal; pat dry. Season with salt and pepper.
3. Arrange veal scallopini on a cutting board and place a few spinach leaves on each, 3-4 per piece. Top spinach with a slice of mozzarella.
4. Roll each veal scallopini, enclosing spinach and cheese. Secure with a toothpick or with some butcher's string.
5. Heat an oven-proof skillet over a medium-high heat. Add olive oil and garlic, sauté 30 seconds.
6. Add veal rolls (involtini) to pan, sear until lightly brown on all sides, about 2 minutes per side. Pour wine and broth over veal.
7. Put pan in oven to finish cooking, about 15 minutes. Remove from oven, loosely cover with foil; allow to rest 5-10 minutes before serving.

Veal Goulash

1 *serving*

- **SERVING SIZE:** 1 RECIPE
- **COUNTS AS:**
  1 PROTEIN
  2 VEGETABLES
  1 CONDIMENT

❊ Ingredients

5oz (150g) veal (any boneless cut, such as a chop), cubed, into bite-sized pieces

1/8 tsp (.5mL) lite salt

freshly ground pepper

1/2 cup (125mL) white onion, sliced

1 small tomato, seeded and diced

1/2 Tbsp (7.5mL) flour

1/4 cup (50mL) low-sodium beef broth

1 Tbsp (15mL) lemon juice

1/2 tsp (2mL) paprika

1/4 tsp (1mL) caraway seeds

nonfat cooking spray

1. Season veal cubes with salt and pepper.
2. Spray skillet with nonfat cooking spray; brown veal over medium-high heat.
3. Add onion and tomato; cook, uncovered, approximately 15 minutes.
4. Sprinkle veal and vegetables with flour. Stir, while cooking, for about 1 minute.
5. Stir in beef broth, lemon juice, paprika and caraway seeds.
6. Cover and reduce heat. Simmer 20 minutes or until veal is tender.

Veal ❖ Deal Plus

Balsamic Lamb Chops

4 *servings*

- **SERVING SIZE: 1/4 OF RECIPE**
- **COUNTS AS:**
  - 1 PROTEIN
  - 2 FATS
  - 1 CONDIMENT

☀ Ingredients

1 pound (450g) boneless lamb chops

1/2 tsp (2mL) dried rosemary, minced

1/4 tsp (1mL) dried basil

1/4 tsp (1mL) dried oregano

1/2 tsp (2mL) dried thyme

freshly ground pepper

1 Tbsp (15mL) olive oil

2 shallots, minced

1-2 garlic cloves, minced

1/3 cup (75mL) balsamic vinegar

2/3 cup (150mL) low-sodium chicken broth

1/3 cup (75mL) water

1 Tbsp (15mL) flour

1 tsp (5mL) butter

nonfat cooking spray

fresh rosemary

lemon, thinly sliced

1. Combine rosemary, basil, oregano, thyme and pepper in a small bowl. Rub herb mixture onto lamb chops, on both sides; allow to rest 15-30 minutes, covered.

2. Heat olive oil in a large skillet or grill pan over medium-high heat.

3. Cook chops, approximately 3-4 minutes per side, for medium-rare doneness, or to desired temperature. Remove from pan and set aside, keeping warm.

4. Coat the same pan with nonfat cooking spray, allowing pan to reheat. Add shallots and garlic; cook over medium-low heat until golden brown.

5. Add in balsamic vinegar, stirring constantly, scraping to remove any browned bits from the bottom of the pan. Combine flour and water. Add in chicken broth and flour mixture, stirring to combine, and continue to cook approximately 5 minutes or until slightly thickened and reduced by half.

6. Remove sauce from heat and stir in butter.

7. Drizzle each chop with sauce; garnish with fresh rosemary and lemon slices.

Buffalo Burgers

4 *servings*

- **SERVING SIZE: 1 BURGER PATTY**
- **COUNTS AS:**
  - 1 PROTEIN

☀ Ingredients

1 pound (450g) ground buffalo

1/2 jalapeño, seeded and minced

1/8 tsp (.5mL) lite salt

freshly ground pepper

dash of garlic powder

1. Combine all ingredients in a large bowl, mix until just combined.

2. Form into 4 patties. Cover and refrigerate until ready to use.

3. Preheat grill or broiler. Cook burgers for approximately 6 minutes on each side, or until desired doneness.

Veal ❖ Deal Plus

Veal Meatloaf

4 *servings*

- **SERVING SIZE: 1/4 RECIPE**
- **COUNTS AS:**
  1 PROTEIN
  1 STARCH

※ Ingredients

1 pound (450g) ground veal

1/2 cup (125mL) egg substitute

1/2 cup (125mL) dry bread crumbs

1/4 cup (50mL) warm water

1/2 (1oz) envelope dry onion
  soup mix

1 large carrot, grated

1 small shiitake mushroom, sliced

1/4 tsp (1mL) freshly ground pepper

1. Preheat oven to 350°F (180°C).

2. In a bowl, mix the ground veal, egg substitute, dry bread crumbs, water, soup mix, carrots, shiitake mushrooms and pepper. Transfer to a 9 x 5 inch (23 X 13cm) loaf pan.

3. Bake 1 hour or to a minimum internal temperature of 160°F (70°C).

Venison Chili

8 *servings*

family fare

- **SERVING SIZE:**
  1 CUP (250ML)
- **COUNTS AS:**
  1 PROTEIN
  2 VEGETABLES

※ Ingredients

2 1/2 pounds (1.3kg) ground
  venison

1 Tbsp (15mL) canola or other
  vegetable oil

4 garlic cloves, minced

2 cups (500mL) chopped yellow
  onion

1 cup (250mL) chopped green
  pepper

1 jalapeño, seeded and chopped

2 Tbsp (30mL) chili powder

1 tsp (5mL) ground cumin

1 (28oz / 784g) can diced
  tomatoes, no salt, undrained

3 cups (750mL) low-sodium chicken
  or beef broth

1 cup (250mL) red kidney beans

2 Tbsp (30mL) tomato paste, no salt

nonfat cooking spray

1. Coat large pot with nonfat cooking spray; heat over medium flame. Add oil and garlic, sauté until just golden.

2. Add onion, green pepper and jalapeño; cook until soft.

3. Stir in venison, chili powder, and cumin. Cook the meat and spices with the vegetables, stirring, until browned, about 5-6 minutes.

4. Add tomatoes and liquid, broth, tomato paste and beans to chili base; stir to combine. Bring to a boil; reduce heat and simmer at least 30-45 minutes before serving.

173

Veal ✤
Deal Plus

Under
the
Sea

There are lots of delicious foods found Under the Sea and you'll find plenty to choose from inside the *L A Lite Cookbook*! From mouthwatering Ginger Salmon to Citrus Grilled Swordfish, you'll want to dive into our unique seafood blends. Plus, you'll discover the numerous health benefits of a variety of fish and the healthiest methods for selection, preparation and cooking.

Shrimp Fried Rice recipe can be found on page 183

Under the Sea

How to select fish

When purchasing whole fish look for:

- Clear, bright eyes, not sunken eyes.

- Bright red gills.

- Intact scales that are firmLy attached to the skin; scales should not be missing.

- Moist, shiny skin, but not slimy.

- Tail should be stiff and the flesh should be firm.

- Should not smell!

- Refrigerate fish for only 1 or 2 days.

When purchasing fish filets, look for:

- White fish should have a white translucent color with no discoloration.

- Flesh should be firm.

- Should not smell!

- Refrigerate fish for only 1 or 2 days.

How to purchase frozen fish:

- Frozen hard with no signs of thawing.

- Packaging should not be damaged.

- No evidence of freezer burn.

When purchasing shellfish/mollusks:

- Clear, bright eyes for crabs or lobsters.

- Shellfish should not smell!

- Check mollusks before cooking for freshness: avoid broken shells. Also the fish or shellfish should be alive — make sure they are responsive if pressure is applied to their shells.

- Once cooked, discard any shells that do not open after adequate cooking.

- Refrigerate shellfish on ice, for only 1-2 days maximum.

TIP!

Fish is a good source of potassium, vitamins, and other minerals. Potassium in your diet will help regulate blood pressure and proper muscle functions.

Cuts of fish

- **Whole dressed** — A whole fish with tail and head still attached, though typically your fish monger will have cleaned it already.

- **Pan dressed** — A whole fish with head, tail and fins removed.

- **Filets** — To filet a fish is to remove the filets from the bones. Typically, it is sold in a full length or may be cut into individual servings.

- **Steaks** — A cross-cut piece of the body of a larger fish. Steaks may contain small pieces of the backbone.

Basic cooking methods

It is important to cook fin fish thoroughly, but do not overcook it. Proper cooking allows the fish to develop the flavors and soften the connective tissue. Cooking fish at too high a temperature and cooking it too long will destroy the flavor, texture, and moisture of the fish. Fish is fully cooked when the flesh becomes opaque. White fish should also flake easily with pressure from a fork. Fish should be cooked to an internal temperature of 130° - 145°F (55 - 65°C).

Common methods for cooking fish

- **Poaching** — Fish simmered in liquid, serve hot or cold.

- **Steaming** — Fish is cooked from the steam of boiling water or any other liquid.

- **Broiling or Grilling** — Fish is broiled by dry heat from above, as in the oven or in a salamander grill. Or placed on a barbecue grill.

- **Oven baking** — Fish is baked in an oven and basted usually with a small amount of fat or liquid, and sometimes in a pouch of paper or foil.

- **Pan-frying** — Cooking fish quickly in a small amount of fat on a skillet over direct heat.

TIP!

• Fish offers the same quality and quantity of protein as meat but often with fewer calories. Fish is generally low in cholesterol and is healthy for the heart.

Under the ❖ Sea

Poached Fish

1 *serving*

- **SERVING SIZE: 1 FILET**
- **COUNTS AS:**
  1 PROTEIN

meals in minutes

☀ Ingredients

5oz (150g) filet of fish, such as cod or halibut

2 cups (500mL) water

1 cup (250mL) white wine

1/4 tsp (1mL) lite salt

2 Tbsp (30mL) white onion, minced

1/4 tsp (1mL) dried thyme

1/4 tsp (1mL) dried tarragon

1 tsp (5mL) peppercorns

4 sprigs of parsley

1 bay leaf

1 Heat water, wine, salt, onion, thyme, tarragon, peppercorns, parsley and bay leaf to a boil in a deep skillet; reduce heat. Cover and simmer 5 minutes.

2 Place fish in skillet; add water, if necessary, to cover. Again, heat to boiling; then reduce heat.

3 Simmer fish, uncovered, until it flakes easily with a fork.

4 Carefully remove fish with slotted spatula, allowing to drain.

Oven Fried Fish

1 *serving*

- **SERVING SIZE: 1 FILET**
- **COUNTS AS:**
  1 PROTEIN
  1 STARCH

meals in minutes

☀ Ingredients

5oz (150g) fish filet, such as flounder or tilapia

1/2 cup (125mL) breadcrumbs (see recipe on pg 154)

1/8 tsp (.5mL) lite salt

1/8 tsp (.5mL) paprika

dash of dried dill

freshly ground pepper

butter flavor cooking spray

nonfat cooking spray

1 Preheat oven to 350°F (180°C).

2 In a shallow bowl, combine breadcrumbs (see recipe on pg 154), salt, paprika, dill and pepper.

3 Rinse fish in cold water. Lightly pat dry.

4 Dredge fish filet in breadcrumb mixture, coating each side.

5 Coat baking pan with nonfat cooking spray. Place fish on baking sheet. Spray fish with nonfat butter spray.

6 Bake fish, uncovered, until easily flakes, approximately 20 minutes.

Under the ✿ Sea

Vegetable Stuffed Sole

1 *serving*

- **SERVING SIZE:**
  1 STUFFED FILET
- **COUNTS AS:**
  1 PROTEIN
  2 VEGETABLES

☀ Ingredients

5oz (150g) sole filet

1/4 tsp (1mL) lite salt

1/2 tsp (2mL) dried dill

1/4 tsp (1mL) freshly ground pepper

1/2 medium carrot, cut into strips

1/2 medium red pepper, cut into strips

1/4 cup (50mL) dry white wine

nonfat cooking spray

1. Preheat oven to 350°F (180°C). Coat a small baking dish with nonfat cooking spray.

2. In a small bowl, mix salt, dill and pepper; season filets with spice mixture. Place in baking dish.

3. Place carrot and pepper strips in the middle of the sole filet.

4. Roll fish, enclosing the vegetables; secure with toothpicks, if necessary. Place seam side down in baking dish. Pour wine over fish. Coat fish with cooking spray.

5. Cover with aluminum foil and bake until opaque, approximately 20 minutes, or until fish flakes easily with a fork.

Baked Stuffed Fish

1 *serving*

- **SERVING SIZE: 2 FILET PIECES**
  WITH STUFFING
- **COUNTS AS:**
  1 PROTEIN
  1 STARCH
  2 VEGETABLES

☀ Ingredients

5oz (150g) fish filet, such as tilapia or flounder

1 slice lite bread, toasted and cut into cubes

1 garlic clove, minced

1 tsp (5mL) dried minced onion

1/2 cup (125mL) mushrooms, chopped

1/2 medium carrot, shredded

1 Tbsp (15mL) lemon juice

1/4 tsp (1mL) dried marjoram

1/4 tsp (1mL) freshly ground pepper

1/4 cup (50mL) lemon juice

nonfat cooking spray

nonfat butter spray

1. Preheat oven to 350°F (180°C) oven. Coat baking dish with nonfat cooking spray.

2. Cut filet into 2 pieces; set aside.

3. Coat skillet with nonfat cooking spray. Add garlic, onions and mushrooms; sauté until tender.

4. Add in carrots, lemon juice, marjoram and pepper; gently toss with bread to combine.

5. Spoon stuffing on top of one piece of filet. Top with remaining piece of filet.

6. Season filet with butter spray; sprinkle with lemon juice. Bake, uncovered, until fish flakes easily with fork, or approximately 30 minutes.

Under the ❖ Sea

Ginger Salmon

- **SERVING SIZE: 1 FILET WITH SAUCE**
- **COUNTS AS:**
  1 PROTEIN
  1 VEGETABLE

☀ Ingredients

4oz (120g) salmon filet

1/2 Tbsp (7.5mL) brown sugar artificial sweetener

1/2 Tbsp (7.5mL) low-sodium soy sauce

1/2 Tbsp (7.5mL) dry white wine

1/2 Tbsp (7.5mL) lemon juice

1/2 tsp (2mL) garlic minced

1/4 tsp (1mL) fresh ginger, grated

dash of hot pepper sauce

5 green onions, sliced

nonfat cooking spray

1 Coat skillet with nonfat cooking spray and heat over medium heat. Add salmon to pan.

2 Cook salmon for 4 minutes on each side.

3 Remove salmon from pan; cover loosely with foil to keep warm.

4 Combine remaining ingredients in a small bowl.

5 Reduce heat to low. Add sauce to skillet and sauté for 1 minute.

6 Return salmon to pan and cook until heated through.

> "Cooking is so easy now with the L A Weight Loss Cookbook."
>
> *- Mandy M.*

Broiled Ginger Scallops

- **SERVING SIZE: 1 RECIPE**
- **COUNTS AS:**
  1 PROTEIN

☀ Ingredients

5oz (150g) scallops

2 Tbsp (30mL) low-sodium soy sauce

1 garlic clove, minced

1 Tbsp (15mL) ginger, minced

2 Tbsp (30mL) lemon juice

1/2 tsp (2mL) brown sugar artificial sweetener

nonfat cooking spray

1 Arrange scallops in a single layer in a baking dish.

2 Heat soy sauce in a small saucepan, over a medium heat. Add garlic, ginger, lemon juice, and brown sugar; simmer 2-3 minutes. Allow to cool to room temperature.

3 Pour cooled sauce over scallops. Cover and refrigerate at least 2 hours.

4 Preheat broiler.

5 Remove scallops from marinade. Place scallops, in a single layer, on a broiler pan coated with nonfat cooking spray.

6 Broil 4 inches (10cm) from heat until opaque, approximately 6-8 minutes, turning once during cooking.

Under the ❖ Sea

Shrimp Jambalaya

(1) *serving*

- **SERVING SIZE: 1 RECIPE**
- **COUNTS AS:**
  - 1 PROTEIN
  - 1 STARCH
  - 3 VEGETABLES

☀ Ingredients

5oz (150g) fresh shrimp, peeled and deveined

1/2 cup (125mL) white onion, chopped

1/2 medium green pepper, chopped

1 garlic clove, minced

1 cup (250mL) low-sodium chicken broth

1/4 tsp (1mL) lite salt

1/8 tsp (.5mL) freshly ground pepper

1/8 tsp (.5mL) ground thyme

1oz (30g) extra lean ham, small dice

1/8 tsp (.5mL) dry oregano

1/8 tsp (.5mL) dry basil

1/8 tsp (.5mL) hot pepper sauce

1 bay leaf

1 small tomato, seeded and chopped

2 Tbsp (30mL) uncooked brown rice

nonfat cooking spray

1. Coat a saucepan with nonfat cooking spray, over medium heat, with nonfat cooking spray. Add onion, green pepper and garlic; cook until tender.

2. Add shrimp; cook until opaque and turning pink. Remove shrimp and vegetables from pan; set aside.

3. Add rice, chicken broth, salt, pepper, thyme, oregano, basil, ham, hot pepper sauce, bay leaf and tomato. Heat to boiling. Reduce heat; cover and simmer, until rice is tender.

4. Return shrimp and vegetables to saucepan oven. Cover again, and cook until heated through.

"The Shrimp Jambalaya is my favorite, flavorful & easy."

- J. DeBow

Broiled Lobster Tails

(1) *serving*

- **SERVING SIZE: 1 TAIL**
- **COUNTS AS:**
  - 1 PROTEIN

☀ Ingredients

1 lobster tail, with shell, to yield 4oz (120g) cooked

2 quarts (2L) water

1/4 tsp (1mL) lite salt

nonfat cooking spray

lemon juice (optional)

1 tsp (5mL) butter (optional)

1. Bring water and salt to a boil in a large pot. Add lobster tail.

2. Return water to boiling. Cover and reduce heat; simmer 10 minutes. Drain.

3. Slice thin under-shell of tail down the middle and gently open tail; trim away shell, as needed. Pull meat out of tail to expose.

4. Place tail on broiler rack. Season with nonfat cooking spray.

5. Broil 3-inches (8cm) from heat until hot, approximately 2-3 minutes.

6. Serve with lemon and 1 tsp (5mL) of melted butter, to count as 1 fat, as desired.

Under the ❈ Sea

Lemon Shrimp Stir-fry

1 *serving*

- **SERVING SIZE: 1 RECIPE**
- **COUNTS AS:**
  1 PROTEIN
  3 VEGETABLES
  1 FRUIT

✳ Ingredients

5oz (150g) fresh or fresh-frozen shrimp, peeled and deveined

1 Tbsp (15mL) cornstarch

1/2 tsp (5mL) artificial sweetener

1 Tbsp (15mL) low-sodium soy sauce

freshly ground pepper

1/2 cup (125mL) water

1/2 tsp (2mL) lemon zest, minced

1 1/2 Tbsp (23mL) lemon juice

1 large celery stalk, sliced on the bias

1/2 medium green or red pepper, sliced

1/2 cup (125mL) mushrooms, sliced

3 green onions, sliced

1/4 cup (50mL) fresh bean sprouts

nonfat cooking spray

1 In a bowl, combine cornstarch, artificial sweetener, soy sauce, pepper, water, lemon zest and lemon juice. Stir to combine; set aside.

2 Spray skillet or wok with nonfat cooking spray. Preheat over medium-high heat. Add celery and cook for 1 minute. Add pepper and mushrooms and cook for another minute. Finally, add green onion. Stir-fry all vegetables for 1-3 minutes or until crisp-tender. Remove from pan and set aside.

3 Add shrimp to skillet or wok. Stir-fry for 2-3 minutes or until shrimp turns pink. Move shrimp to side(s) of skillet or wok, to keep warm.

4 Add sauce to center of pan; cook, stirring, until slightly thickened.

5 Return vegetables to pan. Add bean sprouts. Cook and stir for 1 minute or until heated through.

If desired, serve stir-fry over brown rice. (Optional-please refer to the menu plan for serving and exchanges).

Steamed Crab

1 *serving*

- **SERVING SIZE:**
  2 CUPS (500ML)
- **COUNTS AS:**
  1 PROTEIN
  1 CONDIMENT

✳ Ingredients

5oz (150g) fresh crab meat, picked for shells

1/2 cup (125mL) water

1/2 cup (125mL) white wine

2-3 slices lemon

1 tsp (5mL) peppercorns

1/8 tsp (.5mL) lite salt

1 bay leaf

1 Under a light stream of water, rinse crab in a fine sieve or strainer.

2 Add water, wine, lemon, peppercorns, salt and bay leaf to a medium saucepan. Place steamer basket in pan.

3 Add crab to basket. Gently steam until heated through, about 10 minutes.

Serve hot or cold with cocktail sauce, hot pepper sauce or other desired condiment. (Optional-please refer to the menu plan for serving and exchanges).

Under
the ✤ Sea

Baked Crab & Broccoli

1 *serving*

- **SERVING SIZE: 1 RECIPE**
- **COUNTS AS:**
  - 1 PROTEIN
  - 1 STARCH
  - 2 VEGETABLES
  - 1 DAIRY

good source of fiber

❋ Ingredients

1 cup (250mL) broccoli florets, trimmed

5oz (150g) fresh crab meat, rinsed and picked for shells

1 cup (250mL) fresh mushrooms, sliced

1 garlic clove, minced

1/2 cup (125mL) skim milk

1 Tbsp (15mL) flour

freshly ground pepper

1oz (30g) reduced-fat sharp cheddar cheese, shredded

3 slices Melba toast, finely crushed

nonfat cooking spray

1 Preheat oven to 400°F (200°C).

2 Steam broccoli until crisp-tender, drain. Arrange broccoli and crab meat in a casserole dish, coated with nonfat cooking spray. Set aside.

3 Spray skillet with nonfat cooking spray. Sauté mushrooms and garlic until tender. Sprinkle vegetables with flour and pepper. Stir in milk.

4 Cook sauce, stirring, until thickened. Add cheddar cheese; stir until melted.

5 Spoon sauce on top of broccoli and crabmeat. Cover with foil.

6 Bake for 15-20 minutes, until bubbling. Sprinkle with Melba toast crumbs; return to oven and bake until golden brown.

Shrimp Fried Rice

1 *serving*

- **SERVING SIZE: 1 RECIPE**
- **COUNTS AS:**
  - 1 PROTEIN
  - 1 STARCH
  - 2 VEGETABLES
  - 1 DAIRY

❋ Ingredients

5oz (150g) peeled and deveined raw shrimp

1/2 medium green pepper, diced

2 green onion, diced

1/2 medium carrot, diced

1/2 stalk celery, diced

dash of garlic powder

dash of onion powder

1/4 tsp (1mL) ground ginger

1 Tbsp (15mL) low-sodium soy sauce

1/4 tsp (1mL) lite salt

1/3 cup (75mL) cooked brown rice

1 egg white, scrambled

nonfat cooking spray

1 Spray skillet or wok with nonfat cooking spray. Over medium-high heat, cook shrimp until pink. Remove from pan; set aside.

2 Return pan to heat. Stir-fry vegetables in wok until crisp-tender.

3 Season vegetables with garlic powder, onion powder, ginger, soy sauce and salt.

4 Add rice, scrambled egg white, and shrimp back to wok. Toss to combine; allow to heat through before serving.

Under the ❦ Sea

Tangy Shrimp Skewers

serving

- **SERVING SIZE: 2-3 SKEWERS**
- **COUNTS AS:**
  - 1 PROTEIN
  - 2 VEGETABLES
  - 1 FRUIT

☀ Ingredients

5oz (150g) fresh or fresh-frozen raw shrimp

1/2 cup (125mL) pineapple chunks, canned in juice (drain and reserve juice)

1/2 medium red pepper, cut into 1-inch (2.5cm) pieces

1/4 red onion, cut into 1-inch (2.5cm) pieces

2 Tbsp (30mL) low-sodium soy sauce

1 tsp (5mL) white wine vinegar

1 tsp (5mL) ginger, minced

1-2 garlic clove(s), minced

nonfat cooking spray

1 Preheat broiler or grill.

2 In a small saucepan, combine reserved pineapple juice, soy sauce, vinegar, ginger and garlic, over a medium flame. Cook, stirring, until slightly thickened.

3 Thread shrimp, pineapple, pepper and onions, onto metal skewers, alternating the ingredients.

4 Place skewers onto grill or broiler pan (coated with nonfat cooking spray). Cook, brushing with sauce, approximately 4-5 minutes per side or until shrimp are opaque and cooked through.

Pan Seared Lemon-Pepper Grouper

1 *serving*

- **SERVING SIZE: 1 FILET**
- **COUNTS AS:**
  - 1 PROTEIN

☀ Ingredients

5oz (150g) of fresh grouper

2 Tbsp (30mL) Herb Blend (recipe on page 224)

1 Tbsp (15mL) lemon juice

1 tsp (5mL) lemon zest

nonfat cooking spray

1 Combine lemon zest and Herb Blend together.

2 Sprinkle herb mixture over both sides of fish.

3 Coat medium skillet with nonfat cooking spray.

4 Fry fish over high heat for 1 minute on each side.

5 Turn down heat to low and cook on each side 5-7 minutes, or until fish flakes with a fork.

6 Drizzle lemon juice over fish, serve hot.

Under the ✤ Sea

Orange Sesame Salmon

1 *serving*

- **SERVING SIZE: 1 FILET**
- **COUNTS AS:**
  1 PROTEIN
  1 FRUIT
  1 FAT

❊ Ingredients

4oz (120g) raw salmon filet

1/4 tsp (1mL) ginger, ground

1/3 cup (75mL) orange juice

1/2 cup (125mL) canned mandarin oranges, drained

1 Tbsp (10mL) sesame seeds, toasted

dash lite salt

nonfat cooking spray

1. Sprinkle ginger over salmon filet.

2. Coat medium skillet with nonfat cooking spray.

3. Place salmon in skillet and sear each side 2 minutes over high heat.

4. Pour orange juice over salmon and reduce heat.

5. Simmer 15 minutes, flipping occasionally to cook evenly.

6. Add oranges and sesame seeds, cooking another 1-2 minutes or until oranges are warmed through, season to taste with lite salt.

Serve hot over rice or salad. (Optional-please refer to the menu plan for serving and exchanges).

Salmon Stuffed Tomatoes

1 *serving*

- **SERVING SIZE:**
  2 STUFFED TOMATOES
- **COUNTS AS:**
  1 PROTEIN
  1 VEGETABLE
  1 FAT

❊ Ingredients

4oz (120g) fresh salmon filet

2 small whole tomatoes

1 tsp (5mL) olive oil

2 tsp (10mL) white wine vinegar

2 tsp (10mL) lemon juice

1/4 tsp (1mL) lite salt

freshly ground pepper

1 Tbsp (15mL) chopped cilantro

chopped parsley

1. Cook salmon filet, as desired; chill.

2. Chop cooked salmon into small pieces.

3. In medium bowl combine salmon, oil, vinegar, lemon juice, salt and cilantro. Mix well. Chill.

4. While salmon mixture is chilling, cut tops off of tomatoes. Remove seeds and flesh from tomatoes. Chop 1/4 cup (50mL) of tomato flesh; discard rest.

5. Mix diced tomato into salmon salad.

6. Fill hollowed tomatoes with salmon mixture.

7. Serve chilled, garnish with chopped parsley and ground pepper.

Under the ❖ Sea

Curried Salmon

- **SERVING SIZE:** 1 FILET
- **COUNTS AS:**
  - 1 PROTEIN
  - 1 VEGETABLE
  - 1/2 DAIRY

❊ Ingredients

4oz (120g) fresh salmon filet

2 Tbsp (30mL) fat-free evaporated milk

2 Tbsp (30mL) skim milk

2 tsp (10mL) curry powder

1/8 tsp (.5mL) ground ginger

1/8 tsp (.5mL) lite salt

1/8 tsp (.5mL) coriander

1 packet artificial sweetener

1/2 carrot, thinly sliced

1/2 small tomato, diced

1 In a small saucepan, combine evaporated milk, skim milk, curry powder, ginger, salt, coriander and artificial sweetener. Heat over medium heat.

2 Chop salmon into small pieces. Add to curried milk mixture.

3 Bring mixture to a simmer; reduce heat to low.

4 Add carrot and tomato and cook 5-10 minutes, or until salmon is cooked.

Serve hot over rice or vegetables. (Optional-please refer to the menu plan for serving and exchanges).

Citrus Grilled Swordfish

1 *serving*

meals in minutes

- **SERVING SIZE:**
  1 SWORDFISH STEAK
- **COUNTS AS:**
  - 1 PROTEIN
  - 1 FRUIT

❊ Ingredients

5oz (150g) raw swordfish steak

1/4 cup (50mL) orange juice

1 Tbsp (15mL) lemon juice

1 Tbsp (15mL) lime juice

1 tsp (5mL) low-sodium soy sauce

1/4 tsp (1mL) lite salt

1 tsp (5mL) chopped cilantro

1 Tbsp (15mL) chives

1/4 tsp (1mL) onion powder

1/4 tsp (1mL) garlic powder

1/4 tsp (1mL) white pepper

1/4 tsp (1mL) freshly ground pepper

2 slices orange

1 Sprinkle swordfish with salt, pepper, cilantro, chives, garlic powder and onion powder.

2 In a small bowl, combine juices and soy sauce; brush steak with marinade and set aside.

3 Place steak on grill. Cook steak for 5 minutes per side, or until cooked through. Baste steak with citrus marinade while cooking.

4 Garnish with fresh orange. Squeeze juice for orange wedges over fish for a fresh burst of flavor.

Under
the ❧ Sea

Salmon with Green Beans

4 *servings*

- SERVING SIZE: 3OZ (90G) COOKED SALMON, 1/2 CUP (125ML) GREEN BEANS, 1/4 RECIPE GLAZE
- COUNTS AS:
  1 PROTEIN
  1 VEGETABLE
  1 CONDIMENT

☀ Ingredients

4 salmon filets, 4oz (120g) each

1/2 tsp (2mL) course black pepper

1/2 cup (125mL) dry white wine

1/2 cup (125mL) balsamic vinegar

2 Tbsp (30mL) fresh orange juice

2 tsp (10mL) lemon juice

1 packet artificial sweetener

1 pound (450g) green beans, trimmed

nonfat cooking spray

1/2in (1.5cm) water of orange and lemon rind from 1 piece each of fruit

1. Coat a cast iron pan or heavy bottomed skillet with nonfat cooking spray. Preheat to medium-high heat.
2. Season filets with pepper to taste, then spray with nonfat cooking spray.
3. Cook salmon until just cooked through, about 3 minutes on each side.
4. While salmon cooks, bring wine, vinegar, juices and artificial sweetener to a boil over high heat, in a small saucepan.
5. Cook glaze 3 or 4 minutes, until reduced and thickened.
6. Remove from heat. Stir in 1/2 tsp (2.5mL) coarse black pepper.
7. In a second skillet, bring 1/2-inch (1.5cm) water to a boil with green beans and pieces of orange rind and/or lemon rind.
8. Cover the green beans and cook 3-4 minutes.
9. Drain the beans and toss and season with pepper.
10. Drizzle glaze over salmon filets. Serve with green beans on the side.

Caesar Shrimp Skewers

1 *serving*

- SERVING SIZE: 1 SERVING
- COUNTS AS:
  1 PROTEIN
  1 VEGETABLE
  1 FAT
  1 CONDIMENT

☀ Ingredients

5oz (150g) fresh shrimp peeled and deveined

1 Tbsp (15mL) fat-free Caesar dressing

2 Tbsp (30mL) lemon juice

1 Tbsp (15mL) lite margarine, melted

1 tsp (5mL) garlic powder

1 green onion, chopped

1/4 tsp (1mL) lite salt

1 yellow squash, cubed

nonfat cooking spray

1. In a small bowl, combine dressing, lemon juice, margarine, chopped onion and half of the garlic powder.
2. Place shrimp and squash on skewers.
3. Spray finished kabobs with cooking spray, then sprinkle with salt and remaining garlic powder.
4. Place skewers on grill.
5. Brush with dressing and turn while grilling.
6. Cook until squash begins to soften. Continue to brush with dressing frequently during cooking.

   Serve hot over rice. (Optional-please refer to the menu plan for serving and exchanges).

Under the ♣ Sea

Herb Stuffed Salmon

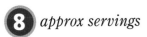

8 *approx servings*

- SERVING SIZE: 3OZ (90G) COOKED
- COUNTS AS:
  1 PROTEIN
  1 CONDIMENT

family fare

☀ Ingredients

2 pounds (900g) salmon filets, skin on, scaled and pin bones removed

freshly ground pepper

1 Tbsp (15mL) olive oil

2 lemons

3 Tbsp (45mL) fresh dill, rough chopped

3 Tbsp (45mL) fresh marjoram, rough chopped

3 Tbsp (45mL) fresh basil, rough chopped

nonfat cooking spray

1. Preheat the oven to 400°F (200°C).

2. Cut 5 lengths of string and lay them out on the work surface next to each another, with less than 1-inch (2.5cm) space between each.

3. Sprinkle pepper over the work surface, then drizzle with olive oil.

4. Lay 1 salmon filet onto work surface, skin side down. Sprinkle pepper over the salmon, then, using fine grater or microplane, grate the zest of 1 lemon over top. Next, season with the marjoram, dill and basil.

5. Season the flesh side of the other salmon filet with pepper, and grate the second lemon.

6. Place 1 filet on top of the other, thin end to thick, skin facing out, then tie them together and trim the strings.

7. Put the fish on a baking sheet coated with nonfat cooking spray.

8. Bake for about 20 minutes, or until fish is flaky.

Fish Tacos

1 *serving*

- SERVING SIZE: 2 TACOS
- COUNTS AS:
  1 PROTEIN
  1 STARCH
  1/2 DAIRY
  1 CONDIMENT

good source of calcium

☀ Ingredients

5oz (150g) mahi-mahi

1 tsp (5mL) hot sauce

1 tsp (5mL) cilantro

1/4 tsp (1mL) chili powder

1/2 whole wheat flour tortilla

1/4 cup (50mL) shredded lettuce

1/2 tomato, seeded and diced

1 Tbsp (15mL) salsa

1 Tbsp (15mL) fat-free sour cream

1oz (30g) reduced-fat shredded cheddar cheese

1. Preheat oven to 375°F (190°C).

2. Sprinkle fish with hot sauce, cilantro and chili powder.

3. Bake until flaky, approximately 15-20 minutes.

4. Slice tortilla in half.

5. Place fish in tortilla. Top with condiments and vegetables.

Under the ♣ Sea

Spinach Stuffed Sole

4 *servings*

good source of calcium

- SERVING SIZE: 1/4 RECIPE
- COUNTS AS:
  1 PROTEIN
  1 VEGETABLE
  1/2 DAIRY

❋ Ingredients

1 pounds (450g) sole filets

1 tsp (5mL) olive oil

1/2 pound (225g) fresh mushrooms, sliced

1/2 pound (225g) fresh spinach, chopped

1/4 tsp (1mL) oregano leaves, crushed

1 garlic clove, minced

2 Tbsp (30mL) sherry

4oz (120g) part-skim mozzarella cheese, grated

nonfat cooking spray

1. Preheat oven to 400°F (200°C).
2. Coat a baking dish with nonfat cooking spray.
3. Heat oil in skillet; sauté mushrooms about 3 minutes or until tender.
4. Add spinach and continue cooking about 1 minute, or until spinach is beginning to wilt.
5. Remove from heat; drain liquid into prepared baking dish.
6. Add oregano and garlic to drained vegetables; stir to mix ingredients.
7. Divide vegetable mixture evenly among filets, placing filling in center of each filet.
8. Roll filet around mixture and place seam-side down in prepared baking dish.
9. Sprinkle with sherry, then grated mozzarella cheese.
10. Bake fish for 15-20 minutes, or until flaky.

Baked Trout

6 *servings*

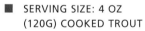
family fare

- SERVING SIZE: 4 OZ (120G) COOKED TROUT
- COUNTS AS:
  1 PROTEIN

❋ Ingredients

2 pounds (900g) trout filet

3 Tbsp (45mL) lime juice (about 2 limes)

1 medium tomato, chopped

5 green onions, chopped

3 Tbsp (45mL) cilantro, chopped

1/2 tsp (2mL) olive oil

1/4 tsp (1mL) freshly ground pepper

1/4 tsp (1mL) cayenne pepper (optional)

nonfat cooking spray

1. Preheat oven to 350°F (180°C).
2. Rinse fish and pat dry.
3. Place in baking dish coated with nonfat cooking spray.
4. In a separate dish, mix remaining ingredients together and pour over fish.
5. Bake for 15-20 minutes or until flaky.

Under the ❦ Sea

Scallops & Mushrooms

1 *serving*

- **SERVING SIZE: 1 RECIPE**
- **COUNTS AS:**
  1 PROTEIN
  2 VEGETABLES
  1 CONDIMENT

☀ Ingredients

5oz (150g) large scallops

12 medium crimini (baby bella) mushroom caps

1 Tbsp (15mL) low-sodium soy sauce

1 garlic clove, finely diced

1 green onion, finely diced

freshly ground pepper

nonfat cooking spray

1. Preheat oven to 325°F (160°C) degrees.

2. Marinate the mushrooms in the soy sauce, garlic and green onion. Let sit for 30 minutes.

3. Grill or broil mushrooms 2 minutes per side; then bake in the oven for 10 minutes. Allow mushrooms to cool slightly before cutting into thin strips.

4. Pat the scallops dry, then season with pepper.

5. Sear the scallops in a large skillet that has been coated with nonfat cooking spray over high heat for about 1 minute per side, or until browned.

6. Add mushrooms. Cook for 1 minute longer, or until warmed through.

Red Snapper

5 *servings*

family fare

- **SERVING SIZE: 4OZ (120G) COOKED**
- **COUNTS AS:**
  1 PROTEIN
  1 VEGETABLE

☀ Ingredients

1 1/2 pound (450g) red snapper filets

2 Tbsp (30mL) low-sodium chicken broth

1 green bell pepper, seeded and cut into thin strips

1 yellow bell pepper, seeded and cut into thin strips

1 onion, sliced

1 garlic clove, crushed

1 can (14.5oz / 406g) canned, diced tomatoes, no salt added

1/4 cup (50mL) sliced pimento-stuffed olives

1/4 cup (50mL) hot sauce

2 Tbsp (30mL) lime juice

1/4 cup (50mL) chopped cilantro

1. In a large skillet, over medium heat, heat the broth to a simmer. Cook peppers and onion until tender-crisp; add garlic.

2. Add diced tomatoes with liquid, olives, hot sauce, lime juice and red snapper filets.

3. Heat to boiling; reduce heat to low.

4. Cover and simmer 5-10 minutes, stirring occasionally until fish is tender.

5. Stir in chopped cilantro.

   Serve with yellow rice. (Optional-please refer to the menu plan for serving and exchanges).

> "The L A Lite Cookbook recipes are such a delight. I savor the dishes bite by bite."
> — *Lynn K.*

Under the ✤ Sea

2 *servings*

- SERVING SIZE: 1 TOSTADA
- COUNTS AS:
  1 PROTEIN
  1 STARCH
  1 DAIRY
  1 FAT
  1 VEGETABLE
  1 CONDIMENT

meals in minutes

Tuna Tostadas

❋ Ingredients

8oz (225g) water-packed, low-sodium tuna, well drained

1-2 tsp (5-10mL) hot sauce

1 small tomato, seeded and chopped

4 (125mL) chopped green onions

1 Tbsp (15mL) finely chopped cilantro

1/4 cup (50mL) fat-free sour cream

2 Tbsp (30mL) fresh lime juice

1/4 ripe avocado, halved and pitted

2 6 inch (15cm) corn tortilla, cut in half

2oz (60g) reduced-fat Mexican-style cheese

nonfat cooking spray

1 Preheat oven to 350°F (180°C).

2 In a bowl, combine tuna and 1 tsp (5mL) hot sauce and mix.

3 Add tomato, onion, cilantro, sour cream and lime juice. Blend and chill.

4 With a spoon, scoop the avocados into a bowl and mash with a fork; add hot sauce and blend.

5 Spray tortilla lightly with nonfat cooking spray on both sides. Place on a baking sheet; bake until crisp.

6 To assemble, spread half of avocado mixture on each tortilla.

7 Add 1/2 of tuna mixture to each tortilla half.

8 Top each tostada with 1oz (30g) cheese.

---

4 *servings*

- SERVING SIZE: 3OZ (90G) COOKED
- COUNTS AS:
  1 PROTEIN

family fare

Swordfish in Lemon Sauce

❋ Ingredients

4 swordfish steaks, 4oz (120g) each

1/2 tsp freshly ground pepper

2 garlic cloves, peeled, crushed

1 tsp (5mL) dried oregano

1/4 tsp (1mL) dried basil

1/3 cup (75mL) fresh lemon juice

3 Tbsp (45mL) low-sodium vegetable broth

nonfat cooking spray

1 Wash fish and dry with paper towels.

2 In a small bowl, combine ground pepper, garlic, oregano and basil. Add lemon juice and broth.

3 Place fish in a shallow dish.

4 Add the marinade; turn to coat both sides.

5 Cover and set aside for 1 hour, turning once.

6 Coat broiling pan with non stick cooking spray and broil 4 inches (10cm) from heat.

7 Broil 4-5 minutes per side, brushing with marinade.

Under the ❖ Sea

Mango Prawns

4 *servings*

- **SERVING SIZE: 1/4 RECIPE**
- **COUNTS AS:**
  1 PROTEIN
  1 FRUIT
  1 FAT

☀ Ingredients

20oz (560g) uncooked prawns

1 egg white

2 tsp (10mL) cornstarch

1 tsp (5mL) sesame oil

1/2 tsp (2mL) white pepper

1 pound (450g) mango

2 cups (500mL) water

1 Tbsp (15mL) fresh ginger, finely chopped

1 Tbsp (15mL) sesame oil

1 Tbsp (15mL) dry sherry

2 Tbsp (30mL) green onion, finely chopped, for garnish

1 garlic clove, minced

1 Peel the prawns, then wash them and pat them dry.

2 Combine the prawns with the egg white, cornstarch, sesame oil and pepper. Mix well and leave in the refrigerator for 20 minutes.

3 Peel the mango and cut the flesh into cubes.

4 Add water to a saucepan, bring to a boil.

5 Remove the saucepan from heat, immediately add the prawns, stirring vigorously to prevent them from sticking.

6 After 2 minutes, when the prawns turn white, quickly drain the prawns in a stainless steel colander.

7 Heat the wok or large frying pan over high flame.

8 Add the oil, when slightly smoking, add the ginger and garlic and fry for 5 seconds.

9 Add the prawns to the wok or pan, together with dry sherry, and white pepper.

10 Stir-fry the mixture for 1 minute.

11 Add the mango pieces and stir gently for 1 minute to warm the mango.

12 Garnish with green onions and serve.

Braised Sea Scallops

2 *servings*

- **SERVING SIZE:**
  1/2 OF RECIPE
- **COUNTS AS:**
  1 PROTEIN
  2 VEGETABLES

☀ Ingredients

10oz (280g) fresh sea scallops

6 mushrooms, sliced

1/2 green pepper, diced

1 tomato, diced

1/4 cup (50mL) dry white wine

2 green onions, chopped

1 tsp (5mL) dill, dried

nonfat cooking spray

1 Rinse scallops and pat dry with a paper towel.

2 Sear the scallops in a skillet that has been coated with nonfat cooking spray. Sear them for one minute per side and remove from pan.

3 Place mushrooms, green pepper, tomato and wine in the same pan; cook 5 minutes until vegetables are tender.

4 Add onions, scallops and dill.

5 Cook another 3 minutes until scallops are opaque.

Under the ♣ Sea

1 *serving*

- SERVING SIZE: 1 FILET
- COUNTS AS:
  1 PROTEIN
  1 FAT

meals in minutes

Lemon Baked Flounder

☀ Ingredients

5oz (150g) flounder filet

1 Tbsp (15mL) lite margarine, melted

1 Tbsp (15mL) lemon juice

1/4 tsp (1mL) lemon zest

1 tsp (5mL) all-purpose flour

2 tsp (10mL) fresh parley, chopped

1/4 tsp (1mL) freshly ground pepper

1/4 tsp (1mL) paprika

nonfat cooking spray

1 Pre-heat oven to 350°F (180°C)

2 Rinse filet thoroughly in cold water; pat dry with paper towels and set aside.

3 Combine melted margarine, lemon juice and lemon zest in a small bowl.

4 Combine flour, chopped parsley, and pepper in a shallow container.

5 Dip filet in margarine mixture, then dredge in flour mixture.

6 Transfer filet to a baking sheet that has been coated with nonfat cooking spray and drizzle any remaining margarine mixture over fish.

7 Sprinkle filets with paprika.

8 Bake in oven for 15 minutes, or until fish is golden brown and flakes easily when tested with a fork.

---

1 *serving*

- SERVING SIZE:
  1 TUNA MELT
- COUNTS AS:
  1 PROTEIN
  1 STARCH
  1 FAT
  1/2 DAIRY

meals in minutes

Tuna Melt

☀ Ingredients

4oz can (120g) waterpacked tuna, drained

1 Tbsp (15mL) lite mayonnaise

1/2 English muffin

1oz (30g) lite shredded cheese

nonfat cooking spray

1 Mix tuna with mayo.

2 Place tuna on top of English muffin.

3 Sprinkle sandwich with cheese.

4 Place in skillet coated with nonfat cooking spray; cover and cook over medium heat until cheese is melted.

5 Serve hot.

Under the ♣ Sea

Tilapia Italiano

1 *serving*

- **SERVING SIZE: 1 FILET**
- **COUNTS AS:**
  - 1 PROTEIN
  - 2 VEGETABLES

☀ Ingredients

5oz (150g) tilapia filet

1 tsp (5mL) crushed garlic

1/4 tsp (1mL) lemon pepper

1/2 tsp (2mL) oregano

dash of lite salt

2 tomatoes, diced

nonfat cooking spray

freshly ground black pepper

1. Rinse tilapia under cold water and pat dry with paper towels.
2. Coat skillet with nonfat cooking spray.
3. Sauté garlic over medium heat for 1 minute.
4. Sprinkle fish with oregano, lemon pepper and salt.
5. Add fish to pan, sauté on each side until opaque. Remove from pan and keep warm.
6. Add tomatoes to pan, heat over medium-high heat for 2 minutes.
7. Return fish to pan and heat.
8. Serve hot. Add ground pepper if desired.

Spiced Shrimp & Rice

1 *serving*

- **SERVING SIZE: 1 RECIPE**
- **COUNTS AS:**
  - 1 PROTEIN
  - 1 STARCH
  - 1 VEGETABLE

☀ Ingredients

5oz (150g) raw shrimp, peeled
  and deveined

5 green onions, sliced

1 garlic clove, minced

1/4 tsp (1mL) grated ginger

1/8 tsp (.5mL) allspice

2 whole cloves

1/2 stick cinnamon

1 cup (250mL) hot water

1/3 cup (75mL) cooked rice

1 green chile, sliced

1/2 tsp (2mL) garam masala
  (Recipe on page 215)

1/4 tsp (1mL) chili powder

1 Tbsp (15mL) cilantro, chopped

nonfat cooking spray

1. Coat a medium saucepan with nonfat cooking spray; heat over a medium-high heat.
2. Cook shrimp, turning once, until pink, approximately 5 minutes. Remove from saucepan and set aside.
3. Add onion, garlic and ginger to saucepan. Cook, stirring, until onion is translucent.
4. Add allspice, cloves and cinnamon stick; cook and stir for 1 minute.
5. Return shrimp to sauce pan. Next add water, rice, green chile, garam masala and chili powder.
6. Bring to a boil. Reduce heat to low and cover; cook for 20 minutes, or until most of the water is absorbed.
7. Remove cloves and cinnamon sticks. Garnish with cilantro, before serving.

Shrimp Creole

4 *servings*

family fare

- **SERVING SIZE:**
  APPROX 1 1/2 CUPS (375ML)
- **COUNTS AS:**
  1 PROTEIN
  2 VEGETABLES

☀ Ingredients

1 Tbsp (15mL) canola oil

1-2 garlic cloves, minced

1/2 cup (125mL) onion, diced

1/2 cup (125mL) green pepper, chopped

1 celery stalk, diced

2 Tbsp (30mL) flour

1/2 cup (125mL) tomato sauce, low-sodium or no salt added

1 1/2 cups (375mL) water

dash of hot pepper sauce

2-3 tomatoes, seeded and chopped

1 1/2 pounds (675g) shrimp, peeled and deveined

1. Heat a large skillet coated with oil over medium heat. Add garlic, onion, pepper and celery; sauté until tender.

2. Sprinkle with flour. Stir to coat all vegetables. Cook, until flour is lightly browned, approximately 5 minutes.

3. Add tomato sauce, water and hot pepper sauce. Stir to combine.

4. Bring to a boil; reduce heat.

5. Add tomatoes and shrimp. Cook, stirring occasionally, until shrimp are pink and cooked through.

Ginger Poached Cod

1 *serving*

- **SERVING SIZE: 1 RECIPE**
- **COUNTS AS:**
  1 PROTEIN
  2 VEGETABLES

☀ Ingredients

5oz (150g) cod filet

2 cups (500mL) water

2 tsp (10mL) lite soy sauce

2 Tbsp (30mL) fresh ginger, thinly sliced

1 small tomato, seeded and chopped

1/4 cup (50mL) white onion, sliced

1 cup (250mL) bok choy, leaves and stems, chopped

lite salt and pepper, to taste

1. In a large saucepan, simmer sliced ginger, tomato, soy sauce and onion in 2 cups (500mL) of water, over medium heat, until onions are tender.

2. Reduce heat to low; add fish and poach for 3-4 minutes, until just becoming opaque.

3. Add bok choy; gently stir while cooking, for approximately 1-2 minutes, allowing bok choy to wilt.

4. Add lite salt and pepper, to taste.

5. Serve immediately.

Under the ❧ Sea

Go Meatless

Vegetarian diets are those that exclude animal products, mainly that of meat, fish or poultry origin. There are several types of diets classified under this term, though the basis of all these diets are plant-based foods, including protein, fruits, vegetables and starches. For vegetarians, the *L A Lite Cookbook* is a fantastic resource of unique food preparation, combinations, storage and more!

◀ Vegetable Ziti Bake recipe can be found on page 208

Complete Proteins and Complementary Proteins

Protein is built of amino acids; there are essential and nonessential amino acids. Essential amino acids cannot be made in the body, therefore it is essential to get these from foods. Nonessential amino acids can be made in the body, so it is not necessary to eat foods containing them. An example of an essential amino acid is tryptophan; tyrosine is a nonessential amino acid.

A complete protein is one that contains all the essential amino acids for the human body in the approximate amounts needed. Most animal proteins are considered complete (with the exception of gelatin). Most plant-based proteins tend to be limiting only in one or two amino acids, such as vegetables, grains and legumes; some plant proteins, like corn, are known to be incomplete, while soy protein is complete.

As you can tell, most vegetable proteins are of lower quality than animal proteins, but if you pair your foods correctly to replace the missing "links" or amino acids, you can create a complete protein. Foods that supply the missing links to each other are complementary proteins; the strategy of combining two complementary proteins in a meal is called mutual supplementation. Some examples are peanut butter and toast and rice and black beans.

But mutual supplementation at every meal is not necessary to achieve optimal health; in most instances, a vegetarian will obtain the essential amino acids over the course of one day, provided he/she eats a variety of foods, such as grains, seeds, legumes, etc.

TIP!

Ever come across a recipe that called for dried herbs when you'd rather use fresh ones? Feel free to use the fresh herbs, just triple the amount that the recipe calls for that specific herb. Better yet, try to add in the herbs in the final cooking stages so their unique flavor stays bold.

Glossary of Vegetarian Cooking

- **Tofu** — Also known as soybean curd or bean curd; produced from curdled soy milk as extracted from ground, cooked soybeans, in which the curds are drained and pressed, similarly done as in cheese-making; it has a bland, nutty flavor that tends to take on the flavor of what it is cooked with or in; may be firm or soft.

- **Tempeh** — A fermented soy bean cake, similar in texture to soft tofu, though with a slightly nuttier flavor.

- **Seitan** — A protein-rich meat substitute made from wheat gluten; it has a firm texture that is chewy and meat-like; also called "wheat meat"; also picks up the flavors that it is cooked in or with; packaged in cakes or tubs.

- **Miso** — A fermented soybean paste that comes in many flavors; its flavor is influenced by the amount of salt and aging, and the amount of koji (mold cultivated in barley, rice or soybean) it contains; can be used in many different menu items: soups, salads, entrees and dips; it is high in protein and B vitamins.

- **Textured Vegetable Protein** — Typically found in powdered form, this is produced by grinding soy beans and extruding them to obtain just protein; appears as a flour and easily prepared by mixing with water; may also be found flaked or in frozen form; make sure to use low-fat version — it is basically defatted soy flour.

- **Edamame** — Japanese name for soybeans; may be fresh or fresh-frozen; may be eaten in the pod or out of the pod; generally steamed or boiled as an appetizer in Japanese restaurants.

☘ TIP!

Want to keep your spices lasting longer? First, move your spice rack from above your stove. Store your spices in a cool, dark place. Humidity, light and heat are all flavor-losing factors in your spice rack. To make the most of your spices, stash them in an airtight container or in the freezer in tightly sealed containers.

Preparing

Use an electric coffee grinder to grind up nuts, seeds and spices. It saves time preparing and cooking so you don't have to crush them yourself. Just make sure to clean it out before you put coffee beans in, or your coffee will go nuts!

When buying garlic for cooking always look for heads that are firm with plenty of flaky paper covering.

Storing

Once you open the tofu package, rinse and cover the leftover with water to store in your refrigerator. Change the water daily and use the food within 7 days.

Keep your fresh herbs staying fresh longer in the refrigerator. Place any stem bunches in water. Store loose leaves in perforated bags in the coldest part of your fridge. Remember to shake them before you store them. To absorb extra moisture place a paper towel in the bag under the herbs.

Cooking

To help the oil heat faster when using a wok, add the oil so that it circles around the sides before reaching the bottom.

When stir-frying vegetables, cook them according to density. Stir-fry the densest veggies, such as carrots and eggplant, first because they take the longest. Green leafy vegetables require less cooking time.

☘ Go
Meatless

1 *serving*

■ **SERVING SIZE: 1 RECIPE**
■ **COUNTS AS:**
  1 PROTEIN
  2 VEGETABLES

good source of fiber

Red Kidney Bean Curry

✳ Ingredients

3/4 cup (175mL) cooked
  red kidney beans

1/4 cup (50mL) white
  onions, chopped

1/2 green chili, sliced

1/2 tsp (2mL) ginger, grated

1/2 tsp (2mL) turmeric

1/2 tsp (2mL) cumin seeds

1 small tomato, seeded and chopped

1 Tbsp (15mL) lemon juice

1/2 tsp (2mL) garam masala
  (Recipe on page 215)

1/4 tsp (1mL) lite salt

1 Tbsp (15mL) chopped cilantro

nonfat cooking spray

1 Coat skillet with nonfat cooking spray. Add onion, chili, ginger, turmeric and cumin seeds. Cook, stirring, until onion is soft and lightly browned. Add tomato; cook until soft.

2 Add beans to onion mixture; toss to combine. Add lemon juice, garam masala and salt. Cook, stirring, uncovered for 5 minutes.

3 Garnish with cilantro.

---

8 *servings*

■ **SERVING SIZE: 1 CUP (250ML) BEANS AND 1/3 CUP (75ML) RICE**
■ **COUNTS AS:**
  1 PROTEIN
  1 VEGETABLE
  1 STARCH

family fare

Red Beans & Rice

✳ Ingredients

3/4 cup (345g) dried red beans,
  rinsed and picked over

1 Tbsp (15mL) olive or canola oil

2 garlic cloves, minced

2 celery stalks, chopped

1 cup (250mL) onion, chopped

1 medium green pepper, chopped

1/4 jalapeño pepper, seeded and
  deveined, chopped

1 Tbsp (15mL) fat-free
  chipotle sauce

2 quarts (2L) low-sodium chicken
  or vegetable broth

1/4 cup (50mL) flat leafed Italian
  parsley, chopped

1/3 cup (75mL) rice, cooked

1 Place beans in a large bowl; cover with water by one inch. Soak overnight. Drain and set aside.

2 In large soup pot, heat oil over medium heat. Add garlic, celery, onion and jalapeño peppers. Sauté until soft, about 10 minutes. Add chipotle sauce.

3 Add broth and beans. Bring to a boil over medium-high heat. Reduce heat.

4 Continue to cook over low heat until beans are soft, about 2 hours. Stir occasionally while cooking.

5 Garnish with parsley and serve over hot cooked rice.

❧ Go
Meatless

Scrambled Tofu

 4 *servings*

- **SERVING SIZE: 1/4 OF RECIPE**
- **COUNTS AS:**
  1 PROTEIN

☀ Ingredients

1/2 cup (125mL) onion, finely chopped

1 pound (450g) firm tofu, crumbled

1 Tbsp (15mL) low-sodium soy sauce

1 tsp (5mL) basil or cilantro

1/4 tsp (1mL) garlic powder

1/4 tsp (1mL) freshly ground pepper

nonfat cooking spray

1 Sauté onions in a skillet coated with nonfat cooking spray until tender; add remaining ingredients.

2 Cook until tofu starts to brown and is heated through.

3 Serve with toast.

Indian-Style Chickpeas

4 *servings*

- **SERVING SIZE: 1/4 OF RECIPE**
- **COUNTS AS:**
  1/2 PROTEIN
  1 VEGETABLE

☀ Ingredients

2 small carrots, diced

1 medium onion

3 garlic cloves, coarsely chopped

1 Tbsp (15mL) cumin seeds

1 Tbsp (15mL) turmeric

2-inch (5cm) long piece of fresh peeled ginger, chopped

1/2 cup (125mL) lite tomato sauce

chilies, cayenne powder, or chopped fresh jalapeños (optional and to taste)

1 can (15.5oz / 434g) chickpeas, rinsed and drained

1 Place the first 6 ingredients and pepper (optional) in a blender and pureé until smooth, add water if it is too thick to mix properly.

2 Pour the paste into a saucepan on medium high heat and stir until it begins to darken and gains aroma.

3 Stir constantly to prevent burning.

4 Add the diced carrots and stir to coat the carrots with the paste; add a small amount of water if there is no liquid at the bottom of the pan and allow the vegetables to steam until nearly done.

5 Add chickpeas and mix well, heating through.

❖ Go Meatless

Vegetarian Chili

10 *servings*

- **SERVING SIZE: 1 CUP (250ML)**
- **COUNTS AS:**
  1/2 PROTEIN
  2 VEGETABLES

✳ Ingredients

1 large onion, finely chopped

1 green pepper, seeded and finely chopped

6 cups (1.5L) canned low sodium stewed tomatoes

2 cups (500mL) canned pinto beans, drained and rinsed

2 cups (500mL) canned kidney beans, drained and rinsed

1/8 tsp (.5mL) ground cloves

dash of allspice

2 Tbsp (30mL) chili powder

1 Tbsp (15mL) cumin

nonfat cooking spray

1. Sauté onion and green pepper in a Dutch oven coated with nonfat cooking spray.

2. Add the remaining ingredients and simmer until flavors are blended.

3. Heat and serve.

Jalapeno Red Bean Burgers

4 *servings*

- **SERVING SIZE: 1 PATTY**
- **COUNTS AS:**
  1/2 PROTEIN
  1 VEGETABLE
  1 CONDIMENT

good source of fiber

✳ Ingredients

1 can (16oz / 450g) kidney beans, drained and rinsed

1 small onion, finely chopped

1 small tomato, chopped

1 jalapeño chili, seeded and chopped

1 garlic clove, finely minced

1 tsp (5mL) chili powder

1/4 cup (50mL) barbecue sauce

1/3 cup (75mL) bread crumbs (see recipe on pg 154)

nonfat cooking spray

1. In a bowl, mash beans with a fork.

2. Add next 6 ingredients to beans.

3. Add bread crumbs, enough so that mixture can be formed into patties that hold together.

4. Make 4 patties.

5. Brown in a skillet coated with nonfat cooking spray, until heated through.

"Try this with the Sweet Cole Slaw."

♣ Go
Meatless

BBQ Tofu

1 *serving*

- **SERVING SIZE: 1 RECIPE**
- **COUNTS AS:**
  1/2 PROTEIN
  1 CONDIMENT

☀ Ingredients

1/2 cup (125mL) firm tofu

1 Tbsp (15mL) low-sodium soy sauce

1 packet artificial sweetener

1 tsp (5mL) water

1/2 tsp (2mL) dry mustard

1 garlic clove, minced

1 tsp (5mL) onion powder

nonfat cooking spray

1 Cut tofu into strips.

2 In medium bowl, combine soy sauce, artificial sweetener, water, mustard, garlic and onion powder.

3 Marinate tofu in sauce 1 hour.

4 Coat wok with nonfat cooking spray and cook tofu until heated through.

Pizza Bagel

1 *serving*

- **SERVING SIZE: 1 RECIPE**
- **COUNTS AS:**
  1 STARCH
  1 VEGETABLE
  1 DAIRY

good source of calcium

☀ Ingredients

1/2 small bagel

1 small tomato

fresh basil

dash dried oregano

2oz (60g) part-skim shredded mozzarella cheese

1 Cut tomato in to 2-3 slices.

2 Place tomato on bagel.

3 Sprinkle basil, oregano and cheese on top of tomato.

4 Place on baking sheet and place in 375°F (190°C) oven, until cheese is melted.

✿ Go
Meatless

Cheesy Delight

4 *servings*

- **SERVING SIZE:**
  1/2 CUP (125ML) COTTAGE CHEESE
- **COUNTS AS:**
  1/2 PROTEIN

good source of calcium

 Ingredients

2 cups (500mL) 1% cottage cheese

3/4 cup (175mL) boiling water

1 envelope sugar-free flavored gelatin*

1/4 cup (50mL) cold water

1 In a small bowl, combine gelatin powder and 1/4 cup (50mL) cold water, allow to soften.

2 In a blender, combine cottage cheese, gelatin mixture and boiling water. Process until smooth.

3 Divide into serving cups and refrigerate until firm.

   Serve with fresh fruit. (Optional-please refer to the menu plan for serving and exchanges.)

*Unflavored gelatin can be used in place of fruit flavored, add 1 tsp vanilla extract and artificial sweetener to add flavor.

Vegetarian Pepper Quesadillas

2 *servings*

- **SERVING SIZE: 1/2 RECIPE**
- **COUNTS AS:**
  1 STARCH
  2 VEGETABLES
  1/2 DAIRY

☀ Ingredients

1/2 green pepper, chopped

1/2 red pepper, chopped

10 small green onions, chopped

1/4 tsp (1mL) lite salt

freshly ground pepper

1/4 tsp (1mL) cumin

2oz (60g) reduced-fat shredded cheese, such as cheddar

2 6 inch (15cm) corn or flour tortilla

4 Tbsp (50mL) salsa

1 Sauté onion and peppers in skillet.

2 Stir in salt, pepper and cumin.

3 Remove from heat.

4 Spoon cheese onto tortilla. Top with pepper mixture, place second tortilla on top.

5 Place on baking sheet and bake in 350°F (180°C) oven for 5-10 minutes until cheese is melted.

6 Top with salsa before serving.

 Go Meatless

4 *servings*

- SERVING SIZE: 1/4 RECIPE
- COUNTS AS:
  1 PROTEIN
  1 CONDIMENT

family fare

Meatless Sloppy Joe

✳ **Ingredients**

1/2 cup (125mL) green onion, chopped

1/2 cup (125mL) green pepper, chopped

1 tsp (5mL) garlic, minced

3/4 cup (175mL) fresh mushroom, sliced

1/2 cup (125mL) reduced-sodium ketchup

2/3 cup (150mL) water

1 Tbsp (15mL) brown sugar artificial sweetener

1 Tbsp (15mL) mustard

1/2 tsp (2mL) celery seed

1/2 tsp (2mL) chili powder

12oz (345g) textured vegetable protein

lite salt and pepper

nonfat cooking spray

1 Coat medium saucepan with nonfat cooking spray; heat over medium flame until hot.

2 Sauté onion, green pepper, and garlic until tender, 5-8 minutes. Stir in mushroom, ketchup, water, brown sugar, mustard, celery seed and chili powder; heat to boiling.

3 Stir in vegetable protein; reduce heat and simmer, covered, 10 minutes.

4 Season to taste with lite salt and pepper.

Tofu-Bacon

4 *servings*

- SERVING SIZE: 1/4 RECIPE
- COUNTS AS:
  1/2 PROTEIN

✳ **Ingredients**

1/3 cup (75mL) low-sodium soy sauce

2 Tbsp (30mL) water

1 Tbsp (15mL) nutritional yeast flakes

1 Tbsp (15mL) maple syrup

1/2 Tbsp (7.5mL) liquid smoke

8oz (225g) extra-firm tofu

1 Mix the soy sauce, water, yeast flakes, maple syrup and liquid smoke together in a shallow, flat container.

2 With a cheese slicer, shave the tofu into thin slices.

3 Marinate in the mixture for 24 hours.

4 To cook, heat a non stick griddle over medium-high heat.

5 Fry the tofu slices until golden brown and almost crispy on both sides, scraping underneath the slices as you turn them with a sturdy spatula.

6 Serve hot.

✤ Go
Meatless

Mediterranean Pasta

1 *serving*

- SERVING SIZE: 1 RECIPE
- COUNTS AS:
  1 STARCH
  1/2 DAIRY
  2 VEGETABLES
  1 FAT

☼ Ingredients

2 garlic cloves, minced

2 Tbsp (30mL) onion, diced

1/4 cup (50mL) thinly sliced zucchini

1/2 tomato, diced

1 tsp (5mL) flour

1/4 cup (50mL) skim milk

1/8 tsp (.5mL) dried oregano

1 Tbsp (15mL) tomato paste

1/3 cup (75mL) cooked pasta

1oz (30g) lite feta cheese

4 kalamata olives, halved

nonfat cooking spray

1 Coat medium skillet with nonfat cooking spray. Sauté garlic and onion over medium heat for 1 minute.

2 Add zucchini and tomato; cook until zucchini is tender.

3 Sprinkle flour into zucchini mixture and mix well.

4 Stir in milk, oregano and tomato paste; heat to a simmer.

5 Toss in pasta. Top with cheese and olives.

Eggplant Parmigiana

2 *servings*

good source of calcium

- SERVING SIZE: 1/2 OF RECIPE
- COUNTS AS:
  1 STARCH
  2 VEGETABLES
  1 DAIRY

☼ Ingredients

1/2 cup (125mL) lite tomato sauce

1 small tomato, diced

1/2 cup (125mL) water

1 tsp (5mL) dried onion

1 tsp (5mL) garlic powder

dash of dried parsley flakes

dash of lite salt

dash of oregano

freshly ground pepper

1/2 eggplant, sliced

1/2 cup (125mL) egg substitute

1/2 cup (125mL) breadcrumbs (see recipe on pg 154)

4oz (120g) part-skim, shredded mozzarella cheese

nonfat cooking spray

1 In small saucepan, combine tomato sauce, diced tomato, water, dried onion, garlic powder, parsley flakes, salt, oregano and pepper. Heat to a simmer and set aside.

2 Dip eggplant slices in egg, then into bread crumbs.

3 Coat skillet with nonfat cooking spray and heat over medium heat. Lightly brown each side of eggplant.

4 Coat casserole dish with nonfat cooking spray. Arrange half of the eggplant slices in a single layer in casserole dish.

5 Top with half of the tomato sauce. Sprinkle with 2oz (60g) of the cheese.

6 Repeat process with remaining eggplant, sauce and cheese.

7 Bake, uncovered, in a 400°F (200°C) oven for 10-15 minutes, or until cheese is melted.

♣ Go
Meatless

Italian Style "Vegetarian Meatballs"

6 *servings*

family fare

■ SERVING SIZE:
4 MEATBALLS AND 1/4 CUP (50ML) SAUCE

■ COUNTS AS:
1 PROTEIN
1 VEGETABLE

☀ Ingredients

12oz (345g) vegetable protein crumbles

1/2 cup (125mL) egg substitute

1/4 cup (50mL) breadcrumbs (see recipe on page 154)

2 garlic cloves, minced

2 Tbsp (30mL) grated reduced-fat parmesan cheese

2 tsp (10mL) Italian herbs

1/2 tsp (2mL) fennel seed, crushed

1 1/2 cups (375mL) lite tomato sauce

1 tomato, chopped

2 Tbsp (30mL) onion, diced

1 tsp (5mL) basil

1/2 tsp (2mL) oregano

1 Combine vegetable protein crumbles, egg substitute, breadcrumbs, garlic, parmesan cheese, Italian herbs and fennel seeds. Mash mixture lightly with fork. Form into 24 balls.

2 Bake in baking pan at 350°F (180°C) until firm, about 15 minutes.

3 To make sauce, combine tomato sauce, chopped tomato, onion, basil and oregano in small saucepan. Bring to a boil, then lower heat and simmer 15 minutes.

4 Serve sauce over hot meatballs.

Mock-Sausage

12 *servings*

■ SERVING SIZE: 1 PATTY
■ COUNTS AS:
1/2 PROTEIN

☀ Ingredients

3/4 cup (175mL) boiling water

2 Tbsp (30mL) low-sodium soy sauce

1 cup (250mL) textured vegetable protein (TVP) granules

1/2 cup (125mL) mashed firm tofu

2 tsp (10mL) marjoram

1/2 tsp (2mL) minced garlic

1/2 tsp (2mL) onion powder

1/2 tsp (2mL) thyme

1/2 tsp (2mL) red cayenne flakes

1/2 tsp (2mL) liquid smoke

1/2 cup (125mL) unbleached flour

nonfat cooking spray

1 In a bowl, pour the water and soy sauce over the TVP.

2 When soft, add the remaining ingredients, except flour and mix well.

3 When the mixture is cooled, add the flour.

4 Mix well with your hands and form into 12 thin patties

5 In a heavy skillet coated with nonfat cooking spray, fry until firm and browned, 7-10 minutes per side.

These can be refrigerated or frozen for later use.

207

♣ Go
Meatless

Vegetable Ziti Bake

2 *servings*

- **SERVING SIZE:**
  1 CUP (250ML)
- **COUNTS AS:**
  1 STARCH
  2 VEGETABLES
  1 DAIRY

good source of calcium

✳ Ingredients

1/4 cup (50mL) diced onion

2 garlic cloves, minced

1/4 cup (50mL) thinly sliced carrots

1/4 cup (50mL) sliced mushrooms

1/4 cup (50mL) thinly sliced zucchini

1/2 tsp (2mL) garlic powder

1/2 cup (125mL) fresh spinach

2/3 cup (150mL) cooked ziti

1/4 cup (50mL) lite tomato sauce

1/2 cup (125mL) part-skim ricotta cheese

1/2 tomato, diced

2oz (60g) part-skim mozzarella cheese

nonfat cooking spray

1 Coat skillet with nonfat cooking spray; heat over medium heat.

2 Add onion, garlic and carrots to skillet and sauté 1-2 minutes, or until onions begin to soften.

3 Add mushrooms, zucchini and garlic powder, and sauté 2 minutes. Add spinach and cook until wilted. Remove vegetables from heat and set aside.

4 In large mixing bowl, combine ziti, ricotta cheese, tomato sauce and vegetable mixture.

5 Coat casserole dish with nonfat cooking spray. Pour ziti mixture into casserole and top with diced tomato.

6 Cover and bake in 350°F (180°C) oven for 20 minutes.

7 Remove from oven and top with mozzarella cheese. Bake, uncovered, 10 minutes, or until cheese is melted.

Edamame

3 *servings*

- **SERVING SIZE: 1 CUP (250ML) COOKED**
- **COUNTS AS:**
  1 PROTEIN

good source of fiber

✳ Ingredients

1 pound (450g) frozen edamame

1 lemon

1 Tbsp (15mL) kosher salt

1 In medium-sized pot, boil edamame for 5-8 minutes until tender, do not overcook.

2 Drain in colander and pat dry.

3 Place edamame in serving bowl.

4 Squeeze lemon juice on edamame and sprinkle with kosher salt.

Tofu Manicotti

1 *serving*

- **SERVING SIZE: 2 MANICOTTI**
- **COUNTS AS:**
  1 PROTEIN
  1 STARCH
  1 DAIRY

good source of calcium

✳ Ingredients

2 manicotti shells

1/4 cup (50mL) fresh mushroom, chopped

1/4 cup green onion (50mL), chopped

1 tsp (5mL) snipped fresh parsley

1/4 tsp (1mL) dried Italian seasoning

dash of paprika

4oz (120g) tofu, drained

1 Tbsp (15mL) reduced-fat parmesan cheese

1/2 cup (125mL) skim milk

1/2 Tbsp (7.5mL) flour

garlic powder

1/8 tsp (.5mL) lite salt

1/8 tsp (.5mL) freshly ground pepper

1oz (30g) reduced-fat mozzarella cheese, shredded

nonfat cooking spray

1. Cook pasta shells according to package directions. Rinse in cold water; drain.

2. Coat medium skillet with nonfat cooking spray. Add mushroom and onion; cook until tender. Stir in parsley, Italian seasoning and paprika. Cool slightly.

3. Mash tofu in a bowl. Stir in parmesan cheese, mushroom and onion mixture.

4. Divide the mixture in half. Stuff each shell with 1/2 of the mixture. Arrange stuffed shells in baking pan.

5. For the sauce, combine milk, flour, garlic powder, salt and pepper in a medium saucepan. Cook, stirring, until slightly thickened. Pour sauce over shells.

6. Bake, covered, in 350°F (180°C) oven for 20-25 minutes, or until heated through.

7. Sprinkle with cheese and bake, uncovered, 2 minutes longer or until cheese is melted.

Baked Macaroni & Cheese

8 *servings*

- **SERVING SIZE:**
  1 CUP (250ML) COOKED
- **COUNTS AS:**
  1 STARCH
  1 FAT
  1 DAIRY

good source of calcium

✳ Ingredients

3 Tbsp (45mL) butter

3 Tbsp (45mL) all-purpose flour

2 1/2 cups (625mL) skim milk

freshly ground pepper

8oz (225g) shredded reduced-fat cheddar cheese

1 pound (450g) macaroni

nonfat cooking spray

1. Over medium heat, melt butter in medium saucepan. Add flour and stir until a paste forms.

2. Remove from heat and add the cold milk a little at a time, stirring well with each addition.

3. Return to heat once all the milk is added and the mixture is smooth. Stir over medium heat until sauce comes to a boil and slightly thickens. Pepper to taste.

4. Remove from heat and add the shredded cheddar. Stir until cheese melts. Preheat broiler.

5. Meanwhile, cook macaroni in rolling boiling water according to package directions. Drain and toss with cheese sauce.

6. Transfer to a medium baking dish that has been coated with nonfat cooking spray.

7. Place under broiler until browned and bubbly, about 3-4 minutes.

✿ Go
Meatless

Vegetable Shepherd's Pie

4 *servings*

- **SERVING SIZE: 1/4 OF RECIPE**
- **COUNTS AS:**
  1/2 PROTEIN
  1 STARCH
  1 VEGETABLE

✳ Ingredients

2 cups (500mL) water, divided

3/4 cup (175mL) cooked
   red lentils

1/4 cup (50mL) uncooked barley

1 medium carrot, diced

1 small onion, finely chopped

8oz (225g) low-sodium canned,
   diced tomatoes

1 garlic clove, crushed

1 tsp (5mL) flour

1 tsp (5mL) parsley

3 small potatoes, cooked and
   mashed

1/2 cup (125mL) skim milk, hot

1 Tbsp (15mL) margarine

1/4 tsp (1mL) lite salt

freshly ground pepper

1. Heat 1-1/4 cups (300mL) water; add lentils and barley; simmer 30 minutes.

2. Heat remaining water in a separate saucepan, add carrot, onion and garlic; cook until tender, then add tomatoes, parsley and pepper, to taste.

3. Mix the flour with a little water and add to saucepan; cook, stirring, over low heat until thickened.

4. Combine the potatoes with the milk and margarine. Season with salt and pepper.

5. Combine vegetable mixture with cooked lentils and barley, place in ovenproof baking dish, cover with mashed potatoes.

6. Bake at 350°F (180°C) for 30 minutes.

Hot & Spicy Dahl

1 *serving*

good source of fiber

- **SERVING SIZE: 1 RECIPE**
- **COUNTS AS:**
  1 PROTEIN
  3 VEGETABLES

✳ Ingredients

3/4 cup (175mL) cooked red lentils

1/2 tsp (2mL) mustard seeds

5 green onions, chopped

2 jalapeños, seeded and chopped

3 garlic cloves, minced

1 Tbsp (15mL) minced ginger

2 tomatoes, seeded and chopped

2 tsp (10mL) ground coriander

2 tsp (10mL) ground cumin

2/3 cup (150mL) water

2 Tbsp (30mL) cilantro

nonfat cooking spray

1. Coat skillet with nonfat cooking spray and heat over medium flame.

2. Add mustard seeds and cook 1-2 minutes.

3. Add onion, ginger, jalapeño and garlic.

4. Cook on medium heat until garlic browns.

5. Add cumin, coriander and tomatoes. Continue to sauté until tomatoes are cooked.

6. Add water, boil 5-6 minutes.

7. Add cooked lentils, stir well.

8. Add cilantro to mixture and remove from heat.

9. Serve immediately.

♣ Go Meatless

Tofu & Vegetable Stir-fry

1 *serving*

meals in minutes

- **SERVING SIZE: 1 RECIPE**
- **COUNTS AS:**
  1/2 PROTEIN
  2 STARCHES
  1 VEGETABLE
  1 FAT

☀ Ingredients

1/2 cup (125mL) water

1/4 cup (50mL) dry sherry

1 Tbsp (15mL) cornstarch

2 Tbsp (30mL) low-sodium soy sauce

1 packet sugar substitute

1 tsp (5mL) very low-sodium bouillon granules

3/4 tsp (3mL) ground ginger

1/2 medium carrot, thinly sliced

1 garlic clove, minced

1 cup (250mL) broccoli florets

1/2 cup (120g) tofu, cubed

1/3 cup (75mL) cooked brown rice

1 Tbsp (15mL) sesame seeds, toasted

nonfat cooking spray

1. For sauce, stir together water, dry sherry, cornstarch, soy sauce, sugar substitute, bouillon and ginger. Set aside.

2. Coat wok or skillet with nonfat cooking spray. Preheat over medium-high heat. Add carrot and garlic and stir-fry for 2 minutes. Add broccoli; stir-fry for another 3-4 minutes, or until all vegetables are crisp-tender. Push vegetables from center of skillet to the side.

3. Stir sauce and add to center of skillet. Cook, stirring, until thickened. Add tofu.

4. Toss ingredients together to coat with sauce.

5. Serve with hot cooked brown rice. Sprinkle with sesame seeds.

Asparagus Soup

4 *servings*

- **SERVING SIZE: 1/4 RECIPE**
- **COUNTS AS:**
  1 STARCH
  1 VEGETABLE
  1 FAT

☀ Ingredients

1 onion, chopped

2 Tbsp (30mL) butter

2 Tbsp (30mL) flour

1 cup (250mL) vegetable broth

1 pound (450g) fresh asparagus, trimmed and coarsely chopped

1 dash garlic powder

1 dash white pepper

1 cup (250mL) 1% milk

1. In a medium sauce pan, melt the butter and add the onion. Cook over medium heat until onion softens.

2. Stir in flour. Add vegetable broth, a little at a time, stirring until smooth.

3. Add asparagus, garlic powder and white pepper. Simmer for 10 minutes. Stir in the milk. Simmer for an additional 5 minutes.

4. Puree in a blender. Serve hot.

♣ Go Meatless

Add
a little
♣ Zest

The *L A Lite Cookbook* shows you just how to add a little spice to life. You'll find all the information you need for increasing flavor and decreasing fat with fresh herbs, spicy sauces and a variety of seasonings. These zesty recipes will keep your appetite satisfied and your taste buds tantalized!

Add a little Zest

Hot Spice Mix (Garam Masala)

Cajun Spice Seasoning

Teriyaki Sauce

Chocolate-Orange Sauce

Seasoned Margarine

Soy-Sesame Marinade

Spicy Curry Powder

Lemon Seasoning

Mushroom Sauce

Italian-Style Tomato Sauce

Margarita Marinade

Orange-Ginger Marinade

Chili Powder

Indian Spice Blend

Hot Citrus Rub

Vegetable Sauce

Plum Sauce

Basil Mayonnaise

Spicy Flavor Blend

Seasoned Salt

Herb Blend

Taco Seasoning Mix

Citrus Rub

Five-Spice Powder

Fajita Seasoning Marinade

Teriyaki Marinade

Add
a little
❋ Zest

Glossary of Sauce Terms

- **Roux** — A cooked mixture of equal parts fat and flour, such as butter and flour, which is cooked until desired color and flavor is reached; used as a base in many sauces and also to thicken soups and stews.

- **Mayonnaise** — An emulsion of egg yolk, oil and lemon juice or vinegar.

- **Aioli** — A garlic mayonnaise, commonly served with fish or vegetables.

- **Pesto** — A puree of fresh herbs, such as basil, with olive oil, pine nuts and garlic; may also be available with sun-dried tomatoes or artichokes.

- **Hollandaise** — A rich sauce blend of egg yolks, butter and tarragon.

- **Bechamel** — A roux-thickened milk sauce.

- **Demi-glace** — A rich reduction of beef or veal broth into a velvety brown sauce.

- **Mornay** — A cheese and milk sauce made by combining a roux with milk and adding parmesan or gruyere cheese.

- **Chutney** — Originated from India; a relish of fruits and spices, such as spicy mango chutney.

- **Tomato** — A common base sauce, in which garlic and vegetables are sautéed in olive oil and then tomatoes are added and simmered together .

- **Salsa** — Spanish for "sauce"; commonly thought of as a raw sauce of tomatoes and/or fruits or other vegetables, combined with garlic, herbs and olive oil.

Cut the fat...

- Choose vegetable or broth-based sauces.

- Keep the sauce on the side to control how much you use with each bite.

- Use sauces and seasonings that are high in flavor—they are more satisfying to the stomach and taste buds.

- Use low-fat milk or evaporated nonfat milk in place of cream.

Increase the flavor...

- Use fresh herbs at the end of the recipe or dried herbs at the beginning for optimum flavor.

- Select herbs and spices that will complement foods, such as rosemary or mint for lamb, nutmeg for spinach or dill for eggs.

- In place of salt, try fresh lemon juice to heighten flavors in a recipe.

- Roast vegetables with olive oil and garlic to bring out the natural sweetness.

Hot Spice Mix (Garam Masala)

✳ Ingredients

4oz (120g) coriander seeds

1oz (30g) cumin seeds

1oz (30g) freshly ground pepper

1/2oz (15g) black cumin seeds

1/4oz (7g) black cardamom

1/4oz (7g) cloves

1/4oz (7g) cinnamon

1/4oz (7g) bay leaves

1/2oz (15g) dry ginger

1. Dry roast all ingredients, except ginger, by cooking the spices in a hot skillet, sliding the spices back and forth over the burner. Cook lightly until aromas are released.

2. Cool to room temperature. Add ginger to mixture; grind to fine powder in a spice/coffee grinder.

3. Store in an air tight container. (Unlimited use)

Cajun Spice Seasoning

✳ Ingredients

3/4 cup (175mL) lite salt

1/4 cup (50mL) ground cayenne pepper

2 Tbsp (30mL) ground white pepper

2 Tbsp (30mL) freshly ground pepper

2 Tbsp (30mL) paprika

2 Tbsp (30mL) onion powder

2 Tbsp (30mL) garlic powder

1. Combine all ingredients and mix well.

2. Place in an airtight container. (Unlimited use)

Spice up Roast Chicken with a Cajun twist.

Add
a little
✣ Zest

Teriyaki Sauce

10 *servings*

- **SERVING SIZE: 2 TBSP (30ML)**
- **COUNTS AS:**
  1 FAT
  1 CONDIMENT

☀ Ingredients
1 cup (250mL) low-sodium soy sauce

1/4 cup (50mL) canola or soybean oil

4 tsp (20mL) ground ginger

4 tsp (20mL) dry mustard

1 garlic clove, minced

1 packet sugar substitute

1 Combine all ingredients and whisk vigorously to combine.

2 Use to flavor beef, chicken, pork or other meats.

Chocolate-Orange Sauce

6 *servings*

- **SERVING SIZE: 3 TBSP (45ML)**
- **COUNTS AS:**
  1 FRUIT
  1 FAT

☀ Ingredients
1/2 cup (125mL) sugar substitute

1 cup (250mL) evaporated skim milk

1 Tbsp (15mL) lite corn syrup

2 squares (1oz / 30g) unsweetened or semi-sweet chocolate (for a sweeter sauce)

2 Tbsp (30mL) butter flavor vegetable shortening

1 Tbsp (15mL) orange zest

1/2 tsp (2mL) orange extract

1 Combine sugar substitute, evaporated milk and corn syrup in a 2 quart (2L) saucepan.

2 Heat to a full boil over medium-high heat; cook for 1 minute, stirring constantly.

3 Reduce heat to low; add chocolate and stir until smooth.

4 Remove from heat.

5 Stir in vegetable shortening, orange zest and extract.

Serve with fruit. (Optional-please refer to the menu plan for serving and exchanges.)

Add a little ♣ Zest

Seasoned Margarine

 4 *servings*

- **SERVING SIZE: 1 TBSP (15ML)**
- **COUNTS AS:**
  - 1 FAT

✻ Ingredients
1/4 cup (50mL) lite margarine, melted

1 Mix margarine with one of the following seasonings, then chill until solid.
- ▶ Basil: 1/4 tsp (1mL) dried basil leaves.
- ▶ Chive-Parsley: 1 Tbsp (15mL) snipped chives and 1 Tbsp (15mL) snipped parsley.
- ▶ Curry: 1/4 tsp (1mL) curry powder.
- ▶ Garlic: 1/4 tsp (1mL) garlic powder.
- ▶ Lemon: 1 Tbsp (15mL) grated lemon peel, 2 Tbsp (30mL) lemon juice.
- ▶ Cinnamon: 1 tsp (5mL) cinnamon and 1 packet of sugar substitute.

Soy-Sesame Marinade

1 *serving*

- **SERVING SIZE: 1 RECIPE**
- **COUNTS AS:**
  - 1 FAT
  - 1 CONDIMENT

✻ Ingredients
2 Tbsp (30mL) low-sodium soy sauce

2 Tbsp (30mL) water

1 tsp (5mL) sesame oil

2 garlic cloves, crushed

1 tsp (5mL) sugar substitute or brown sugar substitute

1 In medium bowl, combine all ingredients; whisk vigorously.

2 Add desired meat, poultry or seafood; toss to combine.(according to menu plan)

3 Cover and marinate in refrigerator 20 minutes before preparing as desired.

Marinate the Chicken Kabobs with this sassy seasoning.

Add
a little
❧ Zest

Spicy Curry Powder

✳ Ingredients

2 cinnamon sticks, broken into pieces

5 bay leaves

1/2 tsp (2mL) whole cloves

1/4 tsp (1mL) grated nutmeg

2 Tbsp (30mL) anise seeds

1 tsp (5mL) black peppercorns

5 dried red chilies

10 dried curry leaves

6 Tbsp (90mL) coriander (cilantro) seeds

3 Tbsp (45mL) cumin seeds

3 Tbsp (45mL) ground turmeric

1 Tbsp (15mL) fenugreek seeds

2 Tbsp (30mL) black mustard seeds

1/2 tsp (2mL) ground white pepper

1 Roast the spices in a small, heavy-bottomed pan over medium heat for 4-5 minutes, stirring constantly until lightly darkened and fragrant.

2 Remove the spices from the pan and grind to a fine powder in a spice or coffee grinder.

3 Store in an airtight container for up to 6 months. (Unlimited use)

Lemon Seasoning

✳ Ingredients

zest from 1/2 of a lemon

2 tsp (10mL) dried parsley

1/2 tsp (2mL) dried dill

1/2 tsp (2mL) garlic powder

1/2 tsp (2mL) dried oregano

1/2 tsp (2mL) dried marjoram leaves, crushed

1/2 tsp (2mL) pepper

1 Combine all ingredients. Toss.

2 Refrigerate in covered, air-tight container. (Unlimited use).

Add a little lemon seasoning to the Herbed Chicken Recipe.

Add
a little
✿ Zest

Mushroom Sauce

4 *servings*

- **SERVING SIZE:**
  1/4 CUP (50ML)
- **COUNTS AS:**
  2 CONDIMENTS

family fare

❊ Ingredients

1 Tbsp (15mL) lite margarine

1 1/2 Tbsp (23mL) flour

1/4 tsp (1mL) lite salt

1/8 tsp (.5mL) white pepper

1 cup (250mL) skim milk

1/2 cup (125mL) cooked
  mushrooms, sliced

1. In a medium saucepan, melt margarine over medium heat.

2. Stir in flour, salt and pepper.

3. Add milk slowly, stirring constantly. Cook, over medium-low heat, until thickened, approximately 10 minutes.

4. Add mushrooms. Continue to cook, until heated through.

Italian-Style Tomato Sauce

8 *servings*

- **SERVING SIZE:**
  1/4 RECIPE (125ML)
- **COUNTS AS:**
  2 VEGETABLES

family fare

❊ Ingredients

1 Tbsp (15mL) olive oil

1/2 cup (125mL) white or yellow
  onion, diced

2 garlic cloves, minced

1 tsp (5mL) dried basil

1 tsp (5mL) dried oregano

1/4 tsp (1mL) lite salt

1 bay leaf

3oz (90mL) full-bodied red wine,
  such as Burgundy

1 (28oz / 825g) can crushed
  tomatoes, no salt added

1. In a large saucepan, heat olive oil over medium heat. Add onion and garlic; sauté until onion is translucent and soft.

2. Add basil, oregano, salt and bay leaf. Cook, stirring constantly, for approximately 1 minute.

3. Add wine, stirring to combine; cook to reduce volume of wine by half.

4. Reduce heat to medium low. Add tomatoes; cook, stirring occasionally, for approximately 20-30 minutes.

Add
a little
❖ Zest

Margarita Marinade

1 *serving*

- **SERVING SIZE: 1 RECIPE**
- **COUNTS AS:**
  - 1 STARCH
  - 1 FAT

☀ Ingredients

- 2 Tbsp (30mL) fresh lime juice
- 1 tsp (5mL) vegetable oil
- 2 Tbsp (30mL) water
- 1oz (30mL) tequila
- 1/2 tsp (2mL) of orange zest
- 1-2 garlic cloves, crushed
- 1/4 tsp (1mL) lite salt

1. In a small bowl, combine all ingredients. Whisk vigorously to combine.
2. Add desired meat, poultry, seafood or vegetables. Toss to coat all pieces.
3. Cover and refrigerate for 20-30 minutes, turning occasionally, before cooking.

Orange-Ginger Marinade

1 *serving*

- **SERVING SIZE: 1 RECIPE**
- **COUNTS AS:**
  - 1 STARCH
  - 1 CONDIMENT

☀ Ingredients

- 1/4 cup (50mL) orange juice
- 1/4 cup (50mL) low-sodium soy sauce
- 2 Tbsp (30mL) dry sherry
- 1-2 garlic cloves, minced
- 1/2 tsp (2mL) ground ginger

1. In a measuring cup, combine all ingredients. Whisk vigorously.
2. Pour marinade into a large zip-top bag; add desired meat, poultry or seafood. Shake to coat. (According to menu plan.)
3. Refrigerate, turning over occasionally, for 20-30 minutes, before cooking.

Try this marinade with the Ginger Chicken with Apricots.

Add a little ❧ Zest

Chili Powder

☀ Ingredients
2 Tbsp (30mL) paprika

2 tsp (10mL) oregano

1 1/4 tsp (6mL) cumin

1 1/4 tsp (6mL) garlic powder

1 1/4 tsp (6mL) cayenne pepper

3/4 tsp (3mL) onion powder

1 Mix all ingredients. Place in an airtight container. (Unlimited use)

Indian Spice Blend

☀ Ingredients
3 Tbsp (45mL) cumin

4 tsp (20mL) ground ginger

2 tsp (10mL) ground coriander

2 tsp (10mL) cayenne pepper

4 tsp (20mL) turmeric

2 tsp (10mL) freshly ground pepper

1 Combine all ingredients in an airtight container. (Unlimited use)

Hot Citrus Rub

☀ Ingredients
1 Tbsp (15mL) lemon zest

1 Tbsp (15mL) orange zest

1 tsp (5mL) sugar substitute

1 tsp (5mL) lite salt

2 tsp (10mL) garlic powder

1 tsp (5mL) cayenne pepper

1 Combine all ingredients in a small bowl.

2 Use to grill all your favorite foods. (Unlimited use)

Add
a little
❖ Zest

Vegetable Sauce

12 *servings*

- SERVING SIZE: 2 TBSP (30ML)
- COUNTS AS:
  1 FAT

☀ Ingredients

1/3 cup (75mL) fat-free sour cream

1/3 cup (75mL) parsley, chopped

2 1/2 Tbsp (37.5mL) red wine vinegar

1 tsp (5mL) Worcestershire sauce

1 tsp (5mL) dry mustard

1 garlic clove, minced

1 cup (250mL) fat-free mayonnaise

2 Tbsp (30mL) chives, chopped

1 Mix all ingredients well.

2 Refrigerate for at least 30-60 minutes before serving.

Use on raw or cooked vegetables. (Optional-please refer to the menu plan for serving and exchanges.)

Plum Sauce

2 *servings*

- SERVING SIZE: 2 TBSP (30ML)
- COUNTS AS:
  1 FRUIT
  1 FAT

☀ Ingredients

2 Tbsp (30mL) plum jam

2 Tbsp (30mL) low-sodium soy sauce

1/2 tsp (2mL) hot chili oil

2 tsp (10mL) sesame oil

1/4 tsp (1mL) ginger, fresh, grated

1 Combine all ingredients and whisk vigorously to combine.

Use to flavor beef, chicken, pork or other meats.

Paint a little Plum Sauce on the Lamb Kabobs to add a little zing.

Add
a little
❧ Zest

Basil Mayonnaise

16 *servings*

- **SERVING SIZE:**
  1 1/2 TBSP (23ML)
- **COUNTS AS:**
  1 FAT

☀ Ingredients

1 cup (250mL) lite mayonnaise

1/2 cup (125mL) fresh basil, roughly chopped

freshly ground pepper

1 Place all ingredients in a blender or food processor. Puree or blend until smooth.

2 Use immediately or refrigerate.

Spicy Flavor Blend

☀ Ingredients

1 Tbsp (15mL) dry mustard

2 1/2 tsp (12.5mL) onion powder

1 3/4 tsp (8mL) curry powder

1 1/4 tsp (6mL) white pepper

1 1/4 tsp (6mL) ground cumin

1 tsp (5mL) garlic powder

1 Mix all ingredients together in a small bowl.

2 Place into shaker and use as desired. (Unlimited use)

Seasoned Salt

☀ Ingredients

1 tsp (5mL) lite salt

1 tsp (5mL) paprika

1 tsp (5mL) turmeric powder

1 tsp (5mL) onion powder

1 tsp (5mL) oregano

1 tsp (5mL) pepper

3/4 tsp (3mL) garlic powder

1/2 packet sugar substitute

1 Mix all ingredients together in a small bowl.

2 Place into shaker and use as desired. (Unlimited use)

Add
a little
❖ Zest

Herb Blend

❋ Ingredients

1 Tbsp (15mL) garlic powder

1 tsp (5mL) dried oregano

1 tsp (5mL) freshly ground pepper

1 Tbsp (15mL) parsley flakes

1 Tbsp (15mL) dried basil

1 Mix all ingredients together.

2 Place in shaker and use as desired. (Unlimited use)

Taco Seasoning Mix

❋ Ingredients

2 Tbsp (30mL) chili powder

2 tsp (10mL) paprika

2 tsp (10mL) cumin

2 tsp (10mL) oregano

1/2 tsp (2mL) onion powder

1/2 tsp (2mL) garlic powder

1/2 tsp (2mL) cayenne pepper

1 Combine all ingredients in an airtight container. (Unlimited use)

Citrus Rub

❋ Ingredients

1 Tbsp (15mL) lemon zest

1 Tbsp (15mL) orange zest

1 tsp (5mL) sugar substitute

1 tsp (5mL) lite salt

1 Combine all ingredients in a small bowl.

2 Use to grill all your favorite foods. (Unlimited use)

Add
a little
 Zest

Five-Spice Powder

☀ Ingredients

2 Tbsp (30mL) black peppercorns

3 star anise

2 tsp (10mL) fennel seeds

2 3-inch (8cm) cinnamon sticks, broken into small pieces

6 whole cloves

1 Dry-roast the peppercorns in a small skillet, sliding the skillet back and forth over the burner to prevent charring, 1-2 minutes.

2 Transfer to a bowl and set aside to cool.

3 Repeat this process, one ingredient at a time, with the remaining ingredients.

4 Put all the ingredients into a spice grinder and grind to a fine powder.

5 Transfer to a glass jar with a tight-fitting lid. Mixture will keep for up to 1 month. (Unlimited use)

Fajita Seasoning Marinade

SERVING SIZE: 2 TBSP (30ML)

COUNTS AS:
FREE FOOD

☀ Ingredients

1/4 cup (50mL) red wine vinegar

1 packet sugar substitute

1/2 tsp (2mL) oregano

1/2 tsp (2mL) chili powder

1/4 tsp (1mL) garlic powder

1/8 tsp (.5mL) freshly ground pepper

1/4 tsp (1mL) lite salt

1 Combine all ingredients.

2 Use as a marinade for chicken or beef.

Teriyaki Marinade

1 *serving*

SERVING SIZE: 1 RECIPE

COUNTS AS:
1 CONDIMENT

☀ Ingredients

1-2 tsp (5-10mL) brown sugar substitute

3 Tbsp (45mL) dry sherry

3 Tbsp (45mL) low-sodium teriyaki sauce

2 tsp (10mL) dark sesame oil

2 garlic cloves, crushed

1/2 tsp (2mL) ground ginger

1 In small bowl, whisk all ingredients to combine.

2 Add desired meat, poultry, fish or vegetables to bowl, tossing to coat.

3 Cover and refrigerate 20 minutes before cooking.

Add a little ✿ Zest

❀ Sweet Surrenders

From smoothies and shakes to pudding, pies and crepes, tasty treats can bring an instant smile to anyone. Unfortunately, many of these treats are high in fat and/or sugar. But there are ways to cut the fat and calories while saving the flavor. For instance, fruit-based desserts that are high in fiber and low in fat are still a sweet treat!

Fruit and Yogurt Parfait recipe can be found on page 233

Sugar Substitutes

■ **Sweet 'N Low**® (Saccharin) — Earliest form of sugar substitute; 300-500 times sweeter than sugar; it is not stable at high temperatures and results in a bitter taste, best used at the end of recipes; 2 teaspoons Sweet 'N Low = 1/4 cup granulated sugar.

■ **Equal**® (Aspartame) — Made of 2 amino acids, the building blocks of protein; 180-200 times sweeter than sugar; breaks down and loses its sweet taste when heated, best for use in cold recipes; in recipes, you may use 1/4 cup Equal in place of 1/4 cup sugar; new Equal Sugar Lite is a product made especially for baking that is half sugar and half encapsulate Equal (making it heat stable).

■ **Splenda**® (Sucralose) — Made from sugar so its taste is closest to sugar; may be used teaspoon for teaspoon in place of sugar; heat stable and may be used in all types of recipes; also available in a sugar blend, called "Splenda for Baking," which is half sugar, half Splenda.

■ **Stevia** — A natural, non-caloric sweetener, derived from the plant, Stevia rebaudiana, which is an herb; native to Paraguay; only can be sold as a "dietary supplement" in the US and therefore is not labeled as a "sweetener"; in its natural state is 300 times sweeter than sugar, and even more so when processed; it is heat stable and may be used in cooking; 1/2 teaspoon stevia is equivalent to 2 teaspoons sugar.

TIP!

Keep brown sugar substitute soft after opening. Store it in a plastic zippered bag to seal in the freshness.

Baking Substitutions

- Use fruit puree, such as unsweetened applesauce or prune puree, in place of some of the fat.

- Replace some of the whole eggs with egg whites or pasteurized egg substitute; it is best to keep some of the whole eggs in the recipe to maintain texture.

- To cut back on sugar, use one-half or one-third sugar substitute — this will maintain flavor but cut back on calories.

- Use evaporated milk in place of heavy cream.

- If cutting out some of the sugar, add extra spices, such as cinnamon, nutmeg, cardamom and ginger to enhance the flavor.

- When making bread, increase the fiber by using whole wheat flour for all or half the flour called for.

TIPS!

• *When baking pies, cover the edges of the crust with foil to prevent the baked edges from browning. If the top of the pie is browning too much, place foil on top but pierce a hole in the center so the crust stays crisp.*

• *For the most delicious desserts, bake cakes, muffins and breads on the middle oven rack. Use the lower rack for yeast breads and pies.*

• *The best way to freeze baked goods is to wrap them in plastic wrap and then in freezer bags or sealed containers. When you want to thaw the dessert, keep it in the bag or container to let any moisture reabsorb if lost during freezing.*

Sweet Surrenders

- Almond Cookies
- Sugarless Heart Cookies
- Grapefruit Watermelon Granita
- Tiramisu-Rice Dessert
- Apple Crisp
- Healthy Pumpkin Bread
- Strawberry Daiquiri
- Spiced Coffee
- Hot Chai Tea
- Pineapple Slush
- Vanilla Nut Milk
- Orange & Spice Tea
- Frozen Mocha Drink
- Classic Strawberry Shake
- Orange Mango Smoothie
- Peanut Butter Shake
- Cranberry Blast
- Coffee Granita
- Chocolate Raspberry Yogurt Shake
- Apple Frappe
- Fresh Fruit Ice

Sweet Surrenders

Applesauce Oatmeal Cookies

2 *dozen cookies*

- **SERVING SIZE: 2 COOKIES**
- **COUNTS AS:**
  1 STARCH

☀ Ingredients

1/4 cup (50mL) packed brown sugar

1/4 cup (50mL) sugar substitute

1/2 cup (125mL) unsweetened applesauce

1/4 cup (50mL) egg substitute

1 cup (250mL) all-purpose flour

1 tsp (5mL) baking powder

1/2 tsp (2mL) low-sodium salt

1 tsp (5mL) cinnamon

1 cup (250mL) oats

1/4 cup (50mL) raisins

1 Preheat oven to 350°F (180°C).

2 In a large mixing bowl, mix together the brown sugar, sugar substitute, egg substitute and applesauce.

3 In a separate bowl, sift the flour, baking powder, salt and cinnamon; stir into the applesauce mixture.

4 Add the rolled oats and raisins. Stir until well combined.

5 Drop by teaspoonful onto the prepared cookie sheet.

6 Bake for 10 minutes. Allow cookies to cool slightly before removing from the baking sheet.

Apricot Custard

1 *serving*

- **SERVING SIZE: 1 RECIPE**
- **COUNTS AS:**
  1/2 PROTEIN
  1 FRUIT
  1/2 DAIRY

good source of fiber

☀ Ingredients

3 medium apricots, chopped

1 egg beaten

1/2 cup (125mL) skim milk

1 packet sugar substitute

1/4 tsp (1mL) vanilla

dash ground nutmeg

1 Preheat oven to 325°F (160°C).

2 Divide chopped apricots into custard cups or soufflé dishes. Place cups in a shallow baking pan.

3 In a small mixing bowl, combine the egg, milk, sugar substitute and vanilla. Pour egg mixture over apricots. Sprinkle with nutmeg.

4 Place the baking pan, containing the cups, on the oven rack. Pour boiling water around custard cups in baking pan to depth of 1 inch (2.5mL).

5 Bake for 30-35 minutes, or until knife inserted in the center comes out clean.

❀ Sweet Surrenders

Sparkling Fruited Gelatin

4 *servings*

family fare

- SERVING SIZE: 1 CUP (250ML)
- COUNTS AS:
  1 FRUIT

✴ Ingredients

2 apples

1/2 cup (125mL) canned, crushed pineapple, drained

1 tsp (5mL) lemon juice

10 grapes

1 package (3oz / 90g) sugar-free mixed fruit flavored gelatin mix

1 cup (250mL) hot water

6oz (175mL) diet ginger ale

1 Peel and core apples; cut into thin slices.

2 Place apple slices in medium bowl. Add pineapple and lemon juice.

3 Slice grapes in half and add to fruit mixture.

4 In a separate bowl, mix gelatin and hot water. Stir until gelatin is dissolved.

5 Once dissolved, pour ginger ale into gelatin.

6 Refrigerate 30 minutes, or until gelatin mixture is the consistency of raw egg whites.

7 Add the fruit mixture to gelatin and fold in gently.

8 Refrigerate until firm.

9 Serve chilled.

Chocolate Banana Crunch Parfait

4 *servings*

- SERVING SIZE: 1 PARFAIT
- COUNTS AS:
  1/2 DAIRY
  1 FRUIT
  1 FAT

✴ Ingredients

2 cups (500mL) skim milk

1 pkg (4 serving) fat-free, sugar-free chocolate pudding dry mix

2 small bananas, sliced

40 peanuts, crushed

1 Place milk into a medium bowl.

2 Slowly whisk in the pudding mix.

3 Spoon half of the pudding mixture into 4 dessert glasses.

4 Divide the banana, nuts and remaining pudding evenly among the glasses.

5 Place in refrigerator for 1 hour before serving.

"These recipes are so much fun to create."

- Bella N.

231

❖ Sweet Surrenders

Chocolate Truffles

1 *serving*

- SERVING SIZE: 6 TRUFFLES
- COUNTS AS:
  1 DAIRY

☀ Ingredients

3 Tbsp (45mL) fat-free cream cheese

2 packets sugar substitute

1 tsp (5mL) rum extract

2 Tbsp (30mL) unsweetened cocoa powder, divided

1. Combine cream cheese, sugar substitute, rum extract, and 1 Tbsp (15mL) cocoa powder.

2. Mix well until all ingredients are blended.

3. Refrigerate 15 minutes.

4. Roll mixture into small balls (approximately 6).

5. Roll balls in remaining 1 Tbsp (15mL) of cocoa powder.

"The desserts definitely satisfied my sweet tooth... and my husband's too."

- Sharon M.

Baked Custard

2 *servings*

- SERVING SIZE: 1/2 CUP (125ML)
- COUNTS AS:
  1/2 DAIRY
  1 FAT

☀ Ingredients

1 egg

1 cup (250mL) skim milk

1 Tbsp (15mL) sugar substitute

1 tsp (5mL) vanilla

1/4 tsp (1mL) low-sodium salt

1-2 Tbsp (15-30mL) orange or lemon zest

nutmeg for garnish, optional

1. Preheat oven to 350°F (180°C).

2. Break egg into small mixing bowl and beat slightly.

3. Add milk, sugar substitute, vanilla, zest and salt; beat well.

4. Pour into damp custard cups and sprinkle with nutmeg.

5. Place cups in a shallow pan of water and bake for 40-50 minutes, or until a knife inserted in the center comes out clean.

❀ Sweet Surrenders

Fruit and Yogurt **Parfait**

2 *servings*

■ SERVING SIZE: 1 PARFAIT
■ COUNTS AS:
  1/2 DAIRY
  1 FRUIT

good source of fiber

✻ Ingredients

12 small strawberries, sliced

8oz (250mL) vanilla nonfat
  lite yogurt

1/2 cup (125mL) blueberries

1/2 cup (125mL) high fiber cereal

1 packet sugar substitute

1 Dice 1 strawberry. Fold into yogurt.

2 In a bowl, toss remaining berries with sugar substitute.

3 In parfait glass layer the yogurt, strawberries, blueberries and cereal.

4 Serve chilled.

Baked Apple **á la Mode**

1 *serving*

■ SERVING SIZE: 1 APPLE
■ COUNTS AS:
  1 STARCH
  1 FRUIT

✻ Ingredients

1 small apple

1/4 cup (50mL) diet black
  cherry soda

1 tsp (5mL) cinnamon

1/2 cup (125mL) fat-free
  sugar-free vanilla ice
  cream or frozen yogurt

1 Core apple and place in microwave-safe dish.

2 Pour soda into middle of apple.

3 Sprinkle cinnamon over top.

4 Cook in microwave, on high, for 3-5 minutes, or until soft.

5 Top with ice cream or frozen yogurt.

"These recipes are just as good as any other cookbook I've used...even better."

- Lauren L.

✿ Sweet
Surrenders

Apple-Raspberry **Crepe**

 serving

- **SERVING SIZE: 1 CREPE**
- **COUNTS AS:**
  1 STARCH
  1 FRUIT

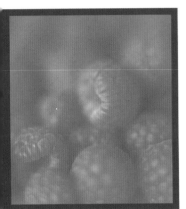

☀ Ingredients

1/4 cup (50mL) raspberries

1 packet sugar substitute

1/4 cup (50mL) unsweetened applesauce

1 crepe (see page 11 for recipe)

1 Place raspberries and sugar substitute in microwave-safe dish.

2 Heat on high 2-3 minutes, or until hot.

3 Stir in applesauce.

4 Place filling over one half of crepe and fold over filling.

> "The cookbook desserts are so delicious, I feel guilty eating them."
>
> *- Lynn K.*

Frozen Fruit **Pops**

 family fare

3 servings

- **SERVING SIZE: 1 POP**
- **COUNTS AS:**
  1 FRUIT

☀ Ingredients

24 strawberries

1/4 cup (50mL) apple juice

1 packet sugar substitute

1/2 cup (125mL) boiling water

1/2 tsp (2mL) sugar-free cherry gelatin mix

1 Place strawberries, apple juice and sweetener in blender. Puree 1 minute. There may still be small chunks of fruit in the mixture.

2 In medium mixing bowl, dissolve gelatin in boiling water.

3 Once dissolved, add gelatin to fruit mixture and toss to combine.

4 Pour mixture into plastic ice pop molds.*

5 Place in freezer. Serve frozen.

* If ice pop molds are unavailable, pour mixture into plastic cups and place in freezer. Once mixture begins to freeze, place ice pop sticks into cups.

 ❖ Sweet Surrenders

Peanut Butter Sundae Parfait

4 *servings*

- SERVING SIZE: 1 PARFAIT
- COUNTS AS:
  - 1/2 DAIRY
  - 1/2 PROTEIN
  - 1 CONDIMENT

☀ Ingredients

1pkg (4 serving) fat-free sugar-free chocolate pudding dry mix

2 cups (500mL) cold skim milk

1/2 cup (125mL) fat-free whipped topping

1/4 cup (50mL) peanut butter

1. Whisk pudding mix and milk together until smooth.

2. In a separate bowl, mix together peanut butter and fat-free whipped topping.

3. Layer pudding and peanut butter mixture in four dessert glasses.

4. Chill at least 1 hour before serving.

> "When it comes to desserts, these are guilt-free."
>
> *- Karen D.*

Rice Pudding

2 *servings*

- SERVING SIZE: 1/2 OF RECIPE
- COUNTS AS:
  - 2 STARCHES
  - 1 FRUIT
  - 1/2 DAIRY

☀ Ingredients

1 Tbsp (15mL) lite margarine

1 Tbsp (15mL) flour

1/2 cup (125mL) raw rice

1 cup (250mL) skim milk

1 tsp (5mL) vanilla extract

4-6 packets of sugar substitute

1/4 cup (50mL) raisins

dash of allspice

1/4 tsp (1mL) cinnamon

1. In medium saucepan melt margarine; add flour to melted margarine, stirring constantly to make a roux.

2. Gradually stir in 1/2 cup (125mL) milk, mix well; heat over medium flame until warm.

3. Add rice, sugar substitute, allspice and cinnamon.

4. Reduce heat and simmer.

5. Slowly add remaining milk during cooking until rice is tender.

6. Add vanilla and cook additional 1-2 minutes on low heat.

7. Remove from stove and add raisins.

8. Pour into bowls and refrigerate.

9. Serve chilled.

❖ Sweet Surrenders

Raspberry Peach Melba Crepe

serving

- SERVING SIZE: 1 CREPE
- COUNTS AS:
  1 STARCH
  1 FRUIT

☀ Ingredients

1/2 peach, diced

1 packet sugar substitute

1/4 tsp (1mL) ginger

1 Tbsp (15mL) sugar-free raspberry jelly or jam

1/4 cup (50mL) raspberries

1 Tbsp (15mL) fat-free whipped topping

1 crepe (see recipe on page 11)

1. Place diced peach, ginger and 1/2 packet of sugar substitute in microwave-safe dish.
2. Heat on high 2-3 minutes, or until hot.
3. Spread raspberry jelly over crepe.
4. Place peach mixture over half of the crepe and fold over filling.
5. Sprinkle remaining sugar substitute over raspberries.
6. Top crepe with raspberries and whipped topping.

Watermelon Ice

serving

- SERVING SIZE: 1 RECIPE
- COUNTS AS:
  1 FRUIT

☀ Ingredients

1 1/2 cups (375mL) watermelon cubes

1 packet sugar substitute

2 Tbsp (30mL) apple juice, chilled

2 ice cubes

1. Freeze watermelon overnight.
2. Once frozen, remove melon from freezer and place in blender.
3. Add remaining ingredients into blender.
4. Blend on medium until smooth.
5. Serve immediately.

> "You can eat desserts on the L A Weight Loss program and still lose weight. I did."
>
> *- Keri K.*

♣ Sweet
Surrenders

Lemon Glazed Cheesecake

6 servings

family fare

- SERVING SIZE: 1 SLICE
- COUNTS AS:
  1 STARCH
  1 DAIRY

☀ Ingredients

Cheesecake

2 - 8oz (225g, each) packages fat-free cream cheese, softened

3/4 cup (175mL) sugar substitute

1 Tbsp (15mL) flour

2 tsp (10mL) vanilla extract

1/2 tsp (2mL) fresh lemon peel, finely grated

1/2 cup (125mL) fat-free sour cream

3 egg whites

1/2 cup (125mL) graham cracker crumbs

nonfat cooking spray

Lemon glaze

1/3 cup (75mL) sugar substitute

1 1/2 Tbsp (23mL) arrowroot or cornstarch

1 1/2 Tbsp (23mL) fresh squeezed lemon juice

1/2 tsp (2mL) fresh lemon peel, finely grated

1/3 cup (75mL) water

2 cups (500mL) berries of choice

1. Blend first 5 ingredients with electric mixer.
2. Blend in sour cream and egg whites.
3. Spray 9-inch (23cm) pie pan with nonfat cooking spray; sprinkle with graham cracker crumbs.
4. Pour in cheese mixture and bake at 325°F (160°C) for 40 minutes.
5. Cool to room temperature, then refrigerate for 3 hours.
6. For glaze, stir sugar substitute and arrowroot or cornstarch together in a small saucepan over medium heat, then add the lemon juice, lemon peel and water.
7. Whisk until smooth.
8. Heat, stirring constantly, until mixture is clear and thick.
9. Spread evenly over cheesecake; allow to set at room temperature, briefly.
10. Top with berries.
11. Slice pie into 8 slices.

Chocolate Covered Cherries

1 serving

- SERVING SIZE: 9 CHERRIES
- COUNTS AS:
  1 FRUIT
  1 L A LITE

☀ Ingredients

1 packet LA Lite Chocolate Shake mix

1/2 cup (125mL) water

9 medium cherries, pitted

1. Mix L A Lite Chocolate Shake Mix with 1/2 cup (125mL) water.
2. Dip cherries into chocolate mixture and place on waxed paper.
3. Chill for 1 hour before serving.

237

Mango-Passion Fruit Frozen Yogurt

servings

- **SERVING SIZE: 3/4 CUP (175ML)**
- **COUNTS AS:**
  1 FRUIT
  1/2 DAIRY

❋ Ingredients

4 medium mangoes, peeled and cubed

1 cup (250mL) passion fruit pulp

1/3 cup (75mL) sugar substitute

1/2 tsp (2mL) vanilla extract

2 cups (500mL) vanilla nonfat yogurt

1 In a food processor or blender, puree the mango; strain through a sieve.

2 Add the remaining ingredients; mix to combine.

3 Pour the mixture into a shallow 9-inch baking pan.

4 Cover with foil or plastic wrap.

5 Freeze until solid (1-2 hours).

6 Break the frozen mixture into pieces.

7 Puree in a food processor, until soft, but not completely melted.

8 Repeat the freezing and pureeing once more.

9 Serve or return to the freezer for later use.

Low-Fat Brownies

servings

- **SERVING SIZE:**
  1/8 OF RECIPE
- **COUNTS AS:**
  1 STARCH

❋ Ingredients

3/4 cup (175mL) sugar

1/2 cup (125mL) flour

1/2 tsp (2mL) baking soda

2 egg whites, lightly beaten

1 tsp (5mL) vanilla

2/3 cup (150mL) unsweetened applesauce

1/4 cup (50mL) unsweetened cocoa powder

nonfat cooking spray

1 Preheat oven to 350°F (180°C).

2 Spray a square nonstick baking pan (8-inch x 8-inch / 20cm x 20cm) with nonfat cooking spray.

3 Combine the ingredients in a large mixing bowl, mix well.

4 Pour batter into pan and bake in preheated oven 20-30 minutes until baked.

5 To test if batter is done, insert a toothpick. If it comes out clean, brownies are done.

6 Remove from oven and let cool for 5 minutes in pan.

7 Gently remove from pan; place on wire rack and cool.

8 Cut into 8 squares.

❋ Sweet
Surrenders

Lemon Sorbet

10 *servings*

- **SERVING SIZE: 1/2 CUP (125ML)**
- **COUNTS AS:**
  2 CONDIMENTS

☀ Ingredients

1 envelope unflavored gelatin

2 1/4 cups (550mL) water, divided

1/3 cup (75mL) granulated sugar, divided

1 Tbsp (15mL) sugar substitute

2/3 cup (150mL) freshly squeezed lemon juice

2 large egg whites

2 tsp (10mL) grated lemon peel

1. In small saucepan, sprinkle gelatin over 1 cup (250mL) water; let stand 5 minutes to soften gelatin. Do not stir.

2. Add 1/3 cup (75mL) sugar and 1 1/4 tsp (6mL) sugar substitute.

3. Cook over low heat, stirring until gelatin and sugar dissolve completely.

4. Pour into large bowl; add remaining water and lemon juice.

5. Chill syrup, about 2 1/2 hours.

6. In a bowl, beat egg whites with remaining sugar substitute, until stiff, but not dry.

7. Fold egg whites into syrup mixture; add lemon peel.

8. Pour into aluminum loaf pan or rectangular baking pan.

9. Cover with foil and freeze 2 hours or until frozen 1-inch (2.5cm) around edges.

10. Spoon into large bowl and beat until smooth.

11. Return to aluminum pan, cover and freeze 3 hours.

12. Transfer to bowl and beat again.

13. Return to pan, cover and freeze, several hours or overnight, until firm.

14. To serve, let sorbet stand at room temperature about 15 minutes for easier scooping.

Bread Pudding

1 *serving*

- **SERVING SIZE: 1 RECIPE**
- **COUNTS AS:**
  1 STARCH

good source of fiber

☀ Ingredients

1/4 cup (50mL) egg substitute

2 tsp (10mL) skim milk

1/2 tsp (2mL) cinnamon

1 tsp (5mL) vanilla extract

1-2 packets of sugar substitute

1 slice of bread

dash of low-sodium salt

1. In a bowl, mix egg substitute, skim milk, cinnamon, sugar substitute, vanilla extract and salt.

2. Tear bread into small pieces and add to mixture.

3. Place in custard cup. Set cup in baking dish containing 1 inch (2.5cm) water.

4. Bake at 350°F (180°C) for 30 minutes.

❖ Sweet Surrenders

1 serving

- **SERVING SIZE: 1 APPLE**
  - 2 FRUITS
  - 1 FAT

good source of fiber

Stuffed Baked Apple

❋ Ingredients

- 1 apple
- 2 Tbsp (30mL) dried oatmeal
- 1 Tbsp (15mL) raisins
- 1 Tbsp (15mL) lite margarine
- 1 Tbsp (15mL) egg substitute
- 1 packet sugar substitute
- 1 tsp (5mL) cinnamon

1. Preheat oven to 350°F (180°C).
2. Core apple and peel a 1-inch (2.5cm) strip of skin around center of apple. Place in a baking dish and set aside.
3. In a medium mixing bowl, combine oatmeal, raisins, egg substitute, sugar substitute and margarine.
4. Stuff mixture into core of apple.
5. Sprinkle with cinnamon.
6. Pour water into baking dish, approximately 1/4-inch (1/2cm) depth.
7. Bake until apple is tender, about 30 minutes.
8. While baking, spoon syrup that forms in pan over the apple.

4 servings

- **SERVING SIZE: 1 PARFAIT**
- **COUNTS AS:**
  - 1/2 DAIRY
  - 1/2 FRUIT
  - 1 CONDIMENT

good source of fiber

Raspberry Vanilla Parfait

❋ Ingredients

- 1 pkg (4 serving) fat-free, sugar-free vanilla pudding dry mix
- 2 cups (500mL) cold skim milk
- 2 cups (500mL) raspberries
- 1/2 cup (125mL) fat-free whipped topping
- Mint (optional)

1. In medium bowl whisk milk and pudding mix until smooth.
2. Rinse raspberries and pat dry.
3. In four dessert glasses, layer pudding and raspberries evenly.
4. Top with a dollop of whipped topping on each.
5. Garnish with mint, if desired.
6. Cool in refrigerator and serve.

❋ Sweet Surrenders

Almond Cookies

dozen cookies

family fare

- SERVING SIZE: 1 COOKIE
- COUNTS AS:
  1 STARCH

☀ Ingredients

1 egg yolk

1/3 (75mL) cup sugar substitute

2 Tbsp (30mL) sugar

1/2 cup (125mL) butter

1 tsp (5mL) almond extract

1 1/2 cups (375mL) flour

1 Preheat oven to 350°F (180°C).

2 Beat the egg yolk, sugar substitute, sugar, butter and almond extract in a large bowl.

3 Blend in flour a little at a time.

4 Shape a tablespoonful of dough into a ball.

5 Repeat with the remaining dough.

6 Place the cookies on an ungreased cookie sheet.

7 Bake for 20 minutes, or until lightly golden brown.

Sugarless Heart Cookies

6 dozen cookies

- SERVING SIZE: 3 COOKIES
- COUNTS AS:
  1 STARCH

☀ Ingredients

3/4 cup (175mL) margarine, softened

1 package (0.3oz) mixed fruit sugar-free gelatin

1/4 cup (50mL) egg substitute

1 tsp (5mL) vanilla extract

1 3/4 cups (425mL) all purpose flour

1/2 tsp (2mL) baking powder

1 In a mixing bowl, cream together the margarine and gelatin.

2 Beat in the egg substitute and vanilla.

3 Mix together the flour and baking powder and add to the egg mixture, mixing well. Chill for 1 hour.

4 Preheat oven to 400°F (204°C). Roll the dough mixture out on a lightly floured surface to 1/4-inch thickness.

5 Cut out cookies with heart-shaped cookie cutter (or any shape you desire).

6 Place the cookies on an ungreased baking sheet and bake for 6-7 minutes or until the bottoms are lightly browned and the cookies are set. Cool on wire racks.

❖Sweet Surrenders

Grapefruit Watermelon Granita

4 *servings*

- SERVING SIZE: 1/4 RECIPE (125ML)
- COUNTS AS:
  1 FRUIT
  IF USING VODKA, COUNTS AS:
  1 FRUIT
  1 STARCH

☀ Ingredients

2 cups (250mL) fresh squeezed grapefruit juice

1/3 cup (75mL) sugar substitute

1 cup (250mL) watermelon pulp, seedless

4oz (125mL) vodka (optional)

1. In a saucepan, bring grapefruit juice and sugar substitute up to a simmer; stir until sugar substitute is dissolved. Remove from heat and cool.
2. Puree grapefruit syrup with watermelon and strain.
3. Stir in vodka (optional) and place in freezer.
4. After an hour, stir granita. Stir 2 more times before frozen-solid.
5. To serve, scrape up granita granules with a fork and spoon into dessert glasses.

Tiramisu-Rice Dessert

family fare

8 *servings*

- SERVING SIZE:
  1 CUP (250ML)
- COUNTS AS:
  1 STARCH
  1 DAIRY

☀ Ingredients

1 cup (250mL) long grain rice

2 1/2 cups (625mL) skim milk

1 Tbsp (15mL) instant coffee granules

2 cups (500mL) frozen fat-free whipped topping, thawed

3/4 cup (200mL) fat-free ricotta cheese

1/2 cup (125mL) sugar substitute

2 Tbsp (30mL) coffee liqueur

unsweetened cocoa

1. In medium saucepan, combine rice, milk and coffee granules, over high heat.
2. Stir occasionally until mixture comes to a boil.
3. Reduce heat to simmer; cover and cook 15 minutes or until rice is tender.
4. Cover and refrigerate until chilled.
5. In large bowl, combine rice mixture, whipped topping, ricotta cheese, sugar substitute and liqueur; mix well.
6. Spoon into individual serving dishes or medium-size serving bowl.
7. Sift cocoa over rice mixture.
8. Cover and refrigerate for at least 1 hour before serving.

❖ Sweet
Surrenders

Apple Crisp

1 *serving*

- **SERVING SIZE: 1 RECIPE**
- **COUNTS AS:**
  1 STARCH
  2 FRUITS
  1 FAT

good source of fiber

☀ Ingredients

2 small apples

2-3 packets sugar substitute

1/4 cup (50mL) oatmeal

1/4 tsp (1mL) ground cinnamon

1/4 tsp (1mL) ground nutmeg

1 Tbsp (15mL) lite margarine **or**

1 tsp (5mL) margarine

nonfat cooking spray

1. Heat oven to 350°F (180°C).

2. Arrange apple slices in baking pan coated with nonfat cooking spray.

3. Mix remaining ingredients; sprinkle over apples. Dot with margarine.

4. Bake until topping is golden brown and apples are tender.

> "Oh, the cookbook was key. There was a recipe for every craving   it really helped me stay on target."
>
> *- M. Norton*

Healthy Pumpkin Bread

10 *servings*

- **SERVING SIZE: 1/10 LOAF**
- **COUNTS AS:**
  2 STARCHES
  1 FAT
  1 CONDIMENT

☀ Ingredients

1 cup (250mL) fresh pumpkin, cooked, puréed

2 cups (500mL) whole wheat flour

1/4 tsp (1mL) low-sodium salt

1/4 tsp (1mL) baking soda

1 tsp (5mL) cinnamon

1/2 tsp (2mL) of cloves, ground

1/2 tsp (2mL) nutmeg

1/2 tsp (2mL) baking powder

1 tsp (5mL) vanilla extract

1/3 cup (75mL) raisins

1/4 cup (50mL) egg substitute

1 cup (250mL) maple syrup

1/4 cup (50mL) safflower oil

1/4 cup (50mL) applesauce

nonfat cooking spray

1. Preheat oven to 350°F (180°C).

2. In a small mixing bowl, blend egg substitute, maple syrup, safflower oil and applesauce.

3. Add the cooked, puréed pumpkin and beat well.

4. In second — larger — bowl, mix whole wheat flour, salt, baking soda, cinnamon, cloves, nutmeg and baking powder.

5. Stir the contents of the first bowl into the dry ingredients in the second.

6. Add vanilla extract and raisins.

7. Grease a standard (3-1/2 x 5 x 9 inch) loaf pan with nonfat cooking spray, and dust lightly with whole wheat flour.

8. Pour the batter into the pan, and bake it for 45 minutes.

9. Turn the oven down to 300°F (150°C) and bake for another 45 minutes.

10. Cool the bread in loaf pan before removing and slicing it.

❋ Sweet Surrenders

Strawberry Daiquiri

1 *serving*

- **SERVING SIZE: 1 RECIPE**
- **COUNTS AS:**
  1 FRUIT
  1 L A LITE
- **IF USING RUM, COUNTS AS:**
  1 STARCH
  1 FRUIT
  1 L A LITE

☼ Ingredients

1 packet L A Lite Vanilla Shake mix

1/2 cup (125mL) water

1 cup (250mL) ice cubes

12 small strawberries

1oz (30mL) rum (optional)

1. Place all ingredients in a blender; puree until smooth.
2. Serve immediately, or freeze until ready to use.

Spiced Coffee

1 *serving*

- **SERVING SIZE: 1 RECIPE**
- **COUNTS AS:**
  1 UNLIMITED BEVERAGE

☼ Ingredients

2 cups (500mL) brewed decaffeinated coffee

1 2-inch (5cm) stick cinnamon

1/4 tsp (1mL) whole allspice

2 strips of orange zest

1. In a saucepan combine coffee, cinnamon stick, allspice and orange zest. Bring to boil, reduce heat.
2. Cover and simmer for 5 minutes.
3. Remove solids from coffee with a slotted spoon or by draining over a sieve. If desired, garnish with cinnamon sticks.

Hot Chai Tea

1 *serving*

- **SERVING SIZE:**
  1 CUP (250ML)
- **COUNTS AS:**
  1/2 DAIRY

☼ Ingredients

1/2 cup (125mL) hot strongly brewed orange spiced tea

1/2 cup (125mL) fat-free milk

1 Tbsp (15mL) sugar substitute

1/4 tsp (1mL) vanilla

1/8 tsp (.5mL) ground cloves

1. Brew tea.
2. Place milk in glass measuring cup and microwave on high for 30-40 seconds.
3. Combine all ingredients in beverage mug and mix until blended.

Sweet Surrenders

Pineapple Slush

3 *servings*

- SERVING SIZE: 1/3 OF RECIPE
- COUNTS AS:
  2 FRUITS

❋ Ingredients

20oz (600g) can crushed pineapple

1 cup (250mL) water

2 Tbsp (30mL) powdered sugar

1 packet sugar substitute

1. Combine pineapple, water, sugar substitute and powdered sugar in a freezer-safe bowl; freeze for a few hours.

2. Remove from freezer and put in a blender.

3. Process at high speed; purée until smooth, about 3 minutes.

Vanilla Nut Milk

1 *serving*

- SERVING SIZE: 1 DRINK
- COUNTS AS:
  1 DAIRY

good source of calcium

❋ Ingredients

8oz (250mL) skim milk

1 tsp (5mL) vanilla extract

1/8 tsp (.5mL) almond extract

1 packet sugar substitute

dash of nutmeg

1. Combine all ingredients in small saucepan.

2. Cook over medium heat until warm, stirring frequently; do not bring to a boil.

3. Serve hot.

Orange & Spice Tea

2 *servings*

- SERVING SIZE: 1 CUP (250ML)
- COUNTS AS:
  1 UNLIMITED BEVERAGE
  1 CONDIMENT

❋ Ingredients

2 cups (500mL) water

1 cinnamon stick, broken into pieces

6 whole cloves

2 decaffeinated tea bags

juice from 1 orange

1. In a saucepan, combine water, cinnamon and cloves. Bring to a boil; remove from heat.

2. Add tea bags; steep for 5 minutes. Remove tea bags.

3. Stir in juice of 1 orange.

4. Sweeten to taste.

❋ Sweet Surrenders

Frozen Mocha Drink

- **SERVING SIZE: 1 DRINK**
- **COUNTS AS:**
  1 DAIRY
  1 L A LITE

good source of calcium

✳ Ingredients

1 packet L A Lite Chocolate Shake mix

1 tsp (5mL) instant coffee (decaf or regular)

1 Tbsp (15mL) hot water

8oz (250mL) plain nonfat yogurt

1/2 tsp (2mL) cinnamon

sugar substitute to taste

1/2 cup (125mL) crushed ice or 4 ice cubes

1 Dissolve coffee in hot water.

2 Add all ingredients to blender.

3 Blend on high until smooth.

4 Pour into container and place in freezer to chill.

Classic Strawberry Shake

1 *serving*

- **SERVING SIZE: 1 SMOOTHIE**
- **COUNTS AS:**
  1 STARCH
  2 FRUITS
  1/2 DAIRY

good source of calcium

✳ Ingredients

1 scoop L A Lite Strawberry-Banana Smoothie mix

12 small strawberries, sliced

4oz (125mL) skim milk

1/2 cup (125mL) sugar-free or fat-free vanilla frozen yogurt

3 ice cubes

1 Place smoothie mix, milk, ice and berries in blender.

2 Blend well.

3 Add yogurt and blend until smooth.

4 Serve immediately.

Sweet Surrenders

Orange Mango Smoothie

2 *servings*

- **SERVING SIZE: 1/2 OF RECIPE**
- **COUNTS AS:**
  1 FRUIT
  1/2 DAIRY

❊ Ingredients

1 cup (250mL) crushed ice

1 cup (250mL) mango, cubed

1 cup (250mL) skim milk

1/2 cup (125mL) fresh squeezed orange juice

1 tsp (5mL) honey

orange slice (optional)

1 In a blender, combine ice, mango, milk, orange juice and honey; blend until smooth.

2 Pour into 2 glasses and garnish with orange slice.

Peanut Butter Shake

1 *serving*

- **SERVING SIZE: 1 SHAKE**
- **COUNTS AS:**
  1/2 PROTEIN
  1 DAIRY
  1 L A LITE

❊ Ingredients

1 Tbsp (15mL) peanut butter

8oz (250mL) skim milk

1 packet L A Lite Vanilla Shake mix

3 ice cubes

1 Combine all ingredients in a blender.

2 Blend together; chill.

Cranberry Blast

1 *serving*

- **SERVING SIZE: 1 SMOOTHIE**
- **COUNTS AS:**
  2 FRUITS

❊ Ingredients

1 scoop L A Lite Mixed Berry Smoothie mix

1/3 cup (75mL) cranberry juice

1/4 cup (50mL) diet cranberry ginger ale

3 ice cubes

1 Place all ingredients in blender, blend until frothy.

2 Serve immediately.

❖ Sweet Surrenders

Coffee Granita

2 *servings*

- SERVING SIZE: 1/2 CUP (125ML)
- COUNTS AS:
  1 CONDIMENT

※ Ingredients

1-2 packets sugar substitute

2 Tbsp (30mL) instant espresso coffee powder

1/2 cup (125mL) cold water

2 Tbsp (30mL) fat-free whipped topping

1 cup boiling water

1. In a bowl, combine sugar substitute and coffee powder. Add boiling water; stir until dissolved. Stir in cold water.

2. Pour mixture into 9 x 5 x 3-inch (23 x 13 x 8cm) loaf pan. Freeze for about 2 hours or until firm.

3. Break frozen mixture into small chunks and place in a small chilled mixer bowl. Beat with electric mixer on low speed until fluffy.

4. Freeze mixture for 2 hours, or until firm.

5. To serve, scrape or scoop ice into small dessert dishes. Top with whipped topping.

Chocolate Raspberry Yogurt Shake

1 *serving*

good source of fiber

- SERVING SIZE: 1 SHAKE
- COUNTS AS:
  1 FRUIT
  1 DAIRY
  1 L A LITE

※ Ingredients

1/2 cup (125mL) skim milk

1/2 cup (125mL) plain fat-free yogurt

1 packet of L A Lite Chocolate Shake mix

1 cup (250mL) raspberries

1. Place skim milk, yogurt, shake mix and raspberries in blender; cover.

2. Blend until smooth.

3. Serve immediately.

"My kids always ask me for snacks from the L A Lite Cookbook."

- Karen T.

Sweet Surrenders

Apple Frappe

1 *serving*

- **SERVING SIZE: 1 DRINK**
- **COUNTS AS:**
  - 1 STARCH
  - 1 FRUIT
  - 1 L A LITE

✳ Ingredients

1/2 cup (125mL) chopped, cored and peeled apples

1/4 cup (50mL) water

ground cinnamon to taste

1/2 cup (125mL) frozen, fat-free and/or sugar-free vanilla yogurt

1 packet L A Lite Vanilla Shake mix

1 In a blender combine the apples, water, cinnamon and vanilla shake mix.

2 Process until smooth.

3 Add the frozen yogurt and mix until well blended.

4 Pour into freezer-safe glass or mug and freeze until ready to use.

5 Serve cold.

Fresh Fruit Ice

1 *serving*

- **SERVING SIZE: 1 DRINK**
- **COUNTS AS:**
  - 1 FRUIT

✳ Ingredients

3/4 cup (200mL) fresh fruit (suggestions: strawberries, raspberries, blueberries, blackberries, mango, watermelon, honeydew and cantaloupe)

1/2 cup (125mL) crushed ice

1 packet sugar substitute

1 Peel, seed and/or core fruit. If necessary, chop roughly.

2 Put fruit, ice and sugar substitute in blender.

3 Blend on high until smooth.

4 Serve in a champagne, cocktail or wine glass.

✤ Sweet Surrenders

Home
❖ for the
Holidays

Hosting a holiday party or going to one? Use these recipes for any special occasion and you'll always have something tasty to serve or bring...plus a clear conscience! All the recipes are healthy, light and nutritious. Your guests will be so pleased — it just might end up being a special recipe request for every holiday!

◀ Roasted Turkey with Mushroom Gravy recipe can be found on page 258

Healthy for the Holidays!

Many people feel that holidays are a time to let loose and forgo any diet or healthful eating habits. The key to successful weight loss and maintenance is moderation, and this includes the holidays. But with weight loss and maintenance, comes self control and reliance to choose the right foods. Some foods will never be low in fat or calories, but there are many that can be altered to meet your needs. You'll find many of these types of recipes in this section. Remember though, these are still more caloric, sometimes higher fat, food choices, and should be limited to special occasions!

But what if you aren't the one cooking? What if you spend all your holidays visiting friends and family and are never home? There are a few tips to take with you:

- Offer to bring a dish — this way you can have control over something that will be on the menu! You will know what you are eating and what went into the dish!

- Make good choices, avoid the things you could have in an everyday setting, such as chips and dip — instead, go for something that is specific to the event or holiday.

- Fill up on veggies or lower fat/calorie items — if you must try a bit of the richer, creamier items, have a little, but fill up on healthier choices, such as vegetables and dip, salads, lean proteins, such as turkey or lean beef and fruit.

- Have a snack before you leave for the party, such as a piece of fruit and a glass of water. If you get to the party and you are hungry, you are more likely to overindulge!

TIP!

Make good choices, such as vegetables and dip, salads, lean proteins, such as turkey or lean beef, and fruit.

Tips for the Perfect Holiday

Looking for a special gift for the holidays? Homemade dishes are a warm, considerate, and much appreciated way to say "happy holidays." You'll find everything you'll need inside the *L A Lite Cookbook* for that special gift. Here are great ways to wrap up a cake, a plate of cookies, an appetizer or any special dish:

- **Gift Basket** — A gift basket makes a beautiful presentation. Purchasing them can be costly so why not make your own? Colorful tins of Almond and Applesauce Oatmeal cookies and Chocolate Truffles placed in a white basket and wrapped in clear wrap with holiday ribbon is a very festive, fun gift.

- **Holiday Dish** — Why not make a Lemon Glazed Cheesecake and place it in a pretty holiday cake dish or plate…the dish will also be a part of the gift!

- **Holiday Canister** — A fun holiday canister filled with cookies and goodies from the *L A Lite Cookbook* is a unique way to spread the holiday cheer!

What wine should I serve when entertaining for the holidays?

Planning a holiday celebration and wondering what wine goes with what entrees? Here's a simple chart to help you remember when to use a Bordeaux and when you should use a Chardonnay!

- **Salmon** — A medium to full-bodied wine, red or white like Pinot Noir or White Burgundy is perfect for salmon.

- **Pork** — For pork, try a medium full-bodied white wine with fruit aromas and strong acidity like Riesling, Pinot Gris or Pinot Blanc.

- **Roast Beef** — A rich full-bodied red wine with substantial tannin like Cabernet Sauvignon or Rivera del Duero Red is ideal for roast beef.

- **Chicken** — Light chicken dishes go great with a Chardonnay or Pinot Grigio.

- **Turkey** — A medium-bodied red wine like Pinot Noir is an excellent accompaniment to roasted turkey.

(When drinking wine, be sure to count one 3oz (89mL) glass of wine as one fruit exchange!)

TIPS!

• Have smaller helpings at dinner so you can try a wider variety of foods and won't feel as bad at the end of the party. Eating only 1/2 as much as you normally would can prevent overeating.

• Save yourself some time by setting the table for the holidays the night before. The holidays can become a little hectic and scrambling for extra place settings and silverware should be the last thing on your mind.

Home
for the
Holidays

Challah

- **SERVING SIZE:**
  1/12 OF BREAD (APPROX 1OZ / 30G)
- **COUNTS AS:**
  2 STARCHES

✳ Ingredients

1 packet or 1 Tbsp (15mL) active
dry yeast

2 Tbsp (30mL) sugar

1/4 cup (50mL) warm water

2 cups (500mL) all-purpose flour

2 cups (500mL) whole
wheat flour

1/2 tsp (2mL) lite salt

1 egg

2 Tbsp (30mL) vegetable oil

1 1/4 cup (300mL) cold water

1 egg, beaten

1 Tbsp (15mL) poppy seeds

nonfat cooking spray

1 Dissolve the yeast and sugar in warm water. Let stand for 5 minutes.

2 Combine flour and salt in a large mixing bowl.

3 Make a well in the center of the flour mixture; add the egg, oil, yeast mixture and cold water. Mix well.

4 Knead the dough on a floured board, adding more whole wheat flour, as needed, until dough is smooth and elastic.

5 Place in an oiled bowl.

6 Cover with a damp towel and let rise until dough has doubled, about 1 hour.

7 Divide the dough into three parts.

8 Roll, by hand, each third into a strip, about 15 inches long.

9 Braid the strips together and place on a baking sheet that has been lightly coated with nonfat cooking spray. Brush with the beaten egg. Sprinkle on the poppy seeds.

10 Cover and let rise until loaf has doubled in size.

11 Bake in a 375°F (190°C) oven for 40-45 minutes, or until golden brown.

Winter Salad

 servings

- **SERVING SIZE:**
  1/4 OF RECIPE
- **COUNTS AS:**
  2 VEGETABLES
  1 FAT

✳ Ingredients

2 heads bibb lettuce

1 bunch watercress

1 apple, chopped

2 Tbsp (30mL) chopped pecans,
toasted

3 Tbsp (45mL) balsamic vinegar

1 Tbsp (15mL) Dijon mustard

1 Tbsp (15mL) olive oil

1 tsp (5mL) honey

freshly ground pepper, to taste

1 Clean and chop lettuces. Toss together and divide among 4 salad plates.

2 Combine apples and pecans; sprinkle over lettuce.

3 Whisk together remaining ingredients; drizzle over salads.

Home
✤ for the
Holidays

Potato Latkes

8 *servings*

- SERVING SIZE: 3 PANCAKES
- COUNTS AS:
  1 STARCH
  2 VEGETABLES

✳ Ingredients

1 pound (450g) zucchini, peeled

1 pound (450g) potatoes, peeled

2 large onions, chopped

1 pound (450g) fresh spinach

1 large egg

2 egg whites

1/2 cup (125mL) flour

1/2 tsp (2mL) ground cumin

1/2 tsp (2mL) dried ground coriander

ground white pepper, to taste

1/4 tsp (1mL) lite salt

nonfat cooking spray

1. Grate potatoes, zucchini and onion in food processor (work quickly to avoid discoloration). Squeeze out any liquid. Place in a large mixing bowl.

2. Add spinach, egg, egg whites, flour, cumin, coriander, salt and pepper; mix well.

3. Coat large skillet with nonfat cooking spray.

4. Spoon batter into pan, being careful not to crowd.

5. Cook until crisp and brown on one side, then turn over and fry on other side.

6. Keep finished pancakes warm in oven until all pancakes are cooked.

7. Makes 24 pancakes.

Baked Stuffed Zucchini

8 *servings*

family fare

- SERVING SIZE: 1/4 ZUCCHINI
- COUNTS AS:
  1 VEGETABLE

✳ Ingredients

2 zucchini, cut in half lengthwise

1 small onion, finely chopped

1/4 cup (50mL) lite tomato sauce

1/2 tsp (2mL) parsley

1 garlic clove, chopped

2 Tbsp (30mL) matzoh meal

1. Preheat oven to 450°F (230°C).

2. Scoop out pulp/flesh of the zucchini halves.

3. Heat pulp, onion, tomato sauce, parsley and garlic in a pan for 5 minutes. Add matzoh meal to mixture and mix well.

4. Stuff the zucchini shells with mixture.

5. Place in a baking dish with a little water on the bottom.

6. Bake for 30 minutes, until zucchini shells are soft.

Home
✤ for the
Holidays

Filet Mignon with Mushroom & Wine Sauce

4 *servings*

- **SERVING SIZE: 1 STEAK AND 1/2 CUP (125ML) SAUCE**
- **COUNTS AS:**
  1 PROTEIN
  2 VEGETABLES

❋ Ingredients

4 filet mignon steaks (4oz / 120g, each)

1/3 cup (75mL) chopped green onion

1/2 pound (225g) fresh shiitake mushrooms, stems removed

1 1/2 cups (375mL) red wine, divided

1 small (10-12fl oz / 300-360mL) can low-sodium beef consommé, undiluted

freshly ground pepper

1 Tbsp (15mL) low-sodium soy sauce

2 tsp (10mL) cornstarch

1 tsp (5mL) dried thyme

nonfat cooking spray

1. Coat a skillet with nonfat cooking spray and heat over medium heat.

2. Add onions and mushrooms; sauté for 4 minutes.

3. Add 1 cup (250mL) red wine and 3/4 cup (175mL) consommé; cook for 5 minutes, stirring frequently. Remove the mushrooms with a slotted spoon; place in a bowl. .

4. Increase heat to high; cook wine mixture until reduced to 1/2 cup (125mL), about 5 minutes.

5. Add reduction to mushrooms; set aside. Wipe pan with paper towel. Sprinkle steaks with pepper.

6. Coat skillet again with nonfat cooking spray and heat over high heat. Add steaks; cook 3 minutes on each side.

7. Reduce heat to medium-low; continue to cook another 2-4 minutes, or until desired level of doneness.

8. Combine soy sauce with cornstarch.

9. Add 1/2 cup (125mL) wine and remaining consommé to skillet; scrape bottom of skillet to loosen browned bits. Bring to a boil; cook 1 minute.

10. Add mushroom mixture, cornstarch mixture, and dried thyme to skillet; bring to a boil, and cook 1 minute, stirring. Serve sauce over steaks.

Glazed Ham

8 *servings*

- **SERVING SIZE: 3OZ (90G) COOKED**
- **COUNTS AS:**
  1 PROTEIN
  1 CONDIMENT

Home
❖ for the
Holidays

❋ Ingredients

2 pound (1kg) ham

1 Tbsp (15mL) Dijon mustard

1 cup (250mL) apricot halves in lite syrup

3 Tbsp (45mL) no sugar added apricot preserves

1/2 tsp (2mL) whole ground cloves

1. Trim all visible fat from ham. Place ham in baking pan. Rub Dijon mustard all over ham.

2. Pour apricot halves and juice over ham. Dot cloves throughout ham, gently pressing into flesh.

3. Cook ham in oven according to package directions.

4. To prepare glaze, place preserves in small dish. Place in microwave 10-20 seconds, until preserves begin to melt.

5. During last 30 minutes of cooking, brush ham with warm glaze. Continue to brush ham every 10 minutes until cooked through.

6. Preserves may need to be re-heated, as needed, before basting.

7. Allow to rest 5 minutes, before slicing.

Crown Roast of Pork

 15 *servings*

- SERVING SIZE: 3 OZ (90G) COOKED PORK ROAST AND 1/2 CUP (125ML) STUFFING
- COUNTS AS:
  1 PROTEIN
  2 CONDIMENTS

❊ Ingredients

27 pounds (12kg) crown pork roast (12 rib)

freshly ground pepper, to taste

Stuffing

5 green onions, chopped

2 celery stalks, finely chopped

1 cup (250mL) red apple, peeled and chopped

1 cup (250mL) green apple, peeled and chopped

6 slices lite bread, cubed and toasted

2 Tbsp (30mL) dried sage leaves

1/2 tsp (2mL) dried rosemary

1/2 tsp (2mL) dried thyme

1/4 cup (50mL) beaten egg substitute

1/4 cup (50mL) skim milk

1/4 tsp (1mL) freshly ground pepper

nonfat cooking spray

Roast

1 Preheat oven to 325°F (160°C).

2 Trim all visible fat from roast; season with pepper

3 Cut a piece of aluminum foil into an 8-inch square; place on rack in roasting pan.

4 Place roast; bone ends up, on foil-lined rack. Wrap bones individually with foil to prevent blackening.

5 Bake for one hour before stuffing.

Stuffing

1 Coat skillet with nonfat cooking spray and heat over medium-high heat; add onion and celery. Cook, stirring, until tender.

2 Combine apples, bread cubes and seasonings in a large bowl; stir in vegetable mixture, egg and remaining ingredients.

3 Spoon stuffing into center of roast; cover with additional foil.

4 Insert oven-proof meat thermometer into roast, taking care not to touch fat or bone. Continue to bake at 325°F (160°C) for 1 1/2 hours, or until thermometer reaches 150°F (65°C). Remove foil from bones before serving.

Minted Leg of Lamb

12 *servings*

- SERVING SIZE: 3 OZ (90G) COOKED LAMB
- COUNTS AS:
  1 PROTEIN

❊ Ingredients

9 pounds (4kg) bone-in leg of lamb

1 tsp (5mL) lite salt

1 1/2 tsp (7mL) dried mint flakes

1/2 tsp (2mL) cayenne pepper

5 green onions, chopped

3 cups (750mL) dry white wine

1/2 cup (125mL) low-sodium chicken broth

1/3 cup (75mL) Dijon mustard

4 garlic cloves, chopped

2 Tbsp (30mL) low-sodium Worcestershire sauce

nonfat cooking spray

1 Preheat oven to 325°F (160°C).

2 Combine first 3 ingredients; rub into lamb.

3 Place chopped onion in center of a roasting pan coated with nonfat cooking spray; place lamb on top of onion.

4 Combine wine and remaining 4 ingredients; pour over lamb.

5 Insert oven-proof meat thermometer into thickest part of lamb, taking care not to touch bone or fat.

6 Roast for 1 hour 45 minutes to 2 hours 30 minutes, or until thermometer registers 150-160°F (65-70°C). Baste lamb every 30 minutes with wine mixture.

7 Let stand 10 minutes before slicing.

Home
❖ for the
Holidays

Roasted Turkey with Mushroom Gravy

10 *servings*

- SERVING SIZE: 4 OZ (120G) COOKED TURKEY AND 1/4 CUP (50ML) GRAVY
- COUNTS AS:
  1 PROTEIN
  1 CONDIMENT

⁕ Ingredients

Turkey

20-22 pound (9-10kg) turkey

3 Tbsp (45mL) chopped fresh rosemary

3 Tbsp (45mL) chopped fresh thyme

3 Tbsp (45mL) chopped fresh tarragon

1 Tbsp (15mL) freshly ground pepper

2 tsp (10mL) lite salt

3 Tbsp (45mL) lite margarine, melted

4 cups (1L) low-sodium chicken broth

Gravy

1/2 cup (125mL) finely chopped green onions

1 cup (250mL) finely chopped fresh mushrooms

2 Tbsp (30mL) chopped fresh parsley

3/4 cups (175mL) low-sodium chicken broth

2 Tbsp (30mL) cornstarch

freshly ground pepper, to taste

Turkey

1 Position rack in lowest third of oven and preheat to 425°F (220°C).

2 Rinse turkey, then pat dry with paper towels; place on rack set in large roasting pan.

3 Mix herb mixture and place into main cavity. Tie legs together loosely to hold the shape of the turkey.

4 Pour 2 cups (500mL) broth into the pan. Drizzle melted margarine over turkey.

5 Roast turkey 45 minutes.

6 Remove turkey from oven and cover breast with foil. Reduce oven temperature to 350°F (180°C).

7 Return turkey to oven; roast for 1 hour.

8 Remove foil from turkey; pour remaining 2 cups (500mL) broth into pan.

9 Continue roasting turkey until meat thermometer, inserted in thickest part of thigh, registers 180°F (85°C) (or until juices run clear when thickest part of thigh is pierced by skewer), basting occasionally with pan juices. Expected cooking time will be about 1-2 hours longer.

10 Transfer turkey to platter; tent with foil.

11 Let stand 30 minutes before slicing.

Gravy

1 In a saucepan, sauté onion, mushrooms, and parsley in 1/4 cup (60mL) broth until vegetables are tender.

2 Combine cornstarch, pepper, and 1/2 cup (125mL) broth; stir until smooth.

3 Add cornstarch mixture to pan and mix well.

4 Bring to a boil, stirring occasionally. Boil for 2 minutes.

Home
⁕ for the
Holidays

Grilled Chicken & Portabellas

4 *servings*

- SERVING SIZE: 1 CHICKEN BREAST, 1 MUSHROOM CAP, AND 2 TBSP (30ML) SAUCE
- COUNTS AS:
  1 PROTEIN
  2 VEGETABLES
  1 FRUIT

☀ Ingredients

4-5oz (120-150g) boneless, skinless chicken breasts

2 1/4 cups (550mL) Marsala wine, divided

2 Tbsp (30mL) reduced/low-sodium Worcestershire sauce

1 pound (450g) portabella mushroom caps

1/4 cup (50mL) diced green onion

nonfat cooking spray

1 Combine 2 cups (500mL) wine, Worcestershire sauce, and chicken breast in a large zip-top bag; seal and marinate in refrigerator 1 hour.

2 Remove chicken from bag, reserving marinade.

3 Prepare grill.

4 Lightly coat mushrooms with nonfat cooking spray.

5 Place mushrooms, top sides down, on grill rack coated with nonfat cooking spray; spoon 1 Tbsp (15mL) wine into each cap.

6 Grill chicken for 6 minutes on each side, or until chicken is done.

7 While the chicken and mushrooms are grilling, place a medium skillet coated with cooking spray over medium-high heat until hot.

8 Add green onions; sauté for 1 minute.

9 Add the reserved marinade and bring to a boil.

10 Reduce heat, and simmer until reduced to 1/2 cup (125mL).

11 Cut mushrooms into 1/2-inch (1.5mL) thick slices.

12 Serve chicken and mushrooms with sauce.

Balsamic Roasted New Potatoes

 10 *servings*

- SERVING SIZE: 2 POTATOES
- COUNTS AS:
  1 STARCH

☀ Ingredients

2 pounds (900g) new potatoes, quartered

1 Tbsp (15mL) minced garlic

1 tsp (5mL) chopped fresh thyme

1 tsp (5mL) chopped fresh rosemary

3 Tbsp (45mL) balsamic vinegar

1/4 tsp (1mL) freshly ground pepper

dash of lite salt

nonfat cooking spray

1 Preheat oven to 425°F (220°C).

1 Coat large cast iron skillet with nonfat cooking spray and heat over medium-high heat.

2 Add potatoes and seasonings and heat through.

3 Remove skillet from heat; place in oven, uncovered, for 30 minutes, or until potatoes are tender, stirring occasionally.

4 Add vinegar, and toss well.

5 Sprinkle with salt and pepper. Roast, uncovered, 6 more minutes.

6 Serve immediately.

Home
❖ for the
Holidays

Zucchini-Carrot Casserole

3 *servings*

- **SERVING SIZE: 1/3 OF RECIPE**
- **COUNTS AS:**
  3 VEGETABLES
  1 DAIRY

☀ Ingredients

1 onion, chopped

2 medium zucchinis, thinly sliced

1 medium carrot, thinly sliced

2 garlic cloves, chopped

1/4 cup (50mL) low-sodium chicken broth

1/4 cup (50mL) fat-free sour cream

4oz (120g) reduced-fat shredded cheddar cheese, divided

1/2 tsp (2mL) basil

1/4 tsp (1mL) oregano

1/4 tsp (1mL) onion powder

1/4 tsp (1mL) lite salt

1/4 tsp (1mL) freshly ground pepper

4 Melba toasts, crushed

nonfat cooking spray

1. Preheat oven to 350°F (180°C)

2. Coat large skillet with nonfat cooking spray and heat over medium-high heat. Add onion to skillet, cook 1 minute.

3. Increase heat to high. Add zucchini, garlic and carrots. Cook 1-2 minutes. Add broth and cook until vegetables are soft and all liquid has evaporated. Remove from heat.

4. Stir in sour cream, 3oz (90g) cheese, salt and pepper.

5. Pour mixture into a large casserole dish, coated in nonfat cooking spray.

6. In separate bowl, combine basil, oregano, onion powder and crushed Melba toast.

7. Top the zucchini mixture with Melba crumb mixture and remaining cheese.

8. Bake for 15 minutes, or until cheese is melted. Serve immediately.

Bread Dressing

12 *servings*

- **SERVING SIZE: 1/2 CUP (125ML)**
- **COUNTS AS:**
  1 STARCH

☀ Ingredients

1 cup (250mL) chopped celery

1 cup (250mL) chopped onion

1 cup (75mL) low-sodium chicken broth

1 tsp (5mL) ground sage or poultry seasoning

dash of lite salt

freshly ground pepper, to taste

12 slices bread cubes (use diet whole wheat bread and lightly toast to remove excess moisture)

1 1/2 Tbsp (23mL) butter

nonfat cooking spray

1. Preheat oven to 350°F (180°C).

2. In medium saucepan, cook celery and onion in 1/3 cup (75mL) of the broth, until tender. Remove from heat.

3. Stir in poultry seasoning or sage, pepper and salt.

4. Place dry bread cubes in a large mixing bowl. Add onion mixture.

5. Drizzle with remaining broth to moisten, add butter and lightly toss.

6. Coat casserole dish with nonfat cooking spray. Place stuffing in dish and bake for 20 minutes, or until browned.

Home
❖ for the
Holidays

Wild Rice Pilaf

 8 *servings*

- **SERVING SIZE: 1/2 CUP (125ML)**
- **COUNTS AS:**
  1 STARCH
  2 VEGETABLES

☀ Ingredients

1 1/4 cups (300mL) water

3 cups (750mL) low-sodium chicken broth

1 1/2 cups (375mL) uncooked wild rice

1 Tbsp (15mL) lite margarine

3 cups (750mL) sliced mushrooms

1 cup (250mL) chopped green onions

1/2 cup (125mL) finely chopped fresh parsley

1/3 cup (75mL) chopped pecans, toasted

3/4 tsp (3mL) poultry seasoning

1/2 tsp (2mL) lite salt

1/4 tsp (1mL) freshly ground pepper

nonfat cooking spray

1. Bring water and broth to a boil in a medium saucepan.

2. Add wild rice; cover, reduce heat, and simmer 1 hour or until tender. Drain any excess liquid.

3. Preheat oven to 325°F (160°C).

4. Melt margarine in a large, nonstick skillet over medium-high heat.

5. Add mushrooms and onion; sauté until tender.

6. Remove from heat; stir in parsley and next 4 ingredients.

7. Combine rice and mushroom mixture in a 2-quart casserole, coated with nonfat cooking spray.

8. Cover and bake for 25 minutes.

Southern Peach Shortcake

9 *servings*

- **SERVING SIZE: 1/9 OF CAKE**
- **COUNTS AS:**
  1 STARCH
  1/2 FAT

☀ Ingredients

3 peaches, sliced

3 packets of sugar substitute

1/2 tsp (2mL) almond extract

1/2 tsp (2mL) cinnamon

1 cup (250mL) flour

1/3 cup (75mL) sugar

2 tsp (10mL) baking powder

2 Tbsp (30mL) oil

2 egg whites

1/4 cup (50mL) skim milk

nonfat cooking spray

1. Preheat oven to 400°F (200°C).

2. Place peaches in bottom of well-greased 8-inch baking dish coated with nonfat cooking spray.

3. Sprinkle with 3 packets of sugar substitute, almond extract and cinnamon.

4. Combine flour, sugar and baking powder in mixing bowl. Add oil, egg whites and milk to flour mixture. Mix well.

5. Spread mixture evenly over peaches. Bake for 30 minutes, or until lightly browned.

6. Cool for 15 minutes. To serve, place large serving plate over top of the cake and invert onto plate.

   Serve with fat-free, no sugar added, ice cream. (Optional-please refer to the menu plan for serving and exchanges.)

Home
❖ for the
Holidays

New York Cheesecake

12 *servings*

- **SERVING SIZE: 1/12 OF CAKE**
- **COUNTS AS:**
  2 STARCHES
  1 FAT

❋ Ingredients

50 reduced-fat vanilla wafers, crumbled

4 Tbsp (60mL) lite margarine, melted

9 Tbsp (135mL) sugar substitute

2 packages (8oz or 225g each) reduced-fat cream cheese, softened

1 cup (250mL) reduced-fat sour cream

6 Tbsp (90mL) sugar

2 eggs

2 egg whites

2 Tbsp (30mL) cornstarch

1 tsp (5mL) vanilla

1 pint (500mL) strawberries, sliced (optional)

hot water

1. Mix 3/4 of vanilla wafer crumbles, margarine and 8 Tbsp (120mL) of sugar substitute. Set aside 1 Tbsp (15mL) of crumb mixture. Pour the rest into a 9-inch (23cm) springform pan.

2. Pat the mixture evenly onto the bottom and 1/2 inch (1.5cm) up the side of the pan.

3. Bake in preheated 350°F (180°C) oven until the crust is lightly browned, about 8 minutes or so. Cool on wire rack.

4. Beat cream cheese, sour cream, sugar and 1 Tbsp (15mL) of sugar substitute in a large bowl until fluffy; then beat in eggs, egg whites, vanilla and cornstarch. Pour mixture into pre-baked crust.

5. Place cheesecake in roasting pan on oven rack; add hot water covering 1 inch (2.5 cm) of the roasting pan.

6. Bake in preheated 300°F (150°C) oven until cheesecake is set in the center, approximately 45-60 minutes.

7. Remove cheesecake from roasting pan, sprinkle with reserved crumbs and return to oven. Turn oven off and let cheesecake cool in oven with door ajar for 3 hours.

8. Refrigerate 8 hours or overnight.

9. Remove sides of pan; place cheesecake on cake plate.

   Serve with strawberries. (Optional-please refer to the menu plan for serving and exchanges.)

Egg Nog

2 *servings*

- **SERVING SIZE: 3/4 CUP (175ML)**
- **COUNTS AS:**
  1/2 PROTEIN
  1 DAIRY

good source of calcium

❋ Ingredients

2 eggs, well beaten

3 packets sugar substitute

dash of vanilla extract

2 cups (500mL) cold skim milk

dash of nutmeg, to taste

1. Combine eggs and sugar substitute.

2. Add vanilla extract and cold milk and beat well.

3. Pour into glasses or mugs and sprinkle with nutmeg.

Home
❖ for the
Holidays

Crustless Pumpkin Pie

8 *servings*

- **SERVING SIZE: 1/8 OF PIE**
- **COUNTS AS:**
  1 STARCH
  1/2 DAIRY

✳ Ingredients

1 can (15oz / 420g) pumpkin, no salt added

1 can (12oz / 360g) evaporated skim milk

1/2 cup (125mL) egg substitute

2 egg whites

3/4 cup (175mL) sugar substitute

1 tsp (5mL) ground cinnamon

1/4 tsp (1mL) ground allspice

1/4 tsp (1mL) ground ginger

1/8 tsp (.5mL) lite salt

1/2 cup (125mL) reduced-fat graham cracker crumbs

nonfat cooking spray

1 Preheat oven to 325°F (160°C).

2 In a mixing bowl, combine the pumpkin, milk, egg substitute, egg whites and sugar substitute, beat until smooth.

3 Add the spices and salt, beat until well combined.

4 Stir in graham cracker crumbs.

5 Pour into a 9-inch (23cm) pie plate coated with nonfat cooking spray.

6 Bake for 50-55 minutes, or until knife inserted near the center comes out clean. Cool before slicing.

Fruit & Nut Crisp

8 *servings*

- **SERVING SIZE: 1-INCH (2.5CM) SQUARE (1/8 OF PAN)**
- **COUNTS AS:**
  1 STARCH
  1 FRUIT

✳ Ingredients

1/4 cup (50mL) flour

1/2 cup (125mL) uncooked instant oatmeal

1/2 tsp (2mL) allspice

3 Tbsp (45mL) lite margarine, softened

2 cups (500mL) canned pineapple chunks, drained

1 mango, peeled and sliced

1/2 banana, peeled and sliced

1 orange, peeled and sliced

3/4 cup (175mL) sliced papaya

1 kiwi, sliced

2 Tbsp (30mL) brown sugar

2 Tbsp (30mL) sugar substitute

3 Tbsp (45mL) almonds, chopped

1 Tbsp (15mL) flour

nonfat cooking spray

1 Preheat oven to 350°F (180°C).

2 In small bowl, combine 1/4 cup (50mL) flour, oatmeal, brown sugar and allspice.

3 Add margarine; mix with fork, until a crumbly dough forms.

4 In large mixing bowl, combine all fruits, sugar substitute and almonds.

5 Sprinkle with 1 Tbsp (15mL) flour and toss to coat.

6 Pour fruit mixture into greased 8-inch (20cm) square baking pan, coated with nonfat cooking spray. Sprinkle oatmeal mixture on top.

7 Bake until crust is brown and fruit mixture begins to bubble, about 20-25 minutes.

Home
❖ for the
Holidays

General Information

The *L A Lite Cookbook* has been designed to spice up your L A Weight Loss program. Eating a variety of foods will not only keep you interested in your program, it will provide your body with the vitamins, minerals and other nutrients that are essential for balanced nutrition and good health. This cookbook will provide you with healthy and delicious recipes that can be used while you are losing weight, and for many years to come. Eating healthy is important both for losing weight and for maintaining your new weight for a lifetime.

Adopting a healthier lifestyle can benefit the entire family. This cookbook includes many popular dishes that everyone will enjoy. Start off any meal with an appetizer, soup or salad. Next, with over a hundred entrée recipes, you will be sure to find a delicious entrée to suit your mood. Finally, conclude your meal with a tantalizing dessert or delicious beverage.

Depending on the situation, it may make sense to adjust the diet and reduce or exclude the intake of some foods. Here are the most common cases for considering dietary modifications:

Dietary Substitutions

▶ Lactose intolerant
Use fat-free or skim Lactaid milk in place of skim milk in recipes. Soymilk may also be used.

▶ Gluten and wheat free
Use rice in recipes that call for pasta. Starches such as winter squash and potatoes are also delicious wheat and gluten-free alternatives.

▶ Vegetarians
Use your favorite vegetarian protein in place of any meat in a recipe. For example, instead of using beef in the beef teriyaki recipe you can use beans, seitan or textured vegetable protein instead. Tofu and tempeh can be used in place of chicken. Make substitutions accordingly.

▶ Vegans
Use soymilk in place of milk in recipes. Cheeses such as mozzarella and cheddar can be replaced with soy cheese. Ricotta and cottage cheese can be substituted with tofu. Animal proteins such as chicken and beef can be substituted with beans, veggie burgers or textured vegetable protein.

To make using this cookbook easier, we have included a number of icons; you will see these throughout the cookbook. Let these icons help guide you in choosing recipes that fit your lifestyle and nutritional needs. An explanation of each is listed below.

Symbol Key

▶ Good Source of Fiber

These recipes contain fiber (a component of foods that cannot be fully digested). Fiber has many health benefits, from improving digestion, relieving constipation, protecting against some types of cancers and lowering blood cholesterol levels. In addition, high fiber foods take longer to digest, keeping you satisfied longer.

▶ Good Source of Calcium

These recipes contain ingredients with calcium. Calcium is an essential mineral used to maintain strong bones and teeth. Adequate calcium intake can help prevent osteoporosis and is important for people of all ages.

▶ Meals in Minutes

Recipes that will take 20 minutes or less to prepare and reach the table. These recipes are great for people with active lifestyles. You will be able to prepare and cook a delectable meal in less time than waiting for take-out to be delivered!

▶ Family Fare

These are recipes that make more than one serving. These recipes were created so everyone can sit down and enjoy a healthy, well-balanced meal together. With this cookbook, you do not need to cook separate meals for your family and yourself to follow the program and achieve the success of your weight loss goals.

Some of the following terms are found in many of our recipes. For your convenience here are some definitions to help in the preparation of the recipes.

Julienne: Slicing foods into thin matchstick-like strips.

Chopped: Cutting food into uniform bite-sized pieces.

Grated: Thin shreds of a food. Large pieces of food are rubbed against a serrated surface such as a grater. A food processor can also grate many foods.

Zest: The colored portion of the skin/peel of a citrus fruit such as an orange, lemon or lime. Removing this outer layer of skin can add great flavor to foods.

Diced: Cutting food into small cubes.

Minced: Cutting food into very small pieces. Minced foods are smaller than chopped foods.

Working the recipes into your meal plan

You may notice that there are some ingredients in some of the recipes in this cookbook that are not on your weight loss plan. It is okay to use these recipes! These ingredients are portion controlled and the calories are factored into the exchanges.

In addition, some recipes do not appear to have the same exchanges and serving sizes as the menu plans. For example, a recipe may call for only half a cup of raw vegetables but may count as a whole vegetable serving. When working out the exchanges, the registered dietitians have looked at the recipe as a whole before determining its exchange value. As long as you measure out the portions of ingredients and count the recipes as indicated, these recipes can all be used on a regular basis.

Want to change the number of servings from a recipe? You can convert your favorite "Family Fare" recipe to a single serving or adjust any single serving recipe so it can make multiple servings. Here are a few examples:

A single serving recipe that calls for 2 Tablespoons (30mL) of skim milk and 1/2cup (125mL) fresh broccoli can be adjusted to make 12 servings. There are 16 Tablespoons (250mL) per cup, so the new 12-serving recipe would have 24 Tablespoons or 1 1/2 cups (375mL) of skim milk. The new recipe would now call for 6 cups (1.5L) of broccoli.

A recipe that yields 12 servings that calls for 1/4 cup (50mL) of juice can also be modified to serve any number of people. 1/4 cup (50mL) is 4

Tablespoons (60mL) or 12 teaspoons (180mL), if changing this recipe to make 4 servings you would need 4 teaspoons or 1 1/3 Tablespoons (20mL) of juice. To make 1 serving you would use only a teaspoon (5mL) of juice.

Use the following conversion charts to help you adjust any of our delicious recipes.

Have you ever been confused by how many teaspoons equal a Tablespoon, or how many grams equal an ounce? With the reference chart below, hopefully, we will answer all those questions about US and metric measurements.

Conversion Chart

1/8 teaspoon (tsp) = .5 milliliters (mL)	1 ounce (oz) = 30 gram (g)
1/4 tsp = 1 mL	2oz = 60 g
1/2 tsp = 2 mL	3oz = 90 g
1 tsp = 5 mL	4oz = 120 g
1 Tablespoon (Tbsp) = 3 tsp = 15 mL	5oz = 150 g
1/4 cup = 50 mL	6oz = 180 g
1/3 cup = 75 mL	8oz = 225 g
1/2 cup = 125 mL	1 pound (lb) = 450 g
2/3 cup = 150 mL	2.2 lb = 1 kg
3/4 cup = 175 mL	
1 cup = 250 mL	
1 quart = 1 Liter (L)	

Metric conversions
1 inch (in) = 2.5 centimeters (cm)

The following are flavorings, spices and herbs that can be used to make foods tastier without adding salt:

Beef: bay leaf, horseradish, marjoram, nutmeg, onion, pepper, sage, thyme.

Lamb: chili powder, curry powder, garlic, lemon juice, rosemary, mint, turmeric.

Pork: garlic, ginger, onion, sage, pepper, oregano.

Veal: bay leaf, curry powder, ginger, marjoram, oregano.

Chicken: cumin, garlic, ginger, lemon juice, marjoram, oregano, paprika, poultry seasoning, rosemary, sage, tarragon, thyme.

Fish: curry powder, dill, dry mustard, lemon juice, marjoram, parsley, paprika, pepper.

Carrots: cinnamon, cloves, chives, coriander, marjoram, nutmeg, parsley, rosemary, sage.

Corn: cumin, curry powder, onion, paprika, parsley.

Green Beans: dill, curry powder, lemon juice, marjoram, oregano, tarragon, thyme.

Peas: ginger, marjoram, mint, onion, pepper, sage.

Potatoes: dill, garlic, onion, paprika, parsley, sage.

Summer Squash: cloves, curry powder, marjoram, nutmeg, rosemary, sage.

Winter Squash: cinnamon, ginger, nutmeg, onion.

Tomatoes: basil, bay leaf, marjoram, onion, oregano, parsley, pepper.

Ingredient substitutions

If you cannot find…

Sugar Twin® Brown Sugar, use Splenda® or other heat-stable artificial sweetener instead.

Herbox® very low-sodium broth and bouillon, then choose a fat-free broth with as little sodium as possible. Some very low-sodium bouillons and broths contain potassium. Try to choose brands that do not have potassium as an ingredient.

Splenda®, use another heat-stable artificial sweetener.

- 1 Tbsp (15mL) flour can be substituted with 1 1/2 tsp (7.5mL) of arrowroot starch or 1 1/2 tsp (7.5mL) of cornstarch

- 1 clove of garlic can be substituted with 1/8 tsp (.5mL) of garlic powder

- 1 tsp lemon zest can be substituted with 1/2 tsp (2mL) lemon extract

- 1/4 cup (50mL) fresh chopped onion can be replaced with 1 Tbsp (15mL) of instant minced onions

- 1 tsp (5mL) of dry mustard can be replaced with 1 Tbsp (15mL) of prepared mustard

- 1 Tbsp (15mL) of finely chopped fresh herbs can be replaced with 1 tsp (5mL) dried leaf herbs or 1/2 tsp (2mL) ground dried herbs

- Egg substitute can be replaced with egg whites. 2 egg whites will replace 1/4 cup (50mL) of egg substitute.

- Fresh vegetables can be substituted with frozen vegetables.

- Vegetarian proteins found in any recipe, including those in the vegetarian section can be substituted with animal proteins. Poultry or beef could be used in place of Tofu in a recipe for BBQ Tofu.

- Meats can be substituted for one another.

Sugar Substitutes

Equal®	1 packet = 2 tsp (10mL) sugar
Equal Spoonful®	1 tsp (5mL) = 1 tsp (5mL) sugar
Equal Tablet®	1 tablet = 1 tsp (5mL) sugar
Splenda®*	1 tsp (5mL) granulated = 1 tsp (5mL) sugar
	1 packet = 2 tsp (10mL) sugar
Sweet 'N Low®	1 packet = 2 tsp (10mL) sugar
Sweet 'N Low® Brown	1 tsp (5mL) = 1/4 cup (50mL) brown sugar
Sugar Twin®*	1 tsp (5mL) granulated = 1 tsp (5mL) sugar
Sugar Twin Brown*	1 tsp (5mL) granulated = 1 tsp (5mL) sugar

1 packet = 2 tsp sugar

*Heat stable, can be used in baking

Artificial sweeteners are a great way to keep the sweet flavors in your favorite recipes and foods. Most of these are non-nutritive sweeteners, meaning that they have no nutritional value, so they do not contain significant calories.

Steps to reduce sugar in the diet

- Read the ingredient list on labels. If sugar is listed as one of the first five ingredients, the product contains a large amount of sugar as a sweetener.

- Use less white and brown sugar, honey, jam or jelly. Try sugar-free jams and jellies.

- Purchase unsweetened cereals.

- Purchase fresh fruits, or choose canned or frozen fruits without added sugar.

- Try to avoid adding sugar to coffee, tea, cereal and fruit.

- Try reducing the amount of sugar in recipes. You can usually cut the sugar by 1/3 in most recipes without compromising flavor. Try introducing spices like cinnamon, cardamom, coriander, nutmeg, ginger and mace to enhance the sweet flavor of foods.

You'll be delighted with your *L A Lite Cookbook*. We have created the recipes that you want and your family will enjoy! In addition, we have included our clients' favorites. This cookbook is great for clients on the program, as a gift for family or friends and can be used to prepare everyday meals or special occasion dishes for a party or get-together! **Bon Appetit!**